Ground Truths for Airmen

Core Readings in Military & Strategic Studies

United States Air Force Academy

Edited by John T. Farquhar

Pearson Learning Solutions, 501 Boylston Street, Suite 900, Boston, MA 02116
A Pearson Education Company
www.pearsoned.com

Printed in the United States of America

7 8 9 10 V202 17 16 15 14 13 12

000200010271718138

CT/TY

ISBN 10: 1-256-93662-6
ISBN 13: 978-1-256-93662-6

CONTENTS

AIR, SPACE, AND CYBERSPACE POWER: THE FOUNDATION FOR MILITARY & STRATEGIC STUDIES 200

Dr. John Farquhar

During Basic Cadet Training at the United States Air Force Academy, aspiring cadets memorize the Air Force mission statement:

The mission of the United States Air Force is to fly, fight, and win . . . in air, space, and cyberspace.

The purpose of MSS 200, "Air, Space, and Cyberspace Power" is to transform this exercise of rote memory into a meaningful, sophisticated comprehension of what air, space, and cyberspace power means. In short, air, space, and cyberspace power comprise vital tools for national policy makers. An older version of the Air Force mission statement presented the idea, "to deliver sovereign options for the defense of the United States."[1] In order to fully comprehend air, space, and cyberspace power as war-fighting domains and as military instruments to achieve national objectives, the course incorporates a process suggested by the mission statement of the Department of Military & Strategic Studies:

. . . to develop professional Air Force officers educated in the context, theory, and application of military and strategic power

The Department of Military & Strategic Studies educates through inquiry, discussion, reading, case studies, and other interactive methods, focusing on the context, theory, and application of military power. Specifically, context means studying the background factors of military power, to include personalities, motivations, outcomes, and consequences. In other words, students explore the context in order to comprehend and appreciate "what" happened in a military action or strategic event. Linked to context, theory refers to the concepts and principles that explain the "how" or "why" behind actions, the intellectual foundation for understanding the causes of events. Both context and theory use methods from history, political science, economics, and other fields to describe and explain the significance of military power. Application of military power is where "the rubber meets the road," that is the planning, command, control, communication, and execution of military force. It involves the deployment of military personnel and equipment, the maneuver of forces in battle space, and combat. Applying military power may require fighting, destruction, and death that should never be minimized, but it can also involve non-lethal, but strategically important, activities that may ultimately determine victory or defeat. Mastering the context, theory, and application of military power requires a life-long commitment. MSS 200 is only a first step, but reflects a belief that even officer candidates should appreciate the breadth and range of military and strategic activities and are capable of developing the thinking skills required for today's complex challenges. MSS 200 seeks to plant the seed of strategic thought.

AIR, SPACE, AND CYBERSPACE

MSS 200 explores the United States Air Force contribution to national security and the broader development of air, space, and cyberspace power as war fighting domains. The first course objective follows this thought:

1. **Appraise the contributions and limitations of air, space, and cyberspace power to warfare**

   - Comprehend the evolving functions, capabilities, theories, and doctrine of air, space, and cyberspace power.
   - Evaluate the unique operating environments, domain characteristics, and integration challenges of air, space, and cyberspace in war fighting.
   - Assess the impact of culture, heritage, and organization upon joint and coalition interoperability.

Subsequent lessons explore the challenge of defining air, space, and cyberspace power and the intellectual process of how best to utilize their respective potential. As an introduction, three definitions of air power may prove useful:

> "Air power may be defined as the ability to do something in the air. It consists of transporting all sorts of things by aircraft from one place to another."
>
> Brig Gen William "Billy" Mitchell[2]

> "Air power is the ability to use the air spaces for offensive, defensive, and supply services, and to deny their use to the enemy."
>
> Air Chief Marshal of the Royal Air Force Lord Arthur Tedder[3]

"Airpower is the ability to project military power or influence·though the control and exploitation of air, space, and cyberspace to achieve strategic, operational, or tactical objectives.

AFDD 1[4]

Likewise, students will find the Department of Defense (DOD) definition of space power as a useful starting point:

Space power – The total strength of a nation's capabilities to conduct and influence activities to, in, through, and from space to achieve its objectives. See also space. JP 3-14.[5]

At the risk of definitional overkill, the Department of Defense defines space as "A medium like the land, sea, and air within which military activities shall be conducted to achieve US national security objectives." Source: JP 3-14.[6]

Finally, the emerging concept of cyberspace will be explored. The DOD currently defines cyberspace as:

"A global domain within the information environment consisting of the interdependent network of information technology infrastructures, including the Internet, telecommunications networks, computer systems, and embedded processors and controllers." Source: CJCS CM-0363-08.[7]

In keeping with MSS 200's integration of the Air Force and Military & Strategic Studies missions, knowing definitions of air, space, and cyberspace without understanding their context in military theory and strategy would be a grave mistake. MSS 200 recognizes that this course is the first formal exposure of officer candidates to a number of fundamental concepts for the profession of arms, including military theory, doctrine, strategy, and tactics. Although not formally a part of the course, MSS 200 will also enhance important aspects of officership through both course content and methods.

MILITARY THEORY AND DOCTRINE

In a general sense, military theory provides a broad conceptual framework that organizes our thinking. More specifically, Webster's dictionary defines a theory as "…a system of assumptions, accepted principles, and rules of procedure devised to analyze, predict, or otherwise explain the nature or behavior of a specified set of phenomena."[8] In other words, theory puts things known into a system. To some extent, theory simplifies the complexities of life and introduces principles and laws of behavior. Thus, good military theory makes sense out of what otherwise would be an incomprehensible mass of observations and anecdotes. Theory also challenges the status quo; it combines things we observe in new ways and in turn, forces a fresh look at current wisdom.[9]

Noted nineteenth-century Prussian military theorist, Carl von Clausewitz states as a matter of fact: "a working theory is an essential basis for criticism."[10] He emphasizes that military theory should inspire inquiry, the asking of questions, which leads to analytical investigation. In turn, the inquirer applies analysis to experience, which results in a "close acquaintance" and "thorough familiarity" with the subject.[11] Note that Clausewitz did not suggest that knowledge of theory alone would result in the mastery of a subject; experience is imperative. Also, he and most military theorists do not consider military theory a rule book or a checklist to be applied to a given situation.

Military theory provides the foundation to weigh opportunities and constraints in strategic processes. It also focuses upon the timeless, unchanging aspects of the nature of war, as well as those dimensions of conflict that do change with societal evolution and advances in technology. To succeed in comprehending military theory, cadets wrestle with concepts articulated by both classic and modern military strategists. MSS 200 examines core ideas from such famous theorists as Sun Tzu, Carl von Clausewitz, Mao Zedong, T. E. Lawrence, Bernard Brodie, John Warden, and others. Contemporary concerns from global terrorism, Afghanistan, China, Iraq, Iran, and other areas challenge these ideas and increase understanding.

Closely related to military theory, military doctrine seeks to capture how best to fight. Military doctrine often follows from military theory, but is tempered in the fires of experience. The current Department of Defense definition presents doctrine as:

> Fundamental principles by which the military forces or elements there of guide their actions in support of national objectives. It is authoritative but requires judgment in application.[12]

Three pithy quotes further refine the concept of doctrine:

"What we believe about the best way to do things." Colonel Dennis M. Drew and Dr. Donald M. Snow

"That mode of approach that repeated experience has shown usually works best." Maj Gen I. B. Holley, Jr.

"The central beliefs for waging war in order to achieve victory; the building material for strategy." General Curtis E. LeMay[13]

Often academic scholars of strategy and war concentrate upon theory and criticize military doctrine, but despite limitations, military doctrine plays a vital intermediary role spanning ideas and behavior. Military organizations rely on doctrine to train large numbers of people to "sing from the same sheet of music." In other words, military doctrine produces reasonably standard behaviors and actions from troops that a commander can use in planning and executing operations and thus transform them into an instrument of his will.[14] A contemporary

British military analyst, Colin S. Gray, links military theory and doctrine in a thought-provoking way:

> If strategic theory educates the mind by providing intellectual organization, defining terms, suggesting connections among apparently disparate matters, and offering speculative...postulates, strategic (and operational, and tactical) doctrine states beliefs. Doctrine teaches what to think and what to do rather than how to think and how to be prepared to do it.[15]

In sum, military organizations need both military theory and doctrine; one expands the intellectual horizons of soldiers, sailors, and airmen and the other provides guidelines for action and enhances interoperability and war fighting. In studying military theory and doctrine, MSS 200 addresses the second course objective:

2. Appraise the value and limitations of military theory.

- Examine the evolution of classic and contemporary military theories
- Comprehend the nature and character of war
- Assess the reasons for war
- Apply concepts of military theory to contemporary conflicts

STRATEGY AND TACTICS

In one sense, strategy applies military theory and doctrine to distinct political problems, but this functional approach also helps define strategy as a concept. Joint Publication 1-02 presents a definition of strategy: "a prudent idea or set of ideas for employing the instruments of power in a synchronized and integrated fashion to achieve theater, national, and/or multinational objectives."[16] Three well-known military theorists further explain strategy:

> ". . . the art of distributing and applying military means to fulfill the ends of policy."[17]
> B. H. Liddell Hart

> "A plan of action designed in order to achieve some end; a purpose together with a system of measures for its accomplishment."[18] J. C. Wylie

> ". . . the use of the engagement for the purpose of war. The strategist must therefore define an aim for the entire operational side of the war that will be in accordance with its purpose. In other words, he will draft the plan of the war, and the aim will determine the series of actions intended to achieve it: he will, in fact, shape the individual campaigns and, within these, decide on the individual engagements. . . ."[19] Carl von Clausewitz

Students notice the subtle differences in these definitions and should be warned that "strategy" has different meanings depending upon both time and author. For example, Clausewitz, Jomini, and other nineteenth-century authors used "strategy" to refer to military campaigns. In the mid-twentieth century, B. H. Liddell Hart coined the term "grand strategy" to correct this narrow military scope and broaden the perspective of strategic thinking:

> For the role of grand strategy—higher strategy—is to co-ordinate (*sic*) and direct all the resources of a nation, or band of nations, towards the attainment of the political object of the war—the goal defined by fundamental policy.[20]

At its simplest, strategy reconciles ends, ways, and means, with "ends" referring to national and military objectives, "ways" meaning national policies and military concepts, and "means" standing for national resources, military forces, and supplies available to the decision makers.[21]

While a definition of strategy provides the student a starting point for study, experts emphasize the limitations of a definitional approach. In *The Making of Strategy: Rulers, States, and War*, Williamson Murray and Mark Grimsley argue:

> . . . straightforward definitions go fundamentally astray, for strategy is a process, a constant adaptation to shifting conditions and circumstances in a world where chance, uncertainty, and ambiguity dominate.[22]

Colin Gray agrees, but reconciles the need for a definition with the process approach in this observation: "Strategy is the bridge that relates military power to political purpose; it is neither military power *per se* nor political purpose. By strategy I mean *the use that is made of force and the threat of force for the ends of policy*."[23]

In contrast to the complexities associated with strategy, the concept of tactics is simple and direct. The current Department of Defense (DOD) military dictionary defines tactics as "the employment and ordered arrangement of forces in relation to each other."[24] A slightly older version states, "1. The employment of units in combat. 2. The ordered arrangement and maneuver of units in relation to each other and/or the enemy to utilize their full potentialities."[25] At the risk of making the concept too complicated, two other observations contribute to our understanding of tactics:

> "A continuous competition of wits." Stefan T. Possony

> "The immediate employment of any force or weapon to attain the objectives of strategy, as opposed to its comprehensive control, which is strategy." Rear Admiral Henry E. Eccles[26]

Hence, tactics refers to the battlefield and strategy to the process of attaining objectives (ends) through planning (ways), and applying resources (means). By introducing the concepts of strategy and tactics, MSS 200 explores the third course objective:

3. Appraise the value and limitations of military strategy.

- Comprehend the relationship between war and politics.
- Comprehend the concepts of grand strategy and coercion.
- Comprehend the challenges of creating and executing military strategy (reconciling ends, ways, and means)
- Apply knowledge in scenarios based on current strategic issues

Within MSS, military strategy begins where security studies ends. MSS military strategy is not about the political debate over responding to contemporary regional conflicts, although this debate is important and will be covered in political science or international relations courses. MSS will not explore deeply the background for current strategic events; history courses will explore that vital dimension. Instead, in MSS 200 military strategy examines the overall strategy process, the creating of grand strategy by the national command authority, and the articulation of national military strategy. In addition, it focuses upon what the US ought to do with military forces at an operational level and various approaches to employ military force to achieve strategic ends.[27] MSS 200 considers the strategic, operational, and tactical levels of war, where "strategic" refers to achieving overall war aims, "operational" means campaign planning on a theater level to support a strategy, and "tactical" emphasizes the battlefield dimension of war. In exploring the concept of strategy, MSS 200 examines threats to US national security, the complexities of making strategy in a democratic, open society, and the difficulties inherent when decision makers articulate strategic goals for public approval.

OFFICERSHIP

Although not directly studied in the course, MSS 200 indirectly contributes to cadet understanding of officership. By studying air, space, and cyberspace power, officer candidates better comprehend the Air Force mission and their role in the nation's defense. By examining military theory and strategy, future officers better grasp the big picture, the link between war and politics and the relationship of military and society. While there are no specific lessons dedicated to officership, instructors will discuss leadership, ethics, responsibility, and other concepts central to producing leaders of character, the mission of the Air Force Academy. These ideas contribute to the fourth MSS 200 objective:

4. Value the characteristics and relevance of good officership.

- Embody the concept of "Service to the Nation"
- Demonstrate loyalty to ideals of the Constitution, the Oath of Office, and the Air Force Officer's Commission
- Embrace the concept of becoming a "strategic lieutenant" with the ability to think "big picture"
- Internalize the "Warrior Ethos" – prepared to risk one's life to defend the nation

SUMMARY

Why does Military & Strategic Studies matter? Why should a relatively young officer candidate study advanced concepts as military theory, doctrine, and strategy? At the heart of MSS 200 is the belief that strategic thought requires a lifetime of study and reflection. Yet, regardless of age or experience, Air Force cadets possess the intellect, inspiration, and inquiring minds needed to wrestle with tough, challenging issues. Equally important, cadets bring a fresh perspective and a questioning attitude necessary for insight.

The Department of Military & Strategic Studies at the Air Force Academy focuses upon the context, theory, and application of military power. In MSS 200, cadets explore military theory (teaching how to think about war), doctrine (accepted beliefs about how best to fight), strategy (a process of linking ends, ways, and means), and tactics (employing power on the battlefield and in battle space). Definitions of concepts provide a useful starting point and a necessary common terminology, but represent only the beginning of understanding. Students must read with a critical, discerning mind and be open to applying ideas to current problems.

MSS 200 explains how the Air Force fits into a joint operational environment by not only examining air, space, and cyberspace as war-fighting domains, but how they enhance the "sovereign options" or military instrument available to policy makers for achieving national objectives. By examining the ideas and concepts behind air, space, and cyberspace power, officer candidates will better comprehend the evolution of Air Force theory and doctrine within their careers. Air, space, and cyberspace power are inherently linked to rapidly changing technologies. Air Force doctrine will change during an officer's career, but understanding the core ideas and theory behind the doctrine will serve well. Thus, MSS 200 intentionally integrates air, space, and cyberspace power within a context of military theory and strategy.

NOTES

1. *Contrails,* 2008-2009, Vol. 54 (United States Air Force Academy, CO: USAF Academy Cadet Wing), 107.
2. *William Mitchell, Winged Defense: The Development and Possibilities of Modern Air Power—Economic and Military* (New York: G. P. Putnam's Sons, 1925), xi.

3. Air Chief Marshal of the Royal Air Force [Arthur]Tedder, *Air Power in War* (London: Hodder and Stoughton, 1948), 30. Please note that the official Department of Defense on-line dictionary of military terms does not include a definition for air power. For an excellent essay, exploring essential concept regarding an older term, "aerospace" that explains air power well, see "Aerospace Power," in Air Force Manual 1-1, Volume II, *Basic Aerospace Doctrine of the United States Air Force* (Washington: Headquarters US Air Force, 1992), 71-78.

4. Air Force Doctrine Document 1 (AFDD 1), *Air Force Basic Doctrine, Organization, and Command* (Maxwell Air Force Base, AL: LeMay Center, 14 Oct 2011), 11.

5. *Department of Defense Dictionary of Military and Associated Terms,* http://www.dtic.mil/doctrine/dod_dictionary/ (accessed 6 Jul 2011).

6. Ibid.

7. Ibid.

8. *Webster's II: The New Riverside University Dictionary* (Boston, Mass.: Houghton Mifflin, 1988), 1200.

9. Dr. Dorri Karolick provided this valuable perspective in her review of the first draft on 19 Jul 2005.

10. Carl von Clausewitz, *On War* (Princeton, N. J.: Princeton University Press, 1976), 157; Michael I. Handel, *Masters of War: Classical Strategic Thought,* 3rd rev. ed. (London: Frank Cass, 2001), 19.

11. Clausewitz, *On War,* 141; Handel, *Masters,* 23.

12. Joint Publication 1-02, *Department of Defense Dictionary of Military and Associated Terms.* Available from http://www.dtic.mil/doctrine/dod_dictionary/?zoom_query=doctrine&zoom_sort=0&zoom_per_page=10&zoom_and=1. Accessed 16 May 2012.

13. AFM 1-1, *Basic Aerospace Doctrine of the United States Air Force,* Vol. II, March 1992, 282. Although it is not current, this version of Air Force basic doctrine contains two volumes. Volume I presents a brief synopsis of doctrinal precepts and volume II contains a series of thoughtful essays about the nature of war and air and space power that are still useful.

14. Colin S. Gray, *Modern Strategy* (Oxford: Oxford University Press, 1999), 36.

15. Ibid.

16. Joint Publication 1-02, Department of Defense Dictionary of Military and Associated Terms. Available from http://www.dtic.mil/doctrine/dod_dictionary/?zoom_query=strategy&zoom_sort=0&zoom_per_page=10&zoom_and=1. Accessed 16 May 2012.

17. B. H. Liddell Hart, *Strategy,* 2nd rev. ed. (New York: Frederick A. Praeger, 1967), 335; Gray, *Modern Strategy,* 18.

18. J. C. Wylie, *Military Strategy: A General Theory of Power Control,* (New Brunswick, NJ: Rutgers University Press, 1967), 13; Gray, *Modern Strategy,* 18.

19. Clausewitz, *On War,* 177; Handel, *Masters of War,* 37.

20. Liddell Hart, *Strategy,* 335-336; Gray, *Modern Strategy,* 18.

21. JP 3-0, *Doctrine for Joint Operations,* 10 September 2001, I-4; Arthur F. Lykke, Jr., "Toward an Understanding of Military Strategy," cited in Clayton K. S. Chun, *War, Military Theory, and Strategy: An Introduction* (Boston: Houghton Mifflin, 2002), 84.

22. Williamson Murray and Mark Grimsley, "Introduction: On Strategy," in Williamson Murray, MacGregor Knox, and A. Bernstein, eds., *The Making of Strategy: Rulers, States, and War* (Cambridge: Cambridge University Press, 1994), 1; Gray, *Modern Strategy,* 19.

23. Gray, *Modern Strategy,* 17.

24. JP (Joint Publication) 1-02, *DoD (Department of Defense) Dictionary of Military and Associated Terms.* Available from http://www.dtic.mil/doctrine/dod_dictionary/. Accessed 16 May 2012.

25. JP 1-02, as cited in AFM 1-1, *Basic Aerospace Doctrine of the United States Air Force,* Vol. II, March 1992, 306.

26. Ibid.

27. Colonel Thomas A. Drohan, "Why MSS?"Originally available from http://intraweb.usafa.af.mil/df/dfmi/, Accessed 3 Aug 2006; Department of Military Strategic Studies, Mission Brief, 11 May 2006, 3. The current versions of both documents do not include the background material. The current briefings are available from http://mercury.usafa.edu/dfmi/. Accessed 23 June 2010.

THE NATURE AND CHARACTER OF WAR[1]

This chapter introduces the academic study of war. Granted most people involved in war have never studied it per se and most scholars understand the limitations of an academic study of the subject, but mental preparation is essential for battlefield success. Unlike most professions, the military profession cannot be practiced or adequately simulated in times of peace. Leadership in war allows no "spin up" time; however, history shows that academic study can prepare the mind for many of war's intellectual and emotional challenges. Studying past experiences opens the mind; hence, this lesson introduces students to the writings of Thucydides and Carl von Clausewitz.

By presenting a variety of definitions of war, the lesson hopes to open the cadets to a range of thoughts regarding this complex event. Please note that the current on-line Department of Defense military dictionary (Joint Pub 1-02) has no entry for "war"…truly amazing.[2]

The article presents the nature of war and character of war as two distinct concepts. Most scholars use the terms synonymously or as a single entity (i.e. "the nature and character of war"). Nevertheless, the distinction between the terms is useful for comprehending the subject. Certainly the United States faces the timeless nature of war against insurgencies in Iraq and Afghanistan while encountering changes in the character of war. Comparing a Marine's experience in Ramadi or Kandahar with that of his great-grandfather in the Philippines will reveal uncanny similarities…and striking differences.

This lesson also provides a brief overview of the "principles of war." Many of the subsequent theorists will refer to this phrase in their writings. Keep in mind that the principles of war are not written in stone. Like the word "strategy," the phrase "principles of war" refers to different ideas at different times. Most military thinkers acknowledge the validity of timeless foundational concepts, but their writings do not agree on what those are. Ironically, the "timeless" ideas change over time. Nevertheless, students should be aware of the principles, their value, and limitations. This lesson introduces the principles; subsequent chapters will further develop them, although this text will not have a separate lesson solely devoted to the Principles of War.

TEXT

The mission of the United States Air Force is "to fly, fight, and win...in air, space, and cyberspace."[3] Implicit in accomplishing this mission, Air Force personnel must understand the nature and character of war. Although not stated in the formal mission statement, war provides the reason for the Air Force's existence.

A recent version of the Department of Defense Military Dictionary defines war as:

> Sustained use of armed force between nations or organized groups within a nation involving regular and irregular forces in a series of connected battles and campaigns to achieve vital national objectives. War may be limited, with some self-imposed restraints on resources or objectives. Or, it may be general with the total resources of a nation or nations employed and the national survival of a belligerent at stake.[4]

The current version of Air Force Basic Doctrine states it more simply, "War is a violent struggle between rival parties to attain competing objectives."[5] Although he expressed it many different ways, Prussian military theorist Carl von Clausewitz tried to capture the core idea of warfare: "Essentially war is fighting, the only effective principle in the manifold activities generally designated as war."[6] Since war is one of humankind's oldest and most basic activities, analyzing different attempts to express the essence of war provides value:

> A contest or difference between states or large bodies of people, which, not being determinable by the ordinary measures of justice and equity, is referred to the decision of the sword. Colonel William Duane, 1810

> The process by which a nation endeavors to impose its will on its opponent. Air Marshal Arthur W. Tedder

> As generally understood, armed conflicts on a fairly large scale, usually excluding conflict in which fewer than 50,000 combatants are involved. *Encyclopedia Britannica*, 15th edition, 1988[7]

> ...the application of state violence in the name of policy. It involves killing and wounding people and destroying property until the survivors abandon their military resistance or the belligerents come to a negotiated agreement. Allan R. Millett and Peter Maslowski[8]

Definitions provide only the first step in understanding the complexities of war. Over centuries, soldiers, statesmen, and scholars have written countless books exploring the nature and character of war. Many authors use the terms "nature" and "character" interchangeably, but British analyst Colin S. Gray provides a useful service by separating their meaning. The "nature of war" refers to those elements that are timeless and unchanging, whereas "the character of war" describes those features that do change and transform over time.[9]

Within the Western military tradition, two authors stand unsurpassed in exploring the nature of war: Thucydides, an Athenian Greek who lived from approximately 460 to 404 BCE and Carl von Clausewitz (1780-1831), a German contemporary and opponent of Napoleon. Although separated by time, geography, society, and technology, both men proved astute observers of the greatest wars of their time and wrote from first-hand knowledge of war. Thucydides fought for Athens, advanced to the rank of *strategos* (general) and suffered a twenty-year exile for failing in a campaign.[10] Equally remarkable, Clausewitz first encountered war as a twelve-year-old officer cadet in the Prussian Army; he fought in battles and skirmishes against Napoleon from 1793 until 1815.[11]

Although not considered a military theorist per se, Thucydides captures the human dimension of war in *The History of the Peloponnesian War*. In this first great book of war in Western culture, Thucydides seeks to understand a cataclysmic 27-year war between coalitions led by Athens, a vibrant democracy and maritime power, and Sparta, a conservative, agrarian oligarchy renowned for its militaristic society and prowess in land warfare. Through the use of speeches by the major war leaders, Thucydides emphasizes that war centers upon power and contains both rational and irrational elements at the same time. For example, during a debate in the Spartan assembly prior to hostilities, an Athenian delegation presented these pearls of wisdom:

> Think, too, of the great part that is played by the unpredictable in war: think of it now, before you are actually committed to war. The longer a war lasts, the more things tend to depend on accidents.[12]

> And when people are entering upon a war they do things the wrong way round. Action comes first, and it is only when they have already suffered that they begin to think.[13]

> We have done nothing extraordinary, nothing contrary to human nature in accepting an empire when it was offered to us and then in refusing to give it up. Three powerful motives prevent us from doing so – security, honour (*sic*), and self-interest. And we were not the first to act in this way. Far from it. It has always been a rule that the weak should be subject to the strong…[14]

In fact, security, honor, and self-interest still resound as the essential reasons for why nations go to war.[15] Moreover, Thucydides highlights the cultural aspects of warfare and how societal values influence how, as well as why, a nation fights. In turn, he suggests that a society's moral standards inevitably become a casualty of war:

> What used to be described as a thoughtless act of aggression was now regarded as the courage one would expect to find in a party member; to think of the future and wait was merely another way of saying one was a coward; any idea of moderation was just an

attempt to disguise one's unmanly character; ability to understand a question from all sides meant that one was totally unfitted for action. Fanatical enthusiasm was the mark of a real man, and to plot against an enemy behind his back was perfectly legitimate self-defence (*sic*). Anyone who held violent opinions could always be trusted, and anyone who objected to them became a suspect.... it was equally praise worthy to get one's blow in first against someone who was going to do wrong, and to denounce someone who had no intention of doing any wrong at all....Love of power, operating through greed and through personal ambition, was the cause of all these evils.[16]

In his text, Thucydides richly describes the passions inflamed by civil war; the struggle between morality, justice, and state interests; and human loss whether by death in battle, disease, or economic privation. Additionally, the speakers of the day present rational, sophisticated strategies and argue eloquently to democratic assemblies. For example, the Athenian leader Pericles shows shrewd, patient, strategic thinking equal to that of any modern leader in his vision of the war:

> The [Spartans] cultivate their own land themselves; they have no financial resources as individuals or as states; they have no experience of fighting overseas, nor of any fighting that lasts a long time,...Such people are incapable of often manning a fleet or often sending an army, when that means absence from their own land, expense from their own funds and, apart from this, when we have control of the sea....In a single battle the [Spartans] and their allies could stand up to all the rest of [Greece], but they cannot fight a war against a power unlike themselves, so long as they have no central deliberative authority to produce quick decisive action,...But this is the main point: they will be handicapped by lack of money and delayed by the time they will have to take in procuring it. But in war opportunity waits for no man.[17]

Hence, in a few short lines Pericles and Thucydides display an astute understanding of war, economics, politics, land power, sea power, and time. Yet, in the Peloponnesian War, Spartan campaigns lay waste to Athenian territory and the resulting popular outcry and demands for action overcome Pericles' wise strategic rationale. Thus, Thucydides pits rational thought against the emotions, passion, and suffering of a society at war. In his masterpiece, Thucydides provides the foundation for our understanding of the human dimension of war.

Joining Thucydides as a pillar of Western military thought, Carl von Clausewitz contributes four attributes essential to understanding the nature of war:

- War as a political instrument
- War as a clash of wills
- War as violence
- War tempered by "fog, friction, and chance"

Nations go to war for a reason—a political purpose or objective. This political objective determines both the military objective and the amount of effort devoted by a society.[18] Clausewitz observes astutely that "the same political object can elicit *differing* reactions between different peoples, and even from the same peoples at different times." (emphasis in original)[19] For example, in the recent war with Iraq, the war's political objectives, eliminating weapons of mass destruction, ending the brutal regime of Saddam Hussein, and creating a democratic government may be viewed skeptically, or rejected entirely, by different peoples. Instead, critics cite the spread of American imperialism, the invasion of Islamic lands, or aggression to seize oil as the war's "real" objectives leading to bitter debate, both within American society and internationally. Within a democracy, struggles over war aims and political objectives emerge throughout history; often, the longer the war, the more intense the political battle.

Clausewitz emphasizes the need for a nation's political and military leadership to share a common understanding of a war's political objective:

> The first, the supreme, the most far-reaching act of judgment that the statesman and commander have to make is to establish by that test the kind of war on which they are embarking; neither mistaking it for, nor trying to turn it into, something that is alien to its nature.[20]

Yet, wars have their own dynamic and, as Thucydides chronicled, tend to evolve on their own. Clausewitz also captures this idea: "we must take a broader view because the original political objects can greatly alter during the course of the war and may finally change entirely *since they are influenced by events and their probable consequences*" (emphasis in original).[21]

Unpredictable events and unexpected consequences garble and transform the political objectives of a war. For example, consider the impact of the Abu Ghraib or Guantanamo Bay scandals and their impact upon US objectives in Iraq. Additionally, political objectives determine both the magnitude and duration of a war. As Clausewitz points out, "Once the expenditure of effort exceeds the value of the political object, the object must be renounced and peace must follow."[22] Thus, opponents strive to raise the cost of the struggle to outweigh the value of the enemy's political objectives.

Understanding both your own and your enemy's political objective is paramount. A successful nation must clearly articulate its political objectives not only to win popular support from its own people, but to convince the enemy populace, other governments, and, in today's world, the international community of the validity of one's cause.

The political nature of war leads logically to a second attribute of the nature of war: war represents a clash of opposing wills. In Thucydides, the Athenians emerge as bright, innovative, confident, rash, and ambitious, while their Spartan opponents stand as somewhat simple, cautious, resolute, and steady. Both states transformed these attributes into the will to fight sustained war. The relative balance between the foes and their respective strength of will led to nearly three decades of bitter fighting. Clausewitz adds insight:

> War, however, is not the action of a living force upon a lifeless mass...but always the collision of two living forces.... Once again, there is interaction. So long as I have not overthrown my opponent I am bound to fear he may overthrow me. Thus I am not in control: he dictates to me as much as I dictate to him.[23]

With this in mind, contemporary strategic thinker Edward Luttwak identifies a strategic paradox: "Strategy is paradoxical in that what works well today will not work well tomorrow, precisely because it worked well today."[24] In other words, because your enemy is a living, breathing, intelligent human being, he or she will learn from your clever plans, brilliant tactics, and cunning strategy. Once again, Clausewitz explains this unchanging attribute of war's nature:

> War is nothing but a duel on a larger scale. Countless duels go to make up a war, but a picture of it as a whole can be formed by imagining a pair of wrestlers. Each tries through physical force to compel the other to do his will; his *immediate* aim is to *throw* his opponent in order to make him incapable of further resistance.
>
> *War is thus an act of force to compel our enemy to do our will.* (emphasis in original)[25]

Although wrestling and other sports provide military personnel useful martial training and shape a competitive spirit, peace time activities cannot replicate the violence of war. Violence, the third attribute of the nature of war, is the most difficult to comprehend fully through academic study. Yet, if Clausewitz successfully articulates the theory and intellectual dimension of war and politics, Thucydides captures the hatred, violence, and savagery that comprise the nature of war. At its heart, war requires killing.[26] Throughout *On War*, Clausewitz emphasizes combat in an effort to remind the statesman and arm chair warrior of war's reality:

> Combat is the only effective force in war; its aim is to destroy the enemy's forces as a means to a further end. That holds good even if no actual fighting occurs, because the outcome rests on the assumption that if it came to fighting, the enemy would be destroyed.... The decision by arms is for all major and minor operations in war what cash payment is to commerce.[27]

In today's political, military, and security studies journals, authors explore the concept of non-lethal combat made possible by advancing technology. While their ideas merit attention and debate, Clausewitz offers a warning:

> Kind-hearted people might of course think there was some ingenious way to disarm or defeat an enemy without too much bloodshed, and might imagine this is the true goal of the art of war. Pleasant as it sounds, it is a fallacy that must be exposed: war is such a dangerous business that the mistakes which come from kindness are the very worst.[28]

Contemporary soldiers must never forget the violence that forms·the nature of war. Death's reality and the fear that it inspires change how people act. In the face of battle, courage and cowardice, perseverance and panic are all too real.

Danger, fear, physical exertion, fatigue, and mental stress comprise what Clausewitz calls "friction." This amorphous, difficult-to-measure concept forms the fourth attribute of the nature of war. Bad weather, harsh climate, rugged terrain, and other factors compound friction. Clausewitz explains further: "Everything in war is very simple, but the simplest thing is difficult. The difficulties accumulate and end by producing a kind of friction that is inconceivable unless one has experienced war."[29] He adds that friction separates real war from war on paper. Despite extensive efforts to train soldiers, sailors, and airmen to execute duties correctly, to follow orders, and to perform under fire, military organizations are composed of individual human beings, each capable of failure and, hence, of creating friction.[30] In war, "Murphy's Law" lives: as Clausewitz reminds us, "Countless minor incidents—the kind you can never really foresee—combine to lower the general level of performance, so that one always falls far short of the intended goal."[31]

Closely related to friction, Clausewitz describes the "fog of war"—chance and uncertainty—as timeless and elemental. Commanders face imperfect knowledge of any situation: "The only situation a commander can know fully is his own; his opponent's he can know only from unreliable intelligence."[32] Moreover, experienced commanders realize that often it is difficult to coax an accurate picture from one's own organization. From this imperfect knowledge, leaders confront the pressures of time and consequences.[33] For every intended result, actions produce many unanticipated reactions from the enemy, as well as from friends, allies, the press, and public. Clausewitz reminds us: "No other human activity is so continuously or universally bound up with chance. And through the element of chance, guess work and luck come to play a great part in war."[34]

War represents a dynamic human activity, the interplay of interactive events on a large scale. If the nature of war and politics, clashing wills, violence, and friction, chance, and uncertainty mark the unchanging aspects of war, people must understand that every war is unique. Distinct historical experiences, culture, religion, ideology, alliances, and technology influence the changing character of war. Further adding to change, every war occurs at a different place in time and is affected by previous events. Historians Williamson Murray and Mark Grimsley remark:

> Historical experience creates preconceptions about the nature of war and politics.... And ideology and culture shape the course of decision-makers and their societies in both conscious and unconscious ways."[35]

Changes in individual societies resist generalization. In *Modern Strategy*, Colin S. Gray discusses culture as the context that provides meaning for an event. He states, "No one and no institution can operate 'beyond culture.'"[36] A nation's history, geographic location, political and social structures, prevailing ideologies, attitudes, and traditions combine to shape policy makers and policies, and to provide its distinctive "strategic culture."[37] As stated earlier, every society is unique. Certainly, American, German, and Russian strategic cultures vary dramatically, even only considering the twentieth century. Therefore, policy makers and military officers must study the unique strategic cultures encountered in contemporary crises and wars.

For the United States Air Force, technology dominates the character of war. Although Gray argues, "...historical evidence suggests that the outcomes to none of the wars of modern history among the great powers have plausibly been determined by superiority in weapons technology," prudent analysts acknowledge technology's vital importance and dynamic nature.[38] The history of air warfare links technological superiority to operational success, not to mention the emerging fields of space, cyberspace, information, and biological warfare. Of course, superior technology does not guarantee success; effective leadership, doctrine, training, logistics, maintenance, and motivation weigh heavily upon a war's outcome. Still, a modern, transformational United States Air Force recognizes the truth behind Italian Air Marshal GiulioDouhet's famous assertion: "Victory smiles upon those who anticipate the changes in the character of war; not upon those who wait to adapt themselves after the changes occur."[39]

THE PRINCIPLES OF WAR

Linked to the concepts of the nature and character of war, the principles of war represent fundamental truths in the practice of military art that have stood the test of time. Air Force Basic Doctrine (AFDD 1) describes them as "those aspects of war that are universally true and relevant."[40] Although considered "timeless," both military leaders and civilian scholars have not reached consensus on a single list of principles of war; but most will attest that such principles are a good starting point for evaluating military strategy and tactics, and these principles form the foundation for planning.[41]

According to current joint doctrine, the principles of war guide warfighting at the strategic, operational, and tactical levels. Several principles can be involved in any particular application concerned. Although many are tempted to use "the principles of war" as a checklist or sacred text, astute planners understand their limits. The effective officer uses the principles to guide thinking. The following lists the purposes of each of the nine principles of war recognized by today's US armed forces:

- **Unity of Command** ensures concentration of effort for every objective under one responsible commander.
- **Objective** directs military operations toward a defined and attainable objective that contributes to strategic, operational, and tactical aims.
- **Offensive**: To seize, retain, and exploit the initiative.

- **Mass**: To concentrate the effects of combat power at the most advantageous place and time to achieve decisive results.
- **Maneuver** places the enemy in a position of disadvantage through the flexible application of combat power in a multidimensional combat space.
- **Economy of Force** is the judicious employment and distribution of forces.
- **Security**: To never permit the enemy to acquire unexpected advantage.
- **Surprise** leverages the security principle by attacking the enemy at a time, place, or in a manner for which they are unprepared.
- **Simplicity** calls for avoiding unnecessary complexity in organizing, preparing, planning, and conducting military operations.[42]

Additional Principles of Operations

The recently revised AFDD 1, *Air Force Basic Doctrine, Organization, and Command* adds an additional set of principles as a result of experience in contingency operations:

- **Unity of Effort** becomes critical during interagency operations and can best be achieved through consensus building.
- **Restraint** is the disciplined application of military force appropriate to the situation.
- **Perseverance** encompasses the patient, resolute, and persistent pursuit of national goals and objectives, for as long as necessary to achieve them.
- **Legitimacy,** in order to reduce the threat to US forces and to enable them to work toward their objective, the US should be viewed as a legitimate actor in the mission, working towards multi-lateral interests including our own.

Students recognize the simple, "common sense" associated with the principles of war. Comprehending the concepts proves easy; actually attaining the principles in military operations and strategy can prove immensely difficult.[43]

SUMMARY

Wars are complicated, complex, and defy superficial analysis. Students of war recognize timeless elements known as "the nature of war," including, political objectives, a clash of wills, violence, fog, friction, and chance. Yet, every war is unique. The "character of war" refers to aspects that change over time and space: historical experience, ideology, culture, religion, alliances, and technology among others. The astute leader recognizes the subtleties between the nature and character of war. Over the years, military thinkers struggle to capture essential fundamental truths known as the "principles of war" that offer strategic and operational planning guidance. The classic works of Thucydides and Carl von Clausewitz offer insights into these subtleties and shape the necessary thinking required for successful war aims, policy, and strategy. Although he refers to strategy in this observation, Clausewitz's words also apply to the understanding of war:

> Everything in strategy is very simple, but that does not mean that everything is very easy. Once it has been determined, from the political conditions, what a war is meant to achieve and what it can achieve, it is easy to chart the course. But great strength of character, as well as great lucidity and firmness of mind, is required in order to follow through steadily, to carry out the plan, and to not be thrown off course by thousands of diversions.[44]

Air, Space, and Cyberspace Power fit into the realm of the character of war and, in the view of many theorists, revolutionize war's conduct. Nevertheless, strategy and classical military theory largely define the nature of war. Today's airmen must understand both the nature and character of war and the interplay between the two. It is not enough to comprehend how to employ air, space, and cyberspace assets; today's officer must also understand the broader context.

NOTES

1. Each chapter will include an introduction designed to place the article within the context of the book and highlight major themes; a section of text derived from an original primary source article or book in most cases, edited for length and to reduce redundancy; and a summary intended to emphasize major ideas for the reader and link the article to the study of air, space, and cyberspace power in most cases. For this chapter, the author acknowledges and thanks Dr. Jim Titus for his careful reading and helpful comments. The author also acknowledges the fine work of the unnamed author of "Violence and the Nature of War," an essay in Air Force Manual 1-1, *Basic Aerospace Doctrine of the United States Air Force*, Vol. II, March 1992. Students would benefit from reading the many fine essays in the 1992 version of Air Force basic doctrine.
2. Department of Defense Dictionary, http://www.dtic.mil/doctrine/dod_dictionary/. Accessed 16 May 2012.
3. "Air Force Mission," http://www.af.mil/main/welcome.asp. Accessed 23 June 2010.
4. Joint Test Pub 3-0 as cited in AFM 1-1, *Basic Aerospace Doctrine of the United States Air Force*, Vol. 2, March 1992, 308. As mentioned in the overview, the current on-line Department of Defense dictionary does not contain a specific definition of war.
5. AFDD 1, *Air Force Basic Doctrine, Organization, and Command* (Maxwell AFB, AL: Lemay Center, 14 October 2011), 21. The effect of irregular wars can be seen by comparing the current definition with the preceding version: "Open and often prolonged conflict between nations (or organized groups within nations) to achieve national objectives." AFDD 1, *Air Force Basic Doctrine* (Maxwell Air Force Base, AL: Headquarters Air Force Doctrine Center, 17 Nov 2003), 308.
6. Carl von Clausewitz, *On War*, ed. and trans. Michael Howard and Peter Paret (Princeton, NJ: Princeton University Press, 1976, 1984), 127; AFM 1-1, *Basic Aerospace Doctrine*, Vol. 2, 1992, 308.
7. Ibid.
8. Allan R. Millett and Peter Maslowski, *For the Common Defense: A Military History of the United States of America*, rev. and expanded ed. (New York: Free Press, 1994), xiii.
9. Students should keep in mind that Gray's formulation represents a minority view, but his concept better refines and clarifies the terminology. Colin S. Gray, *Modern Strategy* (Oxford: Oxford University Press, 1999), 1-15.
10. M. I. Finley, "Introduction," in Thucydides, *The History of the Peloponnesian War*, trans. Rex Warner (London and New York: Penguin Books, 1972), 10: Victor Davis Hanson, "Introduction," in *The Landmark Thucydides: A Comprehensive Guide to the Peloponnesian War*, ed. Robert B. Strassler (New York: Touchstone, 1996), ix-x.

11. Peter Paret, "The Genesis of *On War*," in Carl von Clausewitz, *On War*, ed. and trans. Michael Howard and Peter Paret (Princeton, NJ: Princeton University Press, 1976, 1984), 5.

12. Thucydides, *History of the Peloponnesian War*, 82.

13. Ibid., 82.

14. Ibid., 80.

15. Today, some would use "fear" instead of security and "national prestige" for honor. M. I. Finley, "Introduction," in Thucydides, *The History of the Peloponnesian War*, trans. Rex Warner (London and New York: Penguin Books, 1972), 23; Clayton K. S. Chun, *War, Military Theory, and Strategy: An Introduction* (Boston: Houghton Mifflin and Co., 2002), 7, 18.

16. Thucydides, *History of the Peloponnesian War*, 242-243.

17. Thucydides, *History of the Peloponnesian War*, 120.

18. Carl von Clausewitz, *On War*, ed. and trans. Michael Howard and Peter Paret (Princeton, NJ: Princeton University Press, 1976, 1984), 81.

19. Ibid.

20. Clausewitz, *On War*, 88.

21. Ibid., 92.

22. Ibid.

23. Clausewitz, *On War*, 77.

24. Gray, *Modern* Strategy, 42; Edward N. Luttwak, *Strategy: The Logic of War and Peace* (Cambridge, MA: Harvard University Press, Belknap Press, 1987), 4-5.

25. Clausewitz, *On War*, 75.

26. AFM 1-1, *Basic Aerospace Doctrine of the United States Air Force*, Vol. 2, March 1992, viii.

27. Clausewitz, *On War*, 97.

28. Ibid., 75.

29. Ibid., 119; AFM 1-1, *Basic Aerospace*, vol.2, ix.

30. Clausewitz, *On War*, 119; AFM 1-1, *Basic Aerospace*, vol. 2, ix.

31. Clausewitz, *On War*, 119.

32. Ibid., 84.

33. Williamson Murray and Mark Grimsley, "Introduction: On Strategy," in *The Making of Strategy: Rulers, States, and War*, Williamson Murray, MacGregor Knox, and A. Bernstein, eds. (Cambridge: Cambridge University Press, 1994), 2.

34. Clausewitz, *On War*, 85.

35. Murray and Grimsley, "Introduction," 2.

36. Gray, *Modern Strategy*, 129.

37. For a thorough explanation of this concept and the literature surrounding it, please see Colin S. Gray's chapter "Strategic Culture as Context" in *Modern Strategy*, 129-151.

38. In fairness, Gray understands the "permanent significance" of technology as a dimension of strategy and war. Gray, *Modern Strategy*, 37.

39. Giulio Douhet, *The Command of the Air*, trans. Dino Ferrari (New York: Coward-McCann, 1942; reprint, Washington, DC: Office of Air Force History, 1983), 30.

40. AFDD 1, *Air Force Basic Doctrine* (Maxwell Air Force Base, AL: LeMay Center, 14 Oct 2011), 29.

41. In-depth discussions of our current principles of war can be found in joint and Service publications. Joint Pub 1, *Joint Warfare of the U.S. Armed Forces*, 14 November 2000 edition discusses the principles of war and their application in joint warfare and will describe them as "the bedrock US military doctrine." Army Field Manual No. 100-1, *The Army*, Naval Doctrine Publication 1, *Naval Warfare*, Air Force Doctrine Document 1, *Air Force Basic Doctrine*, and Fleet Marine Force Manual FMFM 6-4, *Marine Rifle Company/Platoon*, all contain extensive discussions of the principles of war. In addition, excellent articles about the principles of war can be found in *Military Review* (May 1955 and September 1981) and *U.S. Naval Institute Proceedings* (November 1986).

SECURITY, HONOR, AND SELF INTEREST: WHY NATIONS GO TO WAR

Thucydides

This passage, "The Debate at Sparta and Declaration of War," from Thucydides' *History of the Peloponnesian War* stands as one of the oldest and most famous accounts in Western political and military thought. It articulates the reasons why nations go to war: the moral, political, economic, and emotional elements involved in any momentous decision. Notice that although he does not state it explicitly, Thucydides points out that there are both rational and irrational elements that influence war. Any rational policy considerations that ignore the emotions and passions of the peoples involved are doomed to fail.

Thucydides and the Peloponnesian War pose a challenge to today's students. Greek names pose a great obstacle to contemporary readers. Few Americans speak Greek, and even fewer have studied ancient Greek. Hence, many students are intimidated by the bewildering combinations of letters presented by Thucydides and other names from this period. For students new to the subject, do the best that you can.[1] Fortunately, most students have heard of Athens (a great sea power, center of culture and learning, a vibrant and dynamic business hub) and Sparta (the greatest land power of the age, a militaristic society dedicated to martial prowess and war, disdainful of the arts, commerce, and intellectualism). Athens leads the Delian League, an alliance of city states in theory, but in practice an Athenian empire made possible by its navy and commercial wealth. Sparta is the leading city of the Peloponnese, a peninsula containing a number of smaller city states, but the article will use "Spartans" and "Peloponnesians" interchangeably. To ancient Greeks, the Spartans have a reputation for being conservative, slow to anger, fierce, brave, . . . and for being stupid.

Corinth and Potidaea are also mentioned. Earlier in the book, Thucydides explains that Potidaea is a colony of Corinth. Corinth is allied to Sparta because Corinth is a lively, trading city in economic competition with Athens. The Corinthians have come to Sparta to seek aid: Athenian-backed forces have attacked the Corinthian government of Potidaea.

In this passage, Thucydides will use four speeches to convey his main thoughts. First, the Corinthians make an impassioned speech to sway the Spartans to intervene on their behalf.

A group of Athenian traders happen to be in Sparta at the same time and they ask for a chance to present their views; their speech is the second main section. Notice that the Athenians will frequently refer to the "Hellenes"... this is simply the word the Greeks use to refer to themselves: "Hellas" is the Greek word for Greece. The third speech features the Spartan king, Archidamus, an old, respected warrior. The final speech presents the scariest name, "Sthenelaidas." Do not worry about correct pronunciation, focus instead on his argument and his personality. (Note the first line of his speech.) Sthenelaidas is an ephor, an elected leader of Sparta. The five ephors actually have more political power than the Spartan king and run the assembly.

Between the four speeches, a range of political, moral, economic, ethical, and emotional ideas are discussed. Notice how "contemporary" the arguments are. This lesson captures the "war as politics" theme of the course and the nature of war (both war as politics and the importance of emotion). Try not to get bogged down by unfamiliar names or the specific events of the Peloponnesian War. If students look past these, they will enjoy this lesson. There is a reason people still read and benefit from Thucydides.

THE DEBATE AT SPARTA AND DECLARATION OF WAR[2]

Both the Athenians and the Peloponnesians had already grounds of complaint against each other. The grievance of Corinth was that the Athenians were besieging her own colony of Potidaea, with Corinthians and other Peloponnesians in the place: Athens, on the other hand, had her own grievances against the Peloponnesians; they had supported the revolt of a city which was in alliance with her and which paid her tribute, and they had openly joined the Potidaeans in fighting against her. In spite of this, the truce was still in force and war had not yet broken out. What had been done so far had been done on the private initiative of Corinth.

Now, however, Corinth brought matters into the open. Potidaea was under blockade, some of her own citizens were inside, and she feared that the place might be lost. She therefore immediately urged the allies to send delegates to Sparta. There her own delegates violently attacked the Athenians for having broken the truce and committed acts of aggression against the Peloponnese.... The Corinthians were the last to come forward and speak, having allowed the previous speakers to do their part in hardening Spartan opinion against Athens. The Corinthian speech was as follows:

'Spartans, what makes you somewhat reluctant to listen to us others, if we have ideas to put forward, is the great trust and confidence which you have in your own constitution and in your own way of life. This is a quality which certainly makes you moderate in your judgments; it is also, perhaps, responsible for a kind of ignorance which you show when you are dealing with foreign affairs. Many times before now we have told you what we were likely to suffer from Athens, and on each occasion, instead of taking to heart what we were telling you, you chose instead to suspect our motives and to consider that we were speaking only about our own grievances. The result has been that you did not call together this meeting of our allies before the damage was done; you waited until now, when we are actually suffering from it. And of all these allies, we have perhaps the best right to speak now, since we have the most serious complaints to make. We have to complain of Athens for her insolent aggression and of Sparta for her neglect of our advice.

'If there were anything doubtful or obscure about this aggression on the whole of Hellas, our task would have been to try to put the facts before you and show you something that you did not know. As it is, long speeches are unnecessary. You can see yourselves how Athens has deprived some states of their freedom and is scheming to do the same thing for others, especially among our own allies, and that she herself has for a long time been preparing for the eventuality of war. Why otherwise should she have forcibly taken over from us the control of Corcyra? Why is she besieging Potidaea? Potidaea is the best possible base for any campaign in Thrace, and Corcyra might have contributed a very large fleet to the Peloponnesian League.

'And it is you who are responsible for all this. It was you who in the first place allowed the Athenians to fortify their city and build the Long Walls after the Persian War.[3] Since then and up to the present day you have withheld freedom not only from those who have been enslaved by Athens but even from your own allies. When one is deprived of one's liberty one is right in blaming not so much the man who puts the fetters on as the one who had the power to prevent him, but did not use it – especially when such a one rejoices in the glorious reputation of having been the liberator of Hellas.

'Even at this stage it has not been easy to arrange this meeting, and even at this meeting there are no definite proposals. Why are we still considering whether aggression has taken place instead of how we can resist it? Men who are capable of real action first make their plans and then go forward without hesitation while their enemies have still not made up their minds. As for the Athenians, we know their methods and how they gradually encroach upon their neighbours. Now they are proceeding slowly because they think that your insensitiveness to the situation enables them to go on their way unnoticed; you will find that they will develop their full strength once they realize that you do see what is happening and are still doing nothing to prevent it.

'You Spartans are the only people in Hellas who wait calmly on events, relying for your defence not on action but on making people think that you will act. You alone do nothing in the early stages to prevent an enemy's expansion; you wait until your enemy has doubled his strength. Certainly you used to have the reputation of being safe and sure enough: now one wonders whether this reputation was deserved. The Persians, as we know ourselves, came from the ends of the earth and got as far as the Peloponnese before you were able to put a proper force into the field to meet them. The Athenians, unlike the Persians, live close to you, yet still you do not appear to notice them; instead of going out to meet them, you prefer to stand still and wait till you are attacked, thus hazarding everything by fighting with opponents who have grown far stronger than they were originally.

'In fact you know that the chief reason for the failure of the Persian invasion was the mistaken policy of the Persians themselves; and you know, too, that there have been many occasions when, if we managed to stand up to Athenian aggression, it was more because of Athenian mistakes than because of any help we got from you. Indeed, we can think of instances already where those who have relied on you and remained unprepared have been ruined by the confidence they placed in you.

'We should not like any of you to think that we are speaking in an unfriendly spirit. We are only remonstrating with you, as is natural when one's friends are making mistakes. Real accusations must be kept for one's enemies who have actually done one harm.

'Then also we think we have as much right as anyone else to point out faults in our neighbours, especially when we consider the enormous difference between you and the Athenians. To our minds, you are quite unaware of this difference; you have never yet tried to imagine what sort of people these Athenians are against whom you will have to fight—how much, indeed how completely different from you. An Athenian is always an innovator, quick to form a resolution and quick at carrying it out. You, on the other hand, are good at keeping things as they are; you never originate an idea, and your action tends to stop short of its aim. Then again, Athenian daring will outrun its own resources; they will take risks against their better judgement, and still, in the midst of danger, remain confident. But your nature is always to do less than you could have done, to mistrust your own judgement, however sound it may be, and to assume that dangers will last for ever (*sic*). Think of this, too: while you are hanging back, they never hesitate; while you stay at home, they are always abroad; for they think that the farther they go the more they will get, while you think that any movement may endanger what you have already. If they win a victory, they follow it up at once, and if they suffer a defeat, they scarcely fall back at all. As for their bodies, they regard them as expendable for their city's sake, as though they were not their own; but each man cultivates his own intelligence, again with a view to doing something notable for his city. If they aim at something and do not get it, they think that they have been deprived of what belonged to them already; whereas, if their enterprise is successful, they regard that success as nothing compared to what they will do next. Suppose they fail in some undertaking; they make good the loss immediately by setting their hopes in some other direction. Of them alone it may be said that they possess a thing almost as soon as they have begun to desire it, so quickly with them does action follow upon decision. And so they go on working away in hardship and danger all the days of their lives, seldom enjoying their possessions because they are always adding to them. Their view of a holiday is to do what needs doing; they prefer hardship and activity to peace and quiet. In a word, they are by nature incapable of either living a quiet life themselves or of allowing anyone else to do so.

'That is the character of the city which is opposed to you. Yet you still hang back; you will not see that the likeliest way of securing peace is this: only to use one's power in the cause of justice, but to make it perfectly plain that one is resolved not to tolerate aggression. On the contrary, your idea of proper behaviour is, firstly, to avoid harming others, and then to avoid being harmed yourselves, even if it is a matter of defending your own interests. Even if you had on your frontiers a power holding the same principles as you do, it is hard to see how such a policy could have been a success. But at the present time, as we have just pointed out to you, your whole way of life is out of date when compared with theirs. And it is just as true in politics as it is in any art or craft: new methods must drive out old ones. When a city can live in peace and quiet, no doubt the old-established ways are best: but when one is constantly being faced by new problems, one has also to be capable of approaching them in an original way. Thus Athens, because of the very variety of her experience, is a far more modern state than you are.

'Your inactivity has done harm enough. Now let there be an end of it. Give your allies, and especially Potidaea, the help you promised, and invade Attica at once. Do not let your friends and kinsmen fall into the hands of the bitter enemies. Do not force the rest of us in despair to join a different alliance. If we did so, no one could rightly blame us—neither the gods who witnessed our oaths nor any man capable of appreciating our situation. The people who break a treaty of alliance are the ones who fail to give the help they swore to give, not those who have to look elsewhere because they have been left in the lurch. But if you will only make up your minds to act, we will stand by you. It would be an unnatural thing for us to make a change, nor could we find other allies with whom we have such close bonds. You have heard what we have to say. Think carefully over your decision. From your fathers was handed down to you the leadership of the Peloponnese. Maintain its greatness.'

This was the speech of the Corinthians. There happened to be already in Sparta some Athenian representatives who had come there on other business. When they heard the speeches that had been made, they decided that they, too, ought to claim a hearing. Not that they had any intention of defending themselves against any of the charges that had been made against Athens by the various cities, but they wished to make a general statement and to point out that this was an affair which needed further consideration and ought not to be decided upon at once. They wanted also to make clear how powerful their city was, to remind the elder members of the assembly of facts that were known to them, and to inform the younger ones of matters in which they were ignorant. In this way they hoped to divert their audience from the idea of war and make them incline towards letting matters rest. They therefore approached the Spartans and said that, if there was no objection, they, too, would like to make a speech before the assembly. The Spartans invited them to do so, and they came forward and, spoke as follows:

'This delegation of ours did not come here to enter into a controversy with your allies, but to deal with the business on which our city sent us. We observe, however, that extraordinary attacks have been made on us, and so we have come forward to speak. We shall make no reply to the charges which these cities have made against us. Your assembly is not a court of law, competent to listen to pleas either from them or from us. Our aim is to prevent you from coming to the wrong decision on a matter of great importance through paying too much attention to the views of your allies. At the same time we should like to examine the general principles of the argument used against us and to make you see that our gains have been reasonable enough and that our city is one that deserves a certain consideration.

'There is no need to talk about what happened long ago: there our evidence would be that of hear say rather than that of eyewitnesses amongst our audience. But we must refer to the Persian War, to events well known to you all, even though you may be tired of constantly hearing the story. In our actions at that time we ventured everything for the common good; you have your share in what was gained; do not deprive us of all our share of glory and of the good that it may do us. We shall not be speaking in the spirit of one who is asking a favour, but of one who is producing evidence. Our aim is to show you what sort of a city you will have to fight against, if you make the wrong decision.

'This is our record. At Marathon we stood out against the Persians and faced them single-handed.[4] In the later invasion, when we were unable to meet the enemy on land, we and all our people took to our ships, and joined in the battle at Salamis. It was this battle that prevented the Persians from sailing against the Peloponnese and destroying the cities one by one; for no system of mutual defence could have been organized in face of the Persian naval superiority. The best proof of this is in the conduct of the Persians themselves. Once they had lost the battle at sea they realized that their force was crippled and they immediately withdrew most of their army. That, then was the result, and it proved that the fate of Hellas depended on her navy. Now, we contributed to this result in three important ways: we produced most of the ships, we provided the most intelligent of the generals, and we displayed the most unflinching courage. Out of the 400 ships, nearly two-thirds were ours: the commander was Themistocles, who was mainly responsible for the battle being fought in the straits, and this, obviously, was what saved us. You yourselves in fact, because of this, treated him with more distinction than you have ever treated any visitor from abroad. And the courage, the daring that wes howed were without parallel. With no help coming to us by land, with all the states up to our frontier already enslaved, we chose to abandon our city and to sacrifice our property; then, so far from deserting the rest of our allies in the common cause or making ourselves useless to them by dispersing our forces, we took to our ships and chose the path of danger, with no grudges against you for not having come to our help earlier. So it is that we can claim to have given more than we received. There were still people living in the cities which you left behind you, and you were fighting to preserve them; when you sent out your forces you feared for yourselves much more than for us (at all events, you never put in an appearance until we had lost everything). Behind us, on the other hand, was a city that had ceased to exist; yet we still went forward and ventured our lives for this city that seemed so impossible to recover. Thus we joined you and helped to save not only ourselves but you also. But if we, like others, had been frightened about our land and had made terms with the Persians before you arrived, or if, later, we had regarded ourselves as irretrievably ruined and had lacked the courage to take to our ships, then there would no longer have been any point in your fighting the enemy at sea, since you would not have had enough ships. Instead things would have gone easily and quietly just as the Persians wished.

'Surely, Spartans, the courage, the resolution, and the ability which we showed then ought not to be repaid by such immoderate hostility from the Hellenes—especially so far as our empire is concerned. We did not gain this empire by force. It came to us at a time when you were unwilling to fight on to the end against the Persians. At this time our allies came to us of their own accord and begged us to lead them. It was the actual course of events which first compelled us to increase our power to its present extent: fear of Persia was our chief motive, though afterwards we thought, too, of our own honour and our own interest. Finally there came a time when we were surrounded by enemies, when we had already crushed some revolts, when you had lost the friendly feelings that you used to have for us and had turned against us and begun to arouse our suspicion: at this point it was clearly no longer safe for us to risk letting our empire go, especially as any allies that left us would, go over to you. And when tremendous dangers are involved no one can be blamed for looking to his own interest.

'Certainly you Spartans, in your leadership of the Peloponnese, have arranged the affairs of the various states so as to suit yourselves. And if, in the years of which we were speaking, you had gone on taking an active part in the war and had become unpopular, as we did, in the course of exercising your leadership, we have little doubt that you would have been just as hard upon your allies as we were, and that you would have been forced either to govern strongly or to endanger your own security.

'So it is with us. We have done nothing extraordinary, nothing contrary to human nature in accepting an empire when it was offered to us and then in refusing to give it up. Three very powerful motives prevent us from doing so—security, honour, and self interest. And we were not the first to act in this way. Far from it. It has always been a rule that the weak should be subject to the strong; and besides, we consider that we are worthy of our power. Up till the present moment you, too, used to think that we were; but now, after calculating your own interest, you are beginning to talk in terms of right and wrong. Considerations of this kind have never yet turned people aside from the opportunities of aggrandizement offered by superior strength. Those who really deserve praise are the people who, while human enough to enjoy power, nevertheless pay more attention to justice than they are compelled to do by their situation. Certainly we think that if anyone else was in our position it would soon be evident whether we act with moderation or not. Yet, unreasonably enough, our very consideration for others has brought us more blame than praise. For example, in law-suits with our allies arising out of contracts we have put ourselves at a disadvantage, and when we arrange to have such cases tried by impartial courts in Athens, people merely say that we are over fond of going to law. No one bothers to inquire why this reproach is not made against other imperial Powers, who treat their subjects much more harshly than we do: the fact being, of course, that where force can be used there is no need to bring in the law. Our subjects, on the other hand, are used to being treated as equals; consequently, when they are disappointed in what they think right and suffer even the smallest disadvantage because of a judgement in our courts or because of the power that our empire gives us, they cease to feel grateful to us for all the advantages which we have left to them: indeed, they feel more bitterly over this slight disparity than they would feel if we, from the first, had set the law aside and had openly enriched ourselves at their expense. Under those conditions they would certainly not have disputed the fact that the weak must give in to the strong. People, in fact, seem to feel more strongly about their legal wrongs than about the wrongs inflicted on them by violence. In the first case they think they are being outdone by an equal, in the second case that they are being compelled by a superior. Certainly they put up with much worse sufferings than these when they were under the Persians, but now they think that our government is oppressive. That is natural enough, perhaps, since subject peoples always find the present time most hard to bear. But on one point we are quite certain: if you were to destroy us and to take over our empire, you would soon lose all the goodwill which you have gained because of others being afraid of us—that is, if you are going to stick to those principles of behaviour which you showed before, in the short time when you led Hellas against the Persians. Your own regulated ways of life do not mix well with the ways of others. Also it is a fact that when one of you goes abroad he follows neither his own rules nor those of the rest of Hellas.

'Take time, then, over your decision, which is an important one. Do not allow considerations of other people's opinions and other people's complaints to involve you in difficulties which you will feel yourselves. Think, too, of the great part that is played by the unpredictable in war: think of it now, before you are actually committed to war. The longer a war lasts, the more things tend to depend on accidents. Neither you nor we can see into them: we have to abide their outcome in the dark. And when people are entering upon a war they do things the wrong way round. Action comes first, and it is only when they have already suffered that they begin to think. We, however, are still far removed from such a mistaken attitude; so, to the best of our belief, are you. And so we urge you, now, while we are both still free to make sensible decisions, do not break the peace, do not go back upon your oaths; instead let us settle our differences by arbitration, as is laid down in the treaty. If you will not do so, we shall have as our witnesses the gods who heard our oaths. You will have begun the war, and we shall attempt to meet you in any and every field of action that you may choose.'

The Athenians spoke as I have described. Now the Spartans had heard the complaints made by their allies against Athens and also the Athenian reply. They therefore requested all outsiders to leave and discussed the situation among themselves. Most people's views tended to the same conclusion—namely, that Athens was already acting aggressively and that war should be declared without delay. However, the Spartan King Archidamus, a man who had a reputation for both intelligence and moderation, came forward and made the following speech:

'Spartans, in the course of my life I have taken part in many wars, and I see among you people of the same age as I am. They and I have had experience, and so are not likely to share in what may be a general enthusiasm for war, nor to think that war is a good thing or a safe thing. And you will find, if you look carefully into the matter, that this present war which you are now discussing is not likely to be anything on a small scale. When we are engaged with Peloponnesians and neighbours, the forces on both sides are of the same type, and we can strike rapidly where we wish to strike. With Athens it is different. Here we shall be engaged with people who live far off, people also who have the widest experience of the sea and who are extremely well equipped in all other directions, very wealthy both as individuals and as a state, with ships and cavalry and hoplites, with a population bigger than that of any other place in Hellas, and then, too, with numbers of allies who pay tribute to them.[5] How, then, can we irresponsibly start a war with such a people? What have we to rely upon if we rush into it unprepared? Our navy? It is inferior to theirs, and if we are to give proper attention to it and build it up to their strength, that will take time. Or are we relying on our wealth? Here we are at an even greater disadvantage: we have no public funds, and it is no easy matter to secure contributions from private sources. Perhaps there is ground for confidence in the superiority which we have in heavy infantry and in actual numbers, assets which will enable us to invade and devastate their land. Athens, however, controls plenty of land outside Attica and can import what she wants by sea. And if we try to make her allies revolt from her, we shall have to support them with a fleet, since most of them are on the islands. What sort of war, then, are we going to fight? If we can neither defeat them at sea nor take away from them the resources on which their navy depends, we shall do ourselves more harm than good. We shall then find that we can no longer even make an honourable peace, especially if it is thought that it was we who began the quarrel. For we must not bolster ourselves up with the false hope that if we devastate their land, the war will soon be over. I fear that it is more likely that we shall be leaving it to our children after us. So convinced am I that the Athenians have too much pride to become the slaves of their own land, or to shrink back from warfare as though they were inexperienced in it.

'Not that I am suggesting that we should calmly allow them to injure our allies and should turn a blind eye to their machinations. What I do suggest is that we should not take up arms at the present moment; instead we should send to them and put our grievances before them; we should not threaten war too openly, though at the same time we should make it clear that we are not going to let them have their own way. In the meantime we should be making our own preparations by winning over new allies both among Hellenes and among foreigners—from any quarter, in fact, where we can increase our naval and financial resources. No one can blame us for securing our own safety by taking foreigners as well as Greeks into our alliance when we are, as is the fact, having our position undermined by the Athenians. At the same time we must put our own affairs in order. If they pay attention to our diplomatic protests, so much the better. If they do not, then, after two or three years have passed, we shall be in a much sounder position and can attack them, if we decide to do so. And perhaps when they see that our actual strength is keeping pace with the language that we use, they will be more inclined to give way, since their land will still be untouched and, in making up their minds, they will be thinking of advantages which they still possess and which have not yet been destroyed. For you must think of their land as though it was a hostage in your possession, and all the more valuable the better it is looked after. You should spare it up to the last possible moment, and avoid driving them to a state of desperation in which you will find them much harder to deal with. If now in our present state of unpreparedness we lay their land waste, hurried into this course by the complaints of our allies, I warn you to take care that our action does not bring to the Peloponnese still more shame and still greater difficulties. As for complaints, whether they come from cities or from private individuals, they are capable of arrangement; but when war is declared by our whole confederacy for the sake of the interests of some of us, and when it is impossible to foresee the course that the war will take, then an honourable settlement is not an easy thing at all.

'Let no one call it cowardice if we, in all our numbers, hesitate before attacking a single city. They have just as many allies as we have, and their allies pay tribute. And war is not so much a matter of armaments as of the money which makes armaments effective: particularly is this true in a war fought between a land power and a sea power. So let us first of all see to our finances and, until we have done so, avoid being swept away by speeches from our allies. It is we who shall bear most of the responsibility for what happens later, whether it is good or bad; we should therefore be allowed the time to look into some of these possibilities at our leisure.

'As for being slow and cautious—which is the usual criticism made against us—there is nothing to be ashamed of in that. If you take something on before you are ready for it, hurry at the beginning will mean delay at the end. Besides, the city in which we live has always been free and always famous. "Slow" and "cautious" can equally well be "wise" and "sensible". Certainly it is because we possess these qualities that we are the only people who do not become arrogant when we are successful, and who in times of stress are less likely to give in than others. We are not carried away by the pleasure of hearing ourselves praised when people are urging us towards dangers that seem to us unnecessary; and we are no more likely to give in shamefacedly to other people's views when they try to spur us on by their accusations. Because of our well ordered life we are both brave in war and wise in council. Brave, because self-control is based upon a sense of honour, and honour is based on courage. And we are wise because we are not so highly educated as to look down upon our laws and customs, and are too rigorously trained in self-control to be able to disobey them. We are trained to avoid being too clever in matters that are of no use— such as being able to produce an excellent theoretical criticism of one's enemies' dispositions, and then failing in practice to do quite so well against them. Instead we are taught that there is not a great deal of difference between the way we think and the way others think, and that it is impossible to calculate accurately events that are determined by chance. The practical measures that we take are always based on the assumption that our enemies are not unintelligent. And it is right and proper for us to put our hopes in the reliability of our own precautions rather than in the possibility of our opponent making mistakes. There is no need to suppose that human beings differ very much one from another: but it is true, that the ones who come out on top are the ones who have been trained in the hardest school.

'Let us never give up this discipline which our fathers have handed down to us and which we still preserve and which has always done us good. Let us not be hurried, and in one short day's space come to a decision which will so profoundly affect the lives of men and their fortunes, the fates of cities and their national honour. We ought to take time over such a decision. And we, more than others, can afford to take time, because we are strong. As for the Athenians, I advise sending a mission to them about Potidaea and also about the other cases where our allies claim to have been ill treated. Especially is this the right thing to do since the Athenians themselves are prepared to submit to arbitration, and when one party offers this it is quite illegal to attack him first as though he was definitely in the wrong. And at the same time carry on your preparations for war. This decision is the best one you can make for yourselves, and is also the one most likely to inspire fear in your enemies.'

After this speech of Archidamus, Sthenelaidas, one of the ephors of that year, came forward to make the final speech, which was as follows:

'I do not understand these long speeches which the Athenians make. Though they said a great deal in praise of themselves, they made no attempt to contradict the fact that they are acting aggressively against our allies and against the Peloponnese. And surely, if it is the fact that they had a good record in the past against the Persians and now have a bad record as regards us, then they deserve to pay double for it, since, though they were once good, they have now turned out bad. We are the same then and now, and if we are sensible, we shall not allow any aggression against our allies and shall not wait before we come to their help. They are no longer waiting before being ill treated. Others may have a lot of money and ships and horses, but we have good allies, and we ought not to betray them to the Athenians. And this is not a matter to be settled by law-suits and by words: it is not because of words that our own interests are suffering. Instead we should come to the help of our allies quickly and with all our might. And let no one try to tell us that when we are being attacked we should sit down and discuss matters; these long discussions are rather for those who are meditating aggression themselves. Therefore, Spartans, cast your votes for the honour of Sparta and for war! Do not allow the Athenians to grow still stronger! Do not entirely betray your allies! Instead let us, with the help of heaven, go forward to meet the aggressor!'

After this speech he himself, in his capacity of ephor, put the question to the Spartan assembly. They make their decisions by acclamation, not by voting, and Sthenelaidas said at first that he could not decide on which side the acclamations were the louder. This was because he wanted to make them show their opinions openly and so make them all the more enthusiastic for war. He therefore said: 'Spartans, those of you who think that the treaty has been broken and that the Athenians are aggressors, get up and stand on one side. Those who do not think so, stand on the other side,' and he pointed out to them where they were to stand. They then rose to their feet and separated into two divisions. The great majority were of the opinion that the treaty had been broken.

They then summoned their allies to the assembly and told them that they had decided that Athens was acting aggressively, but that they wanted to have all their allies with them when they put the vote, so that, if they decided to make war, it should be done on the basis of a unanimous resolution.

Afterwards the allied delegates, having got their own way, returned home. Later the Athenian representatives, when they had finished the business for which they had come, also returned. This decision of the assembly that the treaty had been broken took place in the fourteenth year of the thirty years' truce which was made after the affair of Euboea. The Spartans voted that the treaty had been broken and that war should be declared not so much because they were influenced by the speeches of their allies as because they were afraid of the further growth of Athenian power, seeing, as, they did, that already the greater part of Hellas was under the control of Athens.

SUMMARY

Thucydides portrays the multiple, interwoven, contradictory reasons nations (or other groups) go to war. The Corinthians appeal to duty, honor, moral right, loyalty, and freedom from aggression among others. The Athenians mention fear, honor, and self-interest, status, obligation, prestige, and economics. King Archidamus warns against hasty decisions and emphasizes the consequences of war and Sthenelaidas argues that some things are not settled by law suits and words, but by blood.

Like last lesson, timeless elements known as "the nature of war" stand out, including, political objectives, a clash of wills, violence, fog, friction, and chance. Yet, every war is unique. The Spartan decision to go to war and the Athenian will to resist will lead to one of the greatest struggles of all time. And, Thucydides will certainly prove in his narrative the truth of the observation: "The longer a war lasts, the more things tend to depend on accidents."

NOTES

1. For the purpose of this course, consider this unofficial guidance: When pronouncing Greek names, simply pronounce every syllable literally, but donot worry about it.
2. Thucydides, *History of the Peloponnesian War*, trans. Rex Warner (New York: Penguin Classics, 1954), 72-87. Please note Professor Rex Warner's translation features British spellings and punctuation standards throughout.
3. Following the defeat of the Persians in 479 BCE, the Athenians rebuilt the city of Athens and linked the city and the port of Piraeus, the base of Athenian commerce and naval power, with defensive walls spanning about

five miles. Robert B. Strassler, ed., *The Landmark Thucydides: A Comprehensive Guide to the Peloponnesian War* (New York: Touchstone, 1996), 39, 49, 58.

4. The Athenians defeated the first Persian invasion of Greece at the Battle of Marathon, 490 BCE. A messenger, Philippides (or Pheidippides), announced the victory in Athens after running from the battlefield; commemorated today by the race of the same name. Charlie Lovett, *A Centennial history of the Games' Most Storied Race* (Westport, CT: Greenwood Press, 1997) as excerpted by http://www.marathonguide.com/history/olympicmarathons/prologue.cfm (Accessed 6 Jun 2012).

5. A "hoplite" referred to the heavy infantryman of ancient Greece equipped with a bronze helmet, armor, spear, sword, and a round shield known as a *hoplon.* Robert L. O' Connell, *Of Arms and Men: A History of War, Weapons, and Aggression* (New York and Oxford: Oxford University Press, 1989), 50.

DECEPTION, SPEED, AND STRATEGY—THE ART OF WAR

Sun Tzu

Sun Tzu assumes a special place in military theory as the only classic Chinese military text known to most Westerners. Like Clausewitz and Thucydides, Sun Tzu provides pithy, quotable statements that contain genuine pearls of wisdom.[1] Scholars disagree over whether Sun Tzu ("Master Sun") actually constitutes a historical figure (sometimes named Sun Wu, Sun Zi, or other transliterations, who lived between 500 and 200 BCE) or simply a body of knowledge (i.e. the *Sun Tzu* represents observations of a series of scholars assembled over time), but General Tao Hanshang's modern Chinese interpretation treats Sun Tzu as a real person.[2] Again, like Machiavelli of Renaissance Italy, Sun Tzu writes as a learned advisor to a ruler. Translations of Sun Tzu vary widely, but readers will like his brevity, simplicity, and wisdom.[3] Of the classic writers studied in this book, Sun Tzu best articulates the relationship of war, strategy, and economics. Many readers try to use Sun Tzu to contrast Clausewitz in an Eastern vs. Western view of war. Although there is some merit to this as an intellectual exercise, closer examination finds this approach lacking. Sun Tzu complements, rather than contrasts, other classic Western military thinkers. To some readers, Sun Tzu's tendency to present numbered lists (i.e. the five calculations for victory) suggests a formulaic, simplistic approach to warfare, but closer examination reveals unspoken subtle ties and difficulties in attaining his famous aphorisms.

Viewed as a whole, classic military thinkers stimulate our thinking on war, politics, power, strategy, and other topics. Changes in time, technology, and other circumstances limit the "classics" as practical tools for policy makers, but few thinkers would suggest such a use. Instead, understanding classic theory unlocks the mind, raises timeless questions, and begins the process of how to wrestle with war aims, political uncertainties, moral dilemmas, and other real world concerns.

Although General Tao Hanzhang's translation proves the most readable for students, there is a significant text note for the reader. On page 22, the Hanzhang translation states: "The first of these is *politics*, . . . *Politics* means the thing which causes the people to be in harmony with their ruler . . . ." On the other hand, Samuel Griffith translates the same passage: "The first of these is *moral influence* . . . By *moral influence* I mean that which causes the people to be in harmony with their leaders...." Ralph Sawyer uses the word *Tao* (which means "the Way")... "the *Tao* causes the people to be fully in accord with their ruler." Brian Bruya and Tsai Chih Chung also use the *Dao*... "Establishing a moral cause means that there must be a common conviction shared by the both the people and the government." [Italics added in each case.] There is a difference between the word "politics" and the term "Tao" (or Dao) or "moral influence" used by the other translations. Perhaps it is a subtle difference, but the Tao implies a moral, philosophical or spiritual dimension missing from "politics." Although "politics" fits this book and compares to Clausewitz, the "moral influence" or "Tao" concept better captures Sun Tzu's association of harmony between the people and ruler.[4]

* * * *

CHAPTER 1 ESTIMATES

War is a matter of vital importance to the state; a matter of life and death, the road either to survival or to ruin. Hence, it is imperative that it be studied thoroughly.

Therefore, appraise it in terms of the five fundamental factors and make comparisons of the various conditions of the antagonistic sides in order to ascertain the results of a war. The first of these factors is politics; the second, weather; the third, terrain; the fourth, the commander; and the fifth, doctrine. Politics means the thing which causes the people to be in harmony with their ruler so that they will follow him in disregard of their lives and without fear of any danger. Weather signifies night and day, cold and heat, fine days and rain, and change of seasons. Terrain means distances, and refers to whether the ground is traversed with ease or difficulty and to whether it is open or constricted, and influences your chances of life of death. The commander stands for the general's qualities of wisdom, sincerity, benevolence, courage, and strictness. Doctrine is to be understood as the organization of the army, the graduations of rank among the officers, the regulation of supply routes, and the provision of military materials to the army.

These five fundamental factors are familiar to every general. Those who master them win; those who do not are defeated. Therefore, in laying plans, compare the following seven elements, appraising them with the utmost care.

1. Which ruler is wise and more able?
2. Which commander is more talented?
3. Which army obtains the advantages of nature and the terrain?
4. In which army are regulations and instructions better carried out?
5. Which troops are stronger?
6. Which army has the better-trained officers and men?

7. Which army administers rewards and punishments in a more enlightened and correct way?

By means of these seven elements, I shall be able to forecast which side will be victorious and which will be defeated.

The general who heeds my counsel is sure to win. Such a general should be retained in command. One who ignores my counsel is certain to be defeated. Such a one should be dismissed.

Having paid attention to my counsel and plans, the general must create a situation which will contribute to their accomplishment. By "situation" I mean he should take the field situation into consideration and act in accordance with what is advantageous.

All warfare is based on deception. Therefore, when capable of attacking, feign incapacity; when active in moving troops, feign inactivity. When near the enemy, make it seem that you are far away; when far away, make it seem that you are near. Hold out baits to lure the enemy. Strike the enemy when he is in disorder. Prepare against the enemy when he is secure at all points. Avoid the enemy for the time being when he is stronger. If your opponent is of choleric temper, try to irritate him. If he is arrogant, try to encourage his egotism. If the enemy troops are well prepared after reorganization, try to wear them down. If they are united, try to sow dissension among them. Attack the enemy where he is unprepared, and appear where you are not expected. These are the keys to victory for a strategist. It is not possible to formulate them in detail beforehand.

Now, if the estimates made before a battle indicate victory, it is because careful calculations show that your conditions are more favorable than those of the enemy; if they indicate defeat, it is because careful calculations show that favorable conditions for battle are fewer. With more careful calculations, one can win; with less, one cannot. How much less chance of victory has one who makes no calculations at all! By this means, one can foresee the outcome of battle.

CHAPTER 2 WAGING WAR

. . . A speedy victory is the main object in war. If this is long in coming, weapons are blunted and morale depressed. If troops are attacking cities, their strength will be exhausted. When the army engages in protracted campaigns, the resources of the state will fall short. When your weapons are dulled and ardor dampened, your strength exhausted and treasure spent, the chief tains of the neighboring states will take advantage of your crisis to act. In that case, no man, however wise, will be able to avert the disastrous consequences that ensue. Thus, while we have heard of stupid haste in war, we have not yet seen a clever operation that was prolonged. For there has never been a protracted war which benefited a country. Therefore, those unable to understand the evils inherent in employing troops are equally unable to understand the advantageous ways of doing so.

Those adept in waging war do not require a second levy of conscripts or more than two provisioning. They carry military equipment from the homeland, but rely on the enemy for provisions. Thus, the army is plentifully provided with food.

When a country is impoverished by military operations, it is due to distant transportation; carrying supplies for great distances renders the people destitute. Where troops are gathered, prices go up. When prices rise, the wealth of the people is drained away. When wealth is drained away, the people will be afflicted with urgent and heavy exactions. With this loss of wealth and exhaustion of strength, the households in the country will be extremely poor and seven-tenths of their wealth is dissipated....

Hence, a wise general sees to it that his troops feed on the enemy,....

In order to make the solders courageous in overcoming the enemy, they must be roused to anger. In order to capture more booty from the enemy, soldiers must have their rewards....Treat the prisoners of war well, and care for them. This is called "winning a battle and becoming stronger."

Hence, what is valued in war is victory, not prolonged operations. And the general who understands how to employ troops is the minister of the people's fate and arbiter of the nation's destiny.

CHAPTER 3 OFFENSIVE STRATEGY

Generally, in war the best policy is to take a state intact; to ruin it is inferior to this. To capture the enemy's entire army is better than to destroy it;...For to win one hundred victories in one hundred battles is not the acme of skill. To subdue the enemy without fighting is the supreme excellence.

Thus, what is of supreme importance in war is to attack the enemy's strategy. Next best is to disrupt his alliances by diplomacy. The next best is to attack his army. And the worst policy is to attack cities. Attack cities only when there is no alternative because to... make ready the necessary arms and equipment require at least three months, and to pile up earthen ramps against walls requires an additional three months. The general, unable to control his impatience, will order his troops to swarm up the wall like ants, with the result that one-third of them will be killed without taking the city. Such is the calamity of attacking cities.

Thus, those skilled in war subdue the enemy's army without battle. They capture the enemy's cities without assaulting them and overthrow his state without protracted operations. Their aim is to take all under heaven intact by strategic considerations. Thus, their troops are not worn out and their gains will be complete. This is the art of offensive strategy.

Consequently, the art of using troops is this: When ten to the enemy's one, surround him. When five times his strength, attack him. If double his strength, divide him. If equally matched, you may engage him with some good plan. If weaker numerically, be capable of withdrawing.

And if in all respects unequal, be capable of eluding him, for a small force is but booty for one more powerful if it fights recklessly.

Now, the general is the assistant to the sovereign of the state. If this assistance is all-embracing, the state will surely be strong; if defective, the state will certainly be weak.

Now, there are three ways in which a sovereign can bring misfortune upon his army:

1. When ignorant that the army should not advance, to order an advance; or when ignorant that it should not retire, to order a retirement. This is described as "hobbling the army."
2. When ignorant of military affairs, to interfere in their administration. This causes officers to be perplexed.
3. When ignorant of command problems, to interfere with the direction of fighting. This engenders doubts in the minds of the officers.

If the army is confused and suspicious, neighboring rulers will take advantage of this and cause trouble....

Thus, there are five points in which victory may be predicted:

1. He who knows when he can fight and when he cannot will be victorious.
2. He who understands how to fight in accordance with the strength of antagonistic forces will be victorious.
3. He whose ranks are united in purpose will be victorious.
4. He who is well prepared and lies in wait for an enemy who is not well prepared will be victorious.
5. He whose generals are able and not interfered with by the sovereign will be victorious.

It is in these five matters that the way to victory is known.

Therefore, I say: Know the enemy and know yourself; in a hundred battles, you will never be defeated. When you are ignorant of the enemy but know yourself, your chances of winning or losing are equal. If ignorant both of your enemy and of yourself, you are sure to be defeated in every battle.

CHAPTER 4 DISPOSITIONS

The skillful warriors in ancient times first made themselves invincible and awaited the enemy's moment of vulnerability. Invincibility depends on oneself, but the enemy's vulnerability on himself. It follows that those skilled in war can make themselves invincible but cannot cause an enemy to be certainly vulnerable. Therefore, it can be said that, one may know how to win, but cannot necessarily do so.

Defend yourself when you cannot defeat the enemy, and attack the enemy when you can. One defends when his strength is inadequate; he attacks when it is abundant....

To foresee a victory which the ordinary man can foresee is not the acme of excellence. Neither is it if you triumph in battle and are universally acclaimed "expert,"...to distinguish between the sun and moon is no test of vision, to hear the thunderclap is no indication of acute hearing....Therefore, the skillful commander takes up a position in which he cannot be defeated and misses no opportunity to overcome his enemy. Thus, a victorious army always seeks battle after his plans indicate that victory is possible under them, whereas an army destined to defeat fights in the hope of winning, but without any planning. . . .

Now the elements of the art of war are first, the measurement of space; second the estimation of quantities; third, calculations; fourth, comparisons; and fifth, chances of victory. Measurements of space are derived from the ground. Quantities derive from measurement, figures from quantities, comparisons from figures, and victory from comparisons....

It is because of disposition that a victorious general is able to make his soldiers fight with the effect of pent-up waters which, suddenly released, plunge into a bottomless abyss.

CHAPTER 5 POSTURE OF AN ARMY

Generally, management of a large force is the same as management of a few men. It is a matter of organization. And to direct a large force is the same as to direct a few men. This is a matter of formations and signals. That the army is certain to sustain the enemy's attack without suffering defeat is due to operations of the extraordinary and the normal forces....

Generally, in battle, use the normal force to engage and use the extraordinary to win. Now, the resources of those skilled in the use of extraordinary forces are as infinite as the heavens and earth, as inexhaustible as the flow of the great rivers, for they end and recommence—cyclical, as are the movements of the sun and moon....The musical notes are only five in number, but their combination gives rise to so many melodies that one cannot hear them all. The primary colors are only five in number, but their combinations are so infinite that one cannot visualize them all....In battle, there are only the normal and extraordinary forces, but their combinations are limitless; none can comprehend them....

When torrential water tosses boulders, it is because of its momentum: when the strike of a hawk breaks the body of its prey, it is because of timing. Thus, the momentum of one skilled in war is overwhelming, and his attack precisely timed. His potential is that of a fully drawn crossbow; his timing, that of the release of the trigger.

In the tumult and uproar, the battle seems chaotic, but there must be no disorder in one's own troops. The battle field may seem in confusion and chaos, but one's array must be in good order. That will be proof against defeat. Apparent confusion is a product of good order; apparent cowardice, of courage; apparent weakness, of strength. Order or disorder depends on organization and direction; courage or cowardice on circumstances; strength or weakness on tactical dispositions. Thus, one who is skilled at making the enemy move does so by creating a situation, according to which the enemy will act....

Therefore, a skilled commander seeks victory from the situation and does not demand it of his subordinates. He selects suitable men and exploits the situation....Thus, the energy of troops skillfully commanded in battle may be compared to the momentum of round boulders which roll down from a mountain thousands of feet in height.

CHAPTER 6 VOID AND ACTUALITY

Generally, he who occupies the field of battle first and awaits his enemy is at ease, and he who comes later to the scene and rushes into the fight is weary. And, therefore, those skilled in war bring the enemy to the field of battle and are not brought there by him. One able to make the enemy come of his own accord does so by offering him some advantage. ...Thus, when the enemy is at ease be able to tire him, when well fed to starve him, when at rest to make him move.

Appear at places which he is unable to rescue; move swiftly in a direction where you are least expected....

...Therefore, against those skilled in attack, the enemy does not know where to defend, and against the experts in defense, the enemy does not know where to attack.

How subtle and insubstantial, that the expert leaves no trace. How divinely mysterious, that he is inaudible. Thus, he is master of his enemy's fate. His offensive will be irresistible if he makes for his enemy's weak positions; he cannot be overtaken when he withdraws if he moves swiftly....the enemy will be unable to attack me because I divert him from going where he wishes.

If I am able to determine the enemy's dispositions while, at the same time, I conceal my own, then I can concentrate my forces and his must be divided. And if I concentrate while he divides, I can use my entire strength to attack a fraction of his. Therefore, I will be numerically superior.... For if he does not know where I intend to give battle, he must prepare in a great many places. And when he prepares in a great many places, those I have to fight in will be few.... Numerical weakness comes from having to guard against possible attacks; numerical strength from forcing the enemy to make these preparations against us.

If one knows where and when a battle will be fought, his troops can march a thousand *li* and meet on the field. But if one knows neither the battleground nor the day of battle, the left will be unable to aid the right and the right will be unable to aid the left.... Thus, I say that victory can be achieved. For even if the enemy is numerically stronger, I can prevent him from engaging.

Therefore, analyze the enemy's plans so that you will know his shortcomings as well as strong points. Agitate him in order to ascertain the pattern of his movement. Lure him out to reveal his dispositions and ascertain his position. Launch a probing attack in order to learn where his strength is abundant and where deficient. The ultimate in disposing one's troops is to conceal them without ascertainable shape.... Therefore, when a victory is won, one's tactics are not repeated. One should always respond to circumstances in an infinite variety of ways.

Now, an army may be likened to water, for just as flowing water avoids the heights and hastens to the lowlands, so an army should avoid strength and strike weakness. And as water shapes its flow in accordance with the ground, so an army manages its victory in accordance with the situation of the enemy. And as water has no constant form, there are in warfare no constant conditions. Thus, one able to win the victory by modifying his tactics in accordance with the enemy situation may be said to be divine. . . .

SUMMARY

Sun Tzu's *Art of War* presents a host of political, economic, and social observations that describe the character and nature of war. Among the most famous and influential are the following:

- All warfare is based on deception.
- A speedy (or swift) victory is the main object of war.
- "For there has never been a prolonged war which benefited a country."
- "To subdue the enemy without fighting is the supreme excellence."
- Attack the enemy's strategy, alliances, army, and last, his cities.
- Know yourself and know your enemy.

Like Thucydides and Clausewitz, using Sun Tzu as book of pithy quotes actually has value, but limits the potential of this classic text. Better that the student uses the book as a spring board for comprehension and analysis. On the other hand, while scholars who lament reading Sun Tzu without a thorough understanding of the culture, history, and language of ancient China have an important point, even reading a simple translation enhances understanding of fundamental concepts of war and strategy. In today's interconnected, media-saturated, information-focused world, even junior officers face decisions with strategic consequences (hence the phrase, the "strategic lieutenant"). Consequently, today's airman must be able to think at a strategic level and grasp the essentials of war and strategy.

NOTES

1. Although most Western scholars have adopted "Sun Zi" as the most appropriate translation in accordance with the *pinyin* transliteration system, the traditional and most common translation, "Sun Tzu," is used by Yuan Shibing, the translator of General Tao Hanzhang's *Sun Tzu's Art of War: The Modern Chinese Translation*. To avoid student confusion, "Sun Tzu" will be used for this course.

2. In 2009 the National Defense University sponsored a "Teaching Sun Zi" conference where the consensus of American scholars present agreed that *The Art of War* represented the thoughts of a number of different scholars that evolved over time. This contrasts the current Chinese interpretation that stresses Sun Zi as a historical person. Like most things, politics enters this realm. Some in today's China view Western debates over the authenticity of Sun Zi/Sun Tzu as an attempt to rob China of a national hero and to cast doubt on China's historical greatness. Regardless of these issues, our text treats Sun Tzu as a person. Also, the Hanshang text uses the Wade-Giles transliteration of Sun Tzu vs. the Sun Zi of the *pin yin* system.

3. There are 251 editions of Sun Tzu's writings. In addition to this recent Chinese interpretation, the editor recommends Roger T. Ames' *Sun Tzu: The Art of Warfare*, Ralph Sawyer's *Sun Tzu: The Art of War*, and Samuel B. Griffith's *Sun Tzu: The Art of War* as the most readable scholarly versions , as well as a student favorite, Tsai Chih Chung's (translated by Brian Bruya) *Sunzi Speaks: The Art of War*, which is a "comic book" version produced by a respected Taiwanese political cartoonist.

4. Sun Tzu, *The Art of War*, trans. Samuel B. Griffith, paper ed. (London: Oxford University Press, 1977), 63-64; Sun Tzu. *The Art of War*, trans. Ralph D. Sawyer (Boulder, Co.: Westview Press, 1994), 167; Sunzi, *Sunzi Speaks: The Art of War*, adapted Tsai Chih Chung, trans. Brian Bruya (New York: Doubleday, Anchor, 1994), 24-25.

MANEUVER, ALLIANCES, AND CHARACTER: SUN TZU'S INFLUENCE

Sun Tzu

Does the latter half of Sun Tzu's *The Art of War* still apply today? Students will wrestle with this question when reading chapters 7-13. Are there valuable insights in his tactical observations? How can Air Force strategic thinkers benefit from Sun Tzu's ideas? Should an air, space, or cyberspace warrior care about terrain, weather, hunger, or thirst? Does today's Air Force strategist need to understand alliances, morale, or a commander's character? Interested students may wish to explore Ralph Sawyer's explanation of war and politics during Sun Tzu's time. In another recent edition of the *Art of War*, both Roger T. Ames and Ralph Peters provide valuable commentaries: Ames is more historical in focus, while Peters addresses contemporary application.[1]

There is a reason why Sun Tzu's thoughts have endured over two thousand years. Although some aspects seem dated, students will discern the relative strengths and weaknesses of this classic work by reading significant excerpts of the text. They will see the value of Sun Tzu's method of inquiry, as well as his astute observations, that suggest a similar approach to today's problems. Although students might not have time now, they should examine the classics in the various editions available. Many non-Chinese speaking students will gain insights by reading the same passage in different translations. Also, students will discover insights as they gain experience in life. Certain passages will mean nothing to a twenty year-old, but may seem profound a decade or two later. In other words, reading military classics (Sun Tzu in this case) plants the seed for lifelong strategic learning. By providing an overview to Sun Tzu and reading the text, we hope to inspire lifelong intellectual development.

CHAPTER 7 MANEUVERING

Normally, in war, the general receives his commands from the sovereign. During the process from assembling the troops and mobilizing the people to blending the army into a harmonious entity and encamping it, nothing is more difficult than the art of maneuvering for advantageous positions. What is difficult about it is to make the devious route the most direct and to turn disadvantage to advantage. Thus, march by an indirect route and divert the enemy by enticing him with a bait. So doing, you may set out after he does and arrive at the battlefield before him. One able to do this shows the knowledge of the artifice of diversion.

Therefore, both advantage and danger are inherent in maneuvering for an advantageous position. One who sets the entire army in motion with impediments to pursue an advantageous position will not attain it. If he abandons the camp and all the impediments to contend for advantage, the stores will be lost. Thus, if one orders his men to make forced marches without armor, stopping neither day or night, covering double the usual distance at a stretch, ... it is possible that the commander will be captured. The stronger men will arrive first and the feeble ones will struggle along behind; so, if this method is used, only one-tenth of the army will reach its destination. ... It follows that an army which lacks heavy equipment, fodder, food, and stores will be lost.

One who is not acquainted with the designs of his neighbors should not enter into alliances with them. Those who do not know the conditions of the mountains and forests, hazardous defiles, marshes and swamps, cannot conduct the march of an army. Those who do not use local guides are unable to obtain the advantages of ground. Now, war is based on deception. Move when it is advantageous and create changes in the situation by dispersal and concentration of forces. When campaigning, be swift as the wind; in leisurely marching, majestic as the forest; in raiding and plundering, be fierce as fire; in standing, firm as the mountains. ... Weigh the situation before you move. He who knows the artifice of diversion will be victorious. Such is the art of maneuvering.

... As the voice cannot be heard in battle, drums and gongs are used. As troops cannot see each other clearly in battle, flags and banners are used to unify the action of the troops. When the troops can be thus united, the brave cannot advance alone, nor can the cowardly withdraw. This is the art of directing large masses of troops. ...

Now, an army may be robbed of its spirit and its commander deprived of his confidence. At the beginning of a campaign, the spirits of soldiers are keen; after a certain period of time, they flag, and in the later stages thought turn towards home. And therefore, those skilled in war avoid the enemy when his spirit is keen and attack him when he is sluggish and his soldiers homesick. This is control of the moral factor. In good order, they await a disorderly enemy; in serenity, a clamorous one. This is control of the mental factor. Close to the field of battle, they await an enemy coming from afar; at rest, they await an exhausted enemy; with well-fed troops, they await hungry ones. This is control of the physical factor. They do not engage an enemy advancing with well-ordered banners nor one whose formations are in impressive array. This is control of the factor of changing circumstances.

Therefore, the art of employing troops is that when the enemy occupies high ground, do not confront him uphill, and when his back is resting on hills, do not make a frontal attack. When he pretends to flee, do not pursue. Do not attack troops whose spirits are keen. Do not swallow bait. Do not thwart an enemy who is returning homewards.

Leave a way to escape to a surrounded enemy, and do not press a desperate enemy too hard. Such is the art of employing troops.

CHAPTER 8 THE NINE VARIABLES

. . . You should not encamp on grounds hard to approach. Unite with your allies on grounds intersected with highways. Do not linger on desolate ground. In enclosed ground, resort to stratagem. In death ground, fight a last-ditch battle.

There are some roads which must not be followed, some troops which must not be attacked, some cities which must not be assaulted, and some ground which should not be contested. There are also occasions when the commands of the sovereign need not be obeyed. Therefore, a general thoroughly versed in the advantages of the nine variable factors knows how to employ troops. One who does not understand their advantages will not be able to use the terrain to his advantage even though he is well acquainted with it. . . .

And for this reason, a wise general in his deliberations must consider both favorable and unfavorable factors. By taking into account the favorable factors, he makes his plan feasible; by taking into account the unfavorable, he may avoid possible disasters. . . .

It is a doctrine of war not to assume the enemy will not come but rather to rely on one's readiness to meet him, and not to presume that he will not attack but rather to make oneself invincible.

There are five qualities which are fatal in the character of a general: if reckless, he can be killed; if cowardly, captured; if quick-tempered, he can be provoked to rage and make a fool of himself; if he has too delicate a sense of honor, he can be easily insulted; if he is of a compassionate nature, you can harass him.

Now these five traits of character are serious faults in a general and in military operations are calamitous. The ruin of the army and the death of the general are inevitable results of these shortcomings. They must be deeply pondered.

CHAPTER 9 ON THE MARCH

When an army takes up a position and confronts the enemy, it has to observe and judge the enemy situation. In doing so, it should pay attention to the following:

When crossing the mountains, be sure to stay close to valleys; when encamping, select high ground facing the sunny side; when high ground is occupied by the enemy, do not ascend to attack....

After crossing a river, you must move some distance away from it. When an advancing enemy crosses water, do not meet him in midstream. It is advantageous to allow half his force to cross and then strike. If you wish to give battle, do not confront your enemy near the water. Take a position on high ground facing the sun....

Cross salt marshes speedily. Do not linger in them. If you encounter the enemy in the middle of a salt marsh, you must take a position close to grass and water with trees in your rear....

On level ground, occupy a position which facilitates your action. With heights to your rear and right, the field of battle is to the front and the rear is safe....

In battle, all armies prefer high ground to low and sunny places to shady. If an army occupies high ground, which is convenient for living, it will not suffer from countless diseases and this will spell victory....

When the enemy is nearby but remains calm, he is depending on a favorable position. When he challenges battle from afar, he wishes to lure you to advance; when he is on easy ground, he must be in an advantageous position....

Dust spurting upwards in high straight columns indicates the approach of chariots. When it hangs low and is widespread, it be tokens that infantry is approaching.... When the enemy's envoys speak in humble terms, but the army continues preparations, that means it will advance. When their language is strong and the enemy pretentiously advances, these may be signs that the enemy will retreat.... When without a previous understanding the enemy asks for a truce, he must be plotting.... When half his force advances and half withdraws, he is attempting to decoy you. When his troops lean on their weapons, they are famished. When drawers of water drink before carrying it to camp, his troops are suffering from thirst. When the enemy sees an advantage but does not advance to seize it, he is fatigued....

When the troops are disorderly, the general has no prestige.... If the officers are short-tempered, they are exhausted.... When the troops continually gather in small groups and whisper together, the general has lost confidence of the army. Too frequent rewards indicate that the general is at the end of his resources; too frequent punishments that he is in acute distress. If the officers at first treat the men violently and later are fearful of them, it shows supreme lack of intelligence....

In war, numbers alone confer no advantage. It is sufficient if you do not advance relying on sheer military power. If you estimate the enemy situation correctly and then concentrate your strength to overcome the enemy, there is no more to it than this. He who lacks foresight and underestimates his enemy will surely be captured by him.

If troops are punished before their loyalty is secured, they will be disobedient. If not obedient, it is difficult to employ them. If troops have become attached to you, but discipline cannot be enforced, you cannot employ them. Thus, command them with civility but keep them under control by iron discipline, and it may be said that victory is certain. If orders are consistently carried out to instruct the troops, they will be obedient. If orders are not consistently carried out to instruct them, they will be disobedient.

If orders are consistently trustworthy and carried out, it shows that the relationship of a commander with his troops is satisfactory.

CHAPTER 10 TERRAIN

Ground may be classified according to its nature as accessible, entangling, temporizing, precipitous, distant, or having narrow passes....

There are six conditions in which troops fail. These are: flight, insubordination, collapse, distress, disorganization, and rout. None of these disasters can be attributed to natural causes, but to the fault of the general.

Other conditions being equal, if a force attacks one ten times its size, the result is flight. When soldiers are strong and officers weak, the army is insubordinate. When the officers are valiant and the soldiers ineffective, the result is collapse. When officers are angry and insubordinate, and on encountering the enemy rush into battle with no understanding of the feasibility of engaging and without awaiting orders from the commander, the army is in distress. When the general is morally weak and without authority, when his instructions and guidance are not enlightened, when there are no consistent rules to guide the officers and men, and when the formations are slovenly, the result is disorganization. When a commander unable to estimate his enemy uses a small force to engage a large one, or weak troops to strike the strong, or when he fails to select shock troops for the van, the result is rout. When any of these six conditions prevails, the army is on the road to defeat. It is the highest responsibility of the general that he examine them carefully.

Conformation of the ground is of the greatest assistance in battle. Therefore, virtues of a superior general are to estimate the enemy situation and to calculate distances and the degree of difficulty of the terrain so as to control victory. He who fights with full knowledge of these factors is certain to win; he who does not will surely be defeated. If the situation is one of victory, but the sovereign has issued orders not to engage, the general may decide to fight. If the situation is such that he cannot win, but the sovereign has issued orders to engage, he need not do so. And, therefore, the general who in advancing does not seek personal fame, and in retreating is not concerned with disgrace, but whose only purpose is to protect the country and promote the best interests of his sovereign, is the precious jewel of the state.

... If a general indulges his men but is unable to employ them, if he loves them but cannot enforce his commands, if the men are disorderly and he is unable to control them, they may be compared to spoiled children, and are useless.

If I know that my troops are capable of striking the enemy, but do not know that he is invulnerable to attack, my chance of victory is but half. If I know that the enemy is vulnerable to attack, but do not know that my troops are incapable of striking him, my chance of victory is but half. If I know that the enemy can be attacked and that my troops are capable of attacking him, but do not realize that the conformation of the ground makes fighting impracticable, my chance of victory is but half. Therefore, when those experienced in war move, they are never bewildered; when they act, their resources are limitless. And, therefore, I say: Know the enemy, know yourself: your victory will never be endangered. Know the ground, know the weather; your victory will then be complete.

CHAPTER 11 THE NINE VARIETIES OF GROUND

In respect to the employment of troops, ground may be classified as dispersive, frontier, key, open, focal, serious, difficult, encircled, and desperate.

When a feudal lord fights in his own territory, he is in dispersive ground. When he makes but a shallow penetration into enemy territory, he is in frontier ground. Ground equally advantageous to occupy is key ground. Ground equally accessible is open. When a state is enclosed by three other states, its territory is focal. He who first gets control of it will gain the support of the majority of neighboring states. When the army has penetrated deep into hostile territory, leaving far behind many enemy cities and towns, it is in serious ground. When the army traverses mountains, forests, or precipitous country, or marches through defiles, marshlands, or swamps, or any place where the going is hard, it is in difficult ground. Ground to which access is constricted, where the way out is tortuous, and where a small enemy force can strike a larger one is called encircled. Ground in which the army survives only if it fights with the courage of desperation is called desperate. And, therefore, do not fight in dispersive ground; do not stop in the frontier borderlands.

Do not attack an enemy who occupies key ground first; in open ground, do not allow your formations to become separated and your communications to be blocked. In focal ground, ally with neighboring states; in serious ground, gather in plunder. In difficult ground, press on; in encircled ground, devise stratagem; in desperate ground, fight courageously....

. . . Should one ask: "How do I cope with a well-ordered enemy host about to attack me?" I reply: "Seize something he cherishes and he will conform to your desires." Speed is the essence of war. Take advantage of the enemy's unpreparedness, make your way by unexpected routes, and attack him where he has taken no precautions.

. . . Pay heed to nourishing the troops; do not unnecessarily fatigue them. Unite them in spirit; conserve their strength. Make unfathomable plans for the movements of the army. Throw the troops into a position from which there is no escape, and even when faced with death they will not flee. For if prepared to die, what can they not achieve?...

It is the business of a general to be serene and inscrutable, impartial and self-controlled. He should be capable of keeping his officers and men in ignorance of his plans. He changes his methods and alters his plans so that people have no knowledge of what he aims at. He alters his campsites and marches by devious routes, and thus makes it impossible for others to anticipate his purpose. . . . To assemble an army and throw it into a desperate position is the business of the general. To take different measures suited to the nine varieties of ground, to take aggressive or defensive tactics in accordance with different situations, and to understand soldiers' psychological states under different circumstances, are matters that must be studied carefully by a general.

. . . For it is the nature of soldiers to resist when surrounded, to fight to the death when there is no alternative, and when desperate to follow commands implicitly.

One ignorant of the plans of neighboring states cannot make alliances with them; if ignorant of the conditions of mountains, forests, dangerous defiles, swamps, and marshes, he cannot conduct the march of an army; if he fails to make use of native guides, he cannot gain the advantages of the ground. A general ignorant of even one of these nine varieties of ground is unfit to command the armies of a hegemonic king. Now, when a hegemonic king attacks a powerful state, he makes it impossible for the enemy to concentrate his troops. He overawes the enemy and prevents his allies from joining him.

. . . Set the troops to their tasks without imparting your designs; use them to gain advantage without revealing the dangers involved. Throw them into a perilous situation and they will survive; put them in desperate ground and they will live. For when the army is placed in such a situation, it can snatch victory from defeat. Now, the crux of military operations lies in the pretense of following the designs of the enemy; and once there is a loophole that can be used, concentrate your forces against the enemy. . . .

. . . When the enemy presents an opportunity, speedily take advantage of it. Seize the place which the enemy values without making an appointment for battle with him. In executing the plan, you should change according the enemy situation in order to win victory. Therefore, at first you should pretend to be as shy as a maiden. When the enemy gives you an opening, be swift as a hare and he will be unable to withstand you.

CHAPTER 12 ATTACK BY FIRE

. . . Now, to win battles and take your objectives but to fail to consolidate these achievements is ominous and may be described as a waste of time. And, therefore, it is said that enlightened rulers must deliberate upon the plans to go to battle, and good generals carefully execute them. If not in the interests of the state do not act. If you cannot succeed, do not use troops. If you are not in danger, do not fight a war. A sovereign cannot launch a war because he is enraged, nor can a general fight a war because he is resentful. For while an angered man may again be happy, and a resentful man again be pleased, a state that has perished cannot be restored, nor can the dead be brought back to life. Therefore, the enlightened ruler is prudent and the good general is warned against rash action. Thus, the state is kept secure and the army preserved.

CHAPTER 13 USE OF SPIES

Now, when an army of one hundred thousand is raised and dispatched on a distant campaign, the expenses borne by the people together with disbursements of the treasury will amount to a thousand pieces of gold a day. In addition, there will be continuous commotion both at home and abroad, people will be exhausted by the corvée of transport, and the farm work of seven hundred thousand households will be disrupted. [In ancient times, eight families comprised a community. When one family sent a man to the army, the remaining seven contributed to its support. Thus, when an army of one hundred thousand was raised, those unable to attend fully to their own plowing and sowing amounted to seven hundred thousand households.]

Hostile armies confront each other for years in order to struggle for victory in a decisive battle; yet if one who begrudges rank, honors, and a few hundred pieces of gold remains ignorant of his enemy's situation, he is completely unaware of the interests of the state and the people. Such a man is no general, no good assistant to his sovereign, and such a sovereign is no master of victory. Now, the reason a brilliant sovereign and a wise general conquer the enemy whenever they move and their achievements surpass those of ordinary men is their foreknowledge of the enemy situation. This "foreknowledge" cannot be elicited from spirits, nor from gods, nor by analogy with past events, nor by astrologic calculations. It must be obtained from men who know the enemy situation.

Now, there are five sorts of spies. These are native spies, internal spies, double spies, doomed spies, and surviving spies. When all these types of spies are at work and their operations are clandestine, it is called the "divine manipulation of threads" and is the treasure of the sovereign. Native spies are those from the enemy's country people whom we employ. Internal spies are enemy officials whom we employ. Double spies are enemy spies whom we employ. Doomed spies are those of our own spies who are deliberately given false information and told to report it to the enemy. Surviving spies are those who return from the enemy camp to report information.

Of all those in the army close to the commander, none is more intimate than the spies; of all rewards, none more liberal than those given to spies; of all matters, none is more confidential than those relating to spy operations. He who is not sage and wise, humane and just, cannot use spies. And he who is not delicate and subtle cannot get the truth out of them.

Delicate, indeed! Truly delicate! There is no place where espionage is not possible. If plans relating to spy operations are prematurely divulged, the agent and all those to whom he spoke of them should be put to death.

Generally, in the case of armies you wish to strike, cities you wish to attack, and people you wish to assassinate, it is necessary to find out the names of the garrison commander, the aides-de-camp, the ushers, gatekeepers, and bodyguards. You must instruct your spies to ascertain these matters in minute detail. It is essential to seek out enemy spies who have come to conduct espionage against you and to bribe them to serve you. Give them instruction and care for them. Thus, double spies are recruited and used. It is by means of the double spies that native and internal spies can be recruited and employed. And it is by this means that the doomed spies, armed with false information, can be sent to convey it to the enemy. It is by this means also that surviving spies can come back and give information as scheduled.

The sovereign must have full knowledge of the activities of the five sorts of spies. And the key is the skill to use the double spies. Therefore, it is mandatory that they be treated with the utmost liberality.

. . . And, therefore, only the enlightened sovereign and the wise general who are able to use the most intelligent people as spies can achieve great results. Spy operations are essential in war; upon them the army relies to make its every move.

SUMMARY

There is a reason why Sun Tzu's thoughts have endured over two thousand years. Although some aspects of the latter chapters of Sun Tzu seem dated, the following concepts deserve attention by strategic thinkers of air, space, and cyberspace:

- Though different in culture and time, Sun Tzu examines both personal and organizational leadership. A commander's character is crucial for victory.
- Nothing is more difficult than maneuvering for advantage.
- One must know the designs (intentions, aspirations, perspective) of current and potential allies.
- Speed is the essence of war.
- If you cannot succeed, do not use troops. If you are not in danger, do not fight.
- There is no place where espionage is not possible (for your enemy and for yourself).

By understanding Sun Tzu's ideas, today's Air Force officer emerges better equipped to confront both the timeless challenges of the nature of war and the unique obstacles posed by contemporary technological and social change. More than just a repository of traditional wisdom, Sun Tzu's *Art of War* provides a method for critical thinking and deep thought. Like Clausewitz and Thucydides, Sun Tzu inspires reflection and perspective.

NOTES

1. See Roger T. Ames, "Preface to the Ballantine Edition," and Ralph Peters, "The Seeker and the Sage," in Sun Tzu, *The Art of Warfare,* trans. Roger T. Ames, in *The Book of War,* ed. Caleb Carr. (New York: Modern Library, 2000).

WAR & POLITICS—A PARADOXCAL TRINITY?

Carl von Clausewitz

Carl von Clausewitz's book, *On War,* constitutes the greatest single book in Western culture devoted to the theory and practice of warfare. Rivaled only by Thucydides' *History of the Peloponnesian War* for its grasp of both the rational and irrational dimensions of war, Clausewitz's work provides a foundation for comprehending military theory and strategy. Although no single book can cover every aspect of war's complexities, *On War* is an excellent starting point. Acknowledged as a timeless masterpiece, the book discusses a vast range of issues that span the nature of war, military theory, politics, strategy, and tactics. Of equal significance, Clausewitz provides a conceptual framework that promotes an intellectual approach to the study of war and its relationship to the state. Because his book represents a kind of intellectual wrestling match, Clausewitz requires careful reading and deep thinking. Although mastery of his concepts comes with experience, perspective, and maturity, junior officers can still benefit from an overview of Clausewitz's theories on war. Likewise, Clausewitz provides a forum for learning how to think about warfare, arguably the most important subject for a military academy.[1]

At first glance, Carl von Clausewitz appears an unlikely candidate for the title of "greatest military theorist." Born in 1780, the fourth son of a retired Prussian army lieutenant, Clausewitz lacked the social status or political connections for command in a conservative army that lived under the shadow of Frederick the Great.[2] Commissioned as an officer cadet, Clausewitz first saw combat at age twelve when his unit fought the French in a series of minor skirmishes. Educated and mentored by military reformer Gerhard von Scharnhorst, Clausewitz served in a wide variety of staff assignments that developed his considerable intellectual skills. A keen observer and prolific writer, Clausewitz experienced the vast sweep of the Napoleonic Wars that dominated Europe from 1795 to 1815. Although he never commanded a unit in combat, Clausewitz fought a wide range of encounters ranging from small-unit engagements to some of the greatest battles of his era, including the epic Battle of Bordino and the Waterloo campaign. As renowned British historian Michael Howard remarked, "Clausewitz was no desk soldier."[3] His firsthand combat experience, high-level staff duties, and intense military education supported his quest to create a universal military theory.[4]

Clausewitz adopts a dialectical approach in his analysis of issues in *On War*. Initially, he presents an idea in a clear, but extreme, form and then examines it by studying its opposite. In other words, a dialectical argument advances a thesis (central idea) followed by its antithesis (counter argument) and the resulting analysis produces a synthesis, a blending of propositions and observations.[5] In addition, his discussion often transitions abruptly between the theoretical absolute (war in theory) to the realities of war as it occurs in the physical world. These methods reflect the intellectual influence of the philosophies of German Idealism and Romanticism as well as the common scientific practices of his time. The battle, or competition, of ideas provides intellectual depth and multiple insights, but also may prove confusing to those unfamiliar with the technique.[6] Making matters worse, Clausewitz wrestled with the book over many years and never finished the work. He began writing in 1819 and over eight years finished the first six of eight planned parts and drafts for the final two.[7] In 1827 he realized a major flaw of his work; he had failed to make clear his two fundamental points—absolute war versus real war and the supreme importance of politics in war:

> I regard the first six books, which are already in a clean copy, merely as a rather formless mass that must be thoroughly reworked once more. The revision will bring out the two types of war with greater clarity at every point. . . . War can be of two kinds, in the sense that either the objective is to *overthrow the enemy*—to render him politically helpless or militarily impotent, thus forcing him to sign whatever peace we please [absolute war]; or *merely to occupy some of his frontier-districts* so that we can annex them or use them for bargaining at the peace negotiations [real or limited war]. . . . This distinction between the two kinds of war is an actual fact. But no less practical is the importance of another point that must be made absolutely clear, namely that *war is nothing but the continuation of policy with other means*.[8]

Unfortunately, Clausewitz contracted cholera and died in 1831 leaving his masterpiece unfinished. Despite his instructions to burn the manuscript, his wife Marie published *On War* in 1832.[9]

Reflecting his experience in the Napoleonic Wars, Clausewitz argues a thesis that the ideal, or "absolute," form of war is total war. "War is thus an act of force to compel our enemy to do our will. . . . If one side uses force without compunction . . . [it] will force the other side to follow suit; each side will drive the other to extremes. . . ."[10] In its absolute form, "there is no logical limit to the application of . . . force."[11] On the other hand, Clausewitz counters with his antithesis: in reality, political objectives, chance, uncertainty, fatigue, and other factors, he termed as "friction," imposed limits on the violence of war. Therefore, understanding Clausewitz's dialectical approach, or what some scholars refer to as the "dual nature of war," (i.e., absolute vs. real war) provides a key to unlocking Clausewitz's insights.[12]

Clausewitz argues that politics provides the reason for war. His observation, "War Is Merely the Continuation of Policy by Other Means," is probably the single most quoted passage of *On War* and constitutes a fundamental concept.[13] Nations go to war to achieve a political purpose. Scholars point out that Clausewitz's original word *"Politik"* means either "politics" or "policy" in English, where "politics" refers to the conduct of or engaging in political affairs, i.e., the argument, competition, and contention of ideas that make governments work, and "policy" means a course of action or plan—"those political acts that lead to war, determine its purpose, influence its conduct, and bring about its termination."[14] Students should note that both concepts apply: war is a continuation of policy by other means, referring to diplomacy, international affairs, and political objectives as described above, and war is a continuation of politics, both domestic and international. The competition of political leaders, parties, factions, and ideas does not cease during a war. Hence, Clausewitz stresses that war is a political instrument of the policymaker.[15]

Further developing both the nature of war and the political dimension, Clausewitz introduced a theoretical construct known as the "paradoxical trinity":

> War is more than a true chameleon that slightly adapts its characteristics to the given case. As a total phenomenon its dominant tendencies always make war a remarkable trinity—composed of primordial violence, hatred, and enmity, which are to be regarded as a blind natural force; of the play of chance and probability within which the creative spirit is free to roam; and of its element of subordination, as an instrument of policy, which makes it subject to reason alone.
>
> The first of these three aspects mainly concerns the people; the second the commander and army; the third the government. The passions that are to be kindled in war must already be inherent in the people; the scope which the play of courage and talent will enjoy in the realm of probability and chance depends on the particular character of the commander and the army; and the political aims are the business of the government alone.[16]

He emphasizes that a genuine theory of war must address all three aspects and their relationships to each other. He describes the theory as being an object that "maintains a balance between the three entities, like an object suspended between three magnets."[17] While some scholars simplify the trinity as a triangle depicting people, commander and army, and government, others emphasize violence, chance and probability, and reason.[18] Additionally, noted scholar, Michael Handel points out that in a modern democracy the people will influence not only the blind natural force of passion, but the policies of the government.[19] Regardless of interpretation, the remarkable trinity proves a valuable conceptual tool for understanding the way by which the people, the government, and the military interact in war. Hopefully, this overview will make your reading of Carl von Clausewitz's first chapter of *On War* more understandable.

CARL VON CLAUSEWITZ'S *ON WAR*
CHAPTER I: WHAT IS WAR?

1. Introduction

I propose to consider first the various *elements* of the subject, next its *various parts* or *sections,* and finally *the whole* in its internal structure. In other words, I shall proceed from the simple to the complex. But in war more than in any other subject we must begin by looking at the nature of the whole; for here more than elsewhere the part and the whole must always be thought of together.

2. Definition

I shall not begin by expounding a pedantic, literary definition of war, but go straight to the heart of the matter, to the duel. War is nothing but a duel on a larger scale. Countless duels go to make up war, but a picture of it as a whole can be formed by imagining a pair of wrestlers. Each tries through physical force to compel the other to do his will; his *immediate* aim is to *throw* his opponent in order to make him incapable of further resistance.

War is thus an act of force to compel our enemy to do our will.

Force, to counter opposing force, equips itself with the inventions of art and science. Attached to force are certain self-imposed, imperceptible limitations hardly worth mentioning, known as international law and custom, but they scarcely weaken it. Force—that is, physical force, for moral force has no existence save as expressed in the state and the law—is thus the *means* of war; to impose our will on the enemy is its *object*. To secure that object we must render the enemy powerless; and that, in theory, is the true aim of warfare. That aim takes the place of the object, discarding it as something not actually part of war itself.

3. The Maximum Use of Force

Kind-hearted people might of course think there was some ingenious way to disarm or defeat an enemy without too much bloodshed, and might imagine this is the true goal of the art of war. Pleasant as it sounds, it is a fallacy that must be exposed: war is such a dangerous business that the mistakes which come from kindness are the very worst. The maximum use of force is in no way incompatible with the simultaneous use of the intellect. If one side uses force without compunction, undeterred by the bloodshed it involves, while the other side refrains, the first will gain the upper hand. That side will force the other to follow suit; each will drive its opponent toward extremes, and the only limiting factors are the counterpoises inherent in war.

This is how the matter must be seen. It would be futile—even wrong—to try and shut one's eyes to what war really is from sheer distress at its brutality.

If wars between civilized nations are far less cruel and destructive than wars between savages, the reason lies in the social conditions of the states themselves and in their relationships to one another. These are the forces that give rise to war; the same forces circumscribe and moderate it. They themselves however are not part of war; they already exist before fighting starts. To introduce the principle of moderation into the theory of war itself would always lead to logical absurdity.

Two different motives make men fight one another: *hostile feelings* and *hostile intentions*. Our definition is based on the latter, since it is the universal element. Even the most savage, almost instinctive, passion of hatred cannot be conceived as existing without hostile intent; but hostile intentions are often unaccompanied by any sort of hostile feelings—at least by none that predominate. Savage peoples are ruled by passion, civilized peoples by the mind. The difference, however, lies not in the respective natures of savagery and civilization, but in their attendant circumstances, institutions, and so forth. The difference, therefore, does not operate in every case, but it does in most of them. Even the most civilized of peoples, in short, can be fired with passionate hatred for each other.

Consequently, it would be an obvious fallacy to imagine war between civilized peoples as resulting merely from a rational act on the part of their governments and to conceive of war as gradually ridding itself of passion, so that in the end one would never really need to use the physical impact of the fighting forces—comparative figures of their strength would be enough. That would be a kind of war by algebra.

Theorists were already beginning to think along such lines when the recent wars taught them a lesson.[20] If war is an act of force, the emotions cannot fail to be involved. War may not spring from them, but they will still affect it to some degree, and the extent to which they do so will depend not on the level of civilization but on how important the conflicting interests are and on how long their conflict lasts.

If, then, civilized nations do not put their prisoners to death or devastate cities and countries, it is because intelligence plays a larger part in their methods of warfare and has taught them more effective ways of using force than the crude expression of instinct.

The invention of gunpowder and the constant improvement of firearms are enough in themselves to show that the advance of civilization has done nothing practical to alter or deflect the impulse to destroy the enemy, which is central to the very idea of war.

The thesis, then, must be repeated: war is an act of force, and there is no logical limit to the application of that force. Each side, therefore, compels its opponent to follow suit; a reciprocal action is started which must lead, in theory, to extremes. This is the *first case of interaction and the first 'extreme'* we meet with.

4. The Aim Is To Disarm the Enemy

I have already said that the aim of warfare is to disarm the enemy and it is time to show that, at least in theory, this is bound to be so. If the enemy is to be coerced you must put him in a situation that is even more unpleasant than the sacrifice you call on him to make.[21] The hardships of that situation must not of course be merely transient—at least not in appearance. Otherwise the enemy would not give in but would wait for things to improve. Any change that might be brought about by continuing hostilities must then, at least in theory, be of a kind to bring the enemy still greater disadvantages. The worst of all conditions in which a belligerent can find himself is to be utterly defenceless. Consequently, if you are to force the enemy, by making war on him, to do your bidding, you must either make him literally defenceless or at least put him in a position that makes this danger probable. It follows, then, that to overcome the enemy, or disarm him—call it what you will—must always be the aim of warfare.

War, however, is not the action of a living force upon a lifeless mass (total nonresistance would be no war at all) but always the collision of two living forces. The ultimate aim of waging war, as formulated here, must be taken as applying to both sides. Once again, there is interaction. So long as I have not overthrown my opponent I am bound to fear he may overthrow me. Thus I am not in control: he dictates to me as much as I dictate to him. This is the *second case of interaction and it leads to the second 'extreme'.*

5. The Maximum Exertion of Strength

If you want to overcome your enemy you must match your effort against his power of resistance, which can be expressed as the product of two inseparable factors, [namely] *the total means at his disposal* and *the strength of his will.* The extent of the means at his disposal is a matter—though not exclusively—of figures, and should be measurable. But the strength of his will is much less easy to determine and can only be gauged approximately by the strength of the motive animating it. Assuming you arrive in this way at a reasonably accurate estimate of the enemy's power of resistance, you can adjust your own efforts accordingly; .... But the enemy will do the same; competition will again result and, in pure theory, it must again force you both to extremes. This is *the third case of interaction and the third 'extreme'.*

6. Modifications in Practice

Thus in the field of abstract thought the inquiring mind can never rest until it reaches the extreme, for here it is dealing with an extreme: a clash of forces freely operating and obedient to no law but their own. From a pure concept of war you might try to deduce absolute terms for the objective you should aim at and for the means of achieving it; but if you did so the continuous interaction would land you in extremes that represented nothing but a play of the imagination....Any such pronouncement would be an abstraction and would leave the real world quite unaffected.

Even assuming this extreme effort to be an absolute quantity that could easily be calculated, one must admit that the human mind is unlikely to consent to being ruled by such a logical fantasy....An effort of will out of all proportion to the object in view would be needed but would not in fact be realized, since subtle ties of logic do not motivate the human will.

But move from the abstract to the real world, and the whole thing looks quite different. In the abstract world, optimism was all powerful and forced us to assume that both parties to the conflict not only sought perfection but attained it. Would this ever be the case in practice? Yes, it would if: (a) war were a wholly isolated act, occurring suddenly and not produced by previous events in the political world; (b) it consisted of a single decisive act or a set of simultaneous ones; (c) the decision achieved was complete and perfect in itself, uninfluenced by any previous estimate of the political situation it would bring about.

7. War Is Never an Isolated Act

As to the first of these conditions, it must be remembered that neither opponent is an abstract person to the other, not even to the extent of that factor in the power of resistance, namely the will, which is dependent on externals. The will is not a wholly unknown factor; we can base a forecast of its state tomorrow on what it is today. War never breaks out wholly unexpectedly, nor can it be spread instantaneously. Each side can therefore gauge the other to a large extent by what he is and does, instead of judging him by what he, strictly speaking, ought to be or do. Man and his affairs, however, are always something short of perfect and will never quite achieve the absolute best. Such shortcomings affect both sides alike and therefore constitute a moderating force.

8. War Does Not Consist of a Single Short Blow

The second condition calls for the following remarks:

If war, consisted of one decisive act,....preparations would tend toward totality, for no omission could ever be rectified. The sole criterion for preparations which the world of reality could provide would be the measures taken by the adversary—so far as they are known; the rest would once more be reduced to abstract calculations. But if the decision in war consists of several successive acts, then each of them, seen in context, will provide a gauge for those that follow. Here again, the abstract world is ousted by the real one and the trend to the extreme is thereby moderated.

. . .

Yet, as I showed above, as soon as preparations for a war begin, the world of reality takes over from the world of abstract thought; material calculations take the place of hypothetical extremes and, if for no other reason, the interaction of the two sides tends to fall short of maximum effort. Their full resources will therefore not be mobilized immediately.

Besides, the very nature of those resources and of their employment means they cannot all be deployed at the same moment. The resources in question are *the fighting forces proper, the country,* with its physical features and population, and its *allies.*

The country—its physical features and population—is more than just the source of all armed forces proper; it is in itself an integral element among the factors at work in war

. . .

It is possible, no doubt, to use all mobile fighting forces simultaneously; but with fortresses, rivers, mountains, inhabitants, and so forth, that cannot be done; not, in short, with the country as a whole, ... Furthermore, allies do not cooperate at the mere desire of those who are actively engaged in fighting; international relations being what they are, such cooperation is often furnished only at some later stage or increased only when a balance has been disturbed and needs correction.

. . . At this stage it is enough to show that the very nature of war impedes the *simultaneous concentration of all forces.* To be sure, that fact in itself cannot be grounds for making any but a maximum effort to obtain the first decision, for a defeat is always a disadvantage no one would deliberately risk. And even if the first clash is not the only one, the influence it has on subsequent actions will be on a scale proportionate to its own. But it is contrary to human nature to make an extreme effort, ... As a result, for the first decision, effort and concentration of forces are not all they might be. Anything omitted out of weakness by one side becomes a real, *objective* reason for the other to reduce its efforts, and the tendency toward extremes is once again reduced by this interaction.

9. In War the Result Is Never Final

Lastly, even the ultimate outcome of a war is not always to be regarded as final. The defeated state often considers the outcome merely as a transitory evil, for which a remedy may still be found in political conditions at some later date. It is obvious how this, too, can slacken tension and reduce the vigour of the effort.

10. The Probabilities of Real Life Replace the Extreme and the Absolute Required by Theory

Warfare thus eludes the strict theoretical requirement that extremes of force be applied. Once the extreme is no longer feared or aimed at, it becomes a matter of judgement what degree of effort should be made; and this can only be based on the phenomena of the real world and the *laws of probability*. Once the antagonists have ceased to be mere figments of a theory and become actual states and governments, when war is no longer a theoretical affair but a series of actions obeying its own peculiar laws, reality supplies the data from which we can deduce the unknown that lies ahead.

From the enemy's character, from his institutions, the state of his affairs and his general situation, each side, using the *laws of probability,* forms an estimate of its opponent's likely course and acts accordingly.

11. The Political Object Now Comes to the Fore Again

A subject which we last considered in Section 2 now forces itself on us again, namely the *political object of the war*. Hitherto it had been rather overshadowed by the law of extremes, the will to overcome the enemy and make him powerless. But as this law begins to lose its force and as this determination wanes, the political aim will reassert itself. If it is all a calculation of probabilities based on given individuals and conditions, the *political object,* which was the *original motive,* must become an essential factor in the equation. The smaller the penalty you demand from your opponent, the less you can expect him to try and deny it to you; the smaller the effort he makes, the less you need make yourself. Moreover, the more modest your own political aim, the less importance you attach to it and the less reluctantly you will abandon it if you must. *This is another reason why your effort will be modified.*

The political object—the original motive for the war—will thus determine both the military objective to be reached and the amount of effort it requires. The political object cannot, however, in *itself* provide the standard of measurement. Since we are dealing with realities, not with abstractions, it can do so only in the context of the two states at war. The same political object can elicit *differing* reactions from different peoples, and even from the same people at different times. We can therefore take the political object as a standard only if we think of *the influence it can exert upon the forces it is meant to move.* The nature of those forces therefore calls for study. Depending on whether their characteristics increase or diminish the drive toward a particular action, the outcome will vary. Between two peoples and two states there can be such tensions, such a mass of inflammable material, that the slightest quarrel can produce a wholly disproportionate effect—a real explosion.

This is equally true of the efforts a political object is expected to arouse in either state, and of the military objectives which their policies require. Sometimes the *political and military objective is the same*—for example, the conquest of a province. In other cases the political object will not provide a suitable military objective. In that event, another military objective must be adopted that will serve the political purpose and symbolize it in the peace negotiations. But here, too, attention must be paid to the character of each state involved. There are times when, if the political object is to be achieved, the substitute must be a good deal more important. The less involved the population and the less serious the strains within states and between them, the more political requirements in themselves will dominate and tend to be decisive. Situations can thus exist in which the political object will almost be the sole determinant.

Generally speaking, a military objective that matches the political object in scale will, if the latter is reduced, be reduced in proportion; this will be all the more so as the political object increases its predominance. Thus it follows that without any inconsistency wars can have all degrees of importance and intensity, ranging from a war of extermination down to simple armed observation. This brings us to a different question, which now needs to be analysed and answered.

12. An Interruption of Military Activity Is Not Explained by Anything Yet Said

However modest the political demands maybe on either side, however small the means employed, however limited the military objective, can the process of war ever be interrupted, even for a moment? The question reaches deep into the heart of the matter.

Every action needs a certain time to be completed. That period is called its duration, and its length will depend on the speed with which the person acting works....

Now if every action in war is allowed its appropriate duration, we would agree that, at least at first sight, any additional expenditure of time—any suspension of military action—seems absurd. In this connection it must be remembered that what we are talking about is not the progress made by one side or the other but the progress of military interaction as a whole.

13. Only One Consideration Can Suspend Military Action, and It Seems that It Can Never Be Present on More than One Side

If two parties have prepared for war, some motive of hostility must have brought them to that point. Moreover so long as they remain under arms...that motive of hostility must still be active. Only one consideration can restrain it: *a desire to wait for a better moment before acting.* At first sight one would think this desire could never operate on more than one side since its opposite must automatically be working on the other. If action would bring an advantage to one side, the other's interest must be to wait....

But from that moment on, logic would seem to call for action by the other side—the object being to deny the enemy the time he needs for getting ready. Throughout all this I have assumed, of course, that both sides understand the situation perfectly.

14. Continuity Would Thus Be Brought About in Military Action and Would Again Intensify Everything

If this continuity were really to exist in the campaign its effect would again be to drive everything to extremes. Not only would such ceaseless activity arouse men's feelings and inject them with more passion and elemental strength, but events would follow more closely on each other and be governed by a stricter causal chain. Each individual action would be more important, and consequently more dangerous.

But war, of course, seldom if ever shows such continuity. In numerous conflicts only a very small part of the time is occupied by action, while the rest is spent in inactivity. This cannot always be an anomaly. Suspension of action in war must be possible; in other words, it is not a contradiction in terms. Let me demonstrate this point, and explain the reasons for it.

15. Here a Principle of Polarity Is Proposed

By thinking that the interests of the two commanders are opposed in equal measure to each other, we have assumed a genuine *polarity*. . . .

The principle of polarity is valid only in relation to one and the same object, in which positive and negative interests exactly cancel one another out. In a battle each side aims at victory; that is a case of true polarity, since the victory of one side excludes the victory of the other. When, however, we are dealing with two different things that have a common relation external to themselves, the polarity lies not in the *things* but in their relationship.

16. Attack and Defence Being Things Different in Kind and Unequal in Strength, Polarity Cannot Be Applied to Them

If war assumed only a single form, namely, attacking the enemy, and defence were nonexistent; or, to put it in another way, if the only differences between attack and defence lay in the fact that attack has a positive aim whereas defence has not, and the forms of fighting were identical; then every advantage gained by one side would be a precisely equal disadvantage to the other—true polarity would exist.

But there are two distinct forms of action in war: attack and defence. As will be shown in detail later, the two are very different and unequal in strength. Polarity, then, does not lie in attack or defence, but in the object both seek to achieve: the decision. If one commander wants to postpone the decision, the other must want to hasten it, always assuming that both are engaged in the same kind of fighting. If it is in A's interest not to attack B now but to attack him in four weeks, then it is in B's interest not to be attacked in four weeks' time, but now. This is an immediate and direct conflict of interest; but it does not follow from this that it would also be to B's advantage to make an immediate attack on A. That would obviously be quite another matter.

17. The Superiority of Defence over Attack Often Destroys the Effect of Polarity, and This Explains the Suspension of Military Action

As we shall show, defence is a stronger form of fighting than attack. Consequently we must ask whether the advantage of *postponing a decision* is as great for one side as the advantage of *defence* is for the other. Whenever it is not, it cannot balance the advantage of defence and in this way influence the progress of the war. It is clear, then, that the impulse created by the polarity of interests may be exhausted in the difference between the strength of attack and defence, and may thus become inoperative.

Consequently, if the side favored by present conditions is not sufficiently strong to do without the added advantages of the defence, it will have to accept the prospect of acting under unfavorable conditions in the future. To fight a defensive battle under these less favourable conditions may still be better than to attack immediately or to make peace. I am convinced that the superiority of the defensive (if rightly understood) is very great, far greater than appears at first sight. It is this which explains without any inconsistency most periods of inaction that occur in war. The weaker the motives for action, the more will they be overlaid and neutralized by this disparity between attack and defence, and the more frequently will action be suspended—as indeed experience shows.

18. A Second Cause Is Imperfect Knowledge of the Situation

There is still another factor that can bring military action to a standstill: imperfect knowledge of the situation. The only situation a commander can know fully is his own; his opponent's he can know only from unreliable intelligence.[22] His evaluation, therefore, may be mistaken and can lead him to suppose that the initiative lies with the enemy when in fact it remains with him. Of course such faulty appreciation is as likely to lead to ill-timed action as to ill-timed inaction, and is no more conducive to slowing down operations than it is to speeding them up. Nevertheless, it must rank among the natural causes which, *without entailing inconsistency, can bring military activity to a halt.* Men are always more inclined to pitch their estimate of the enemy's strength too high than too low, such is human nature. Bearing this in mind, one must admit that partial ignorance of the situation is, generally speaking, a major factor in delaying the progress of military action and in moderating the principle that underlies it.

The possibility of inaction has a further moderating effect on the progress of the war by diluting it, so to speak, in time by delaying danger, and by increasing the means of restoring a balance between the two sides. The greater the tensions that have led to war, and the greater the consequent war effort, the shorter these periods of inaction. Inversely, the weaker the motive for conflict, the longer the intervals between actions. For the stronger motive increases willpower, and willpower, as we know, is always both an element in and the product of strength.

19. Frequent Periods of Inaction Remove War Still Further from the Realm of the Absolute and Make It Even More a Matter of Assessing Probabilities

The slower the progress and the more frequent the interruptions of military action the easier it is to retrieve a mistake, the bolder will be the general's assessments, and the more likely he will be to avoid theoretical extremes and to base his plans on probability and inference. Any given situation requires that probabilities be calculated in the light of circumstances, and the amount of time available for such calculation will depend on the pace with which operations are taking place.

20. Therefore Only the Element of Chance Is Needed to Make War a Gamble, And That Element Is Never Absent

It is now quite clear how greatly the objective nature of war makes it a matter of assessing probabilities. Only one more element is needed to make war a gamble—chance: the very last thing that war lacks. No other human activity is so continuously or universally bound up with chance. And through the element of chance, guesswork and luck come to play a great part in war.

21. Not Only Its Objective But Also Its Subjective Nature Makes War a Gamble

If we now consider briefly the *subjective nature* of war—the means by which war has to be fought—it will look more than ever like a gamble. The element in which war exists is danger. The highest of all moral qualities in time of danger is certainly *courage*. Now courage is perfectly compatible with prudent calculation but the two differ nonetheless, and pertain to different psychological forces. Daring, on the other hand, boldness, rashness, trusting in luck are only variants of courage, and all these traits of character seek their proper element—chance.

In short, absolute, so-called mathematical, factors never find a firm basis in military calculations. From the very start there is an interplay of possibilities, probabilities, good luck and bad that weaves its way throughout the length and breadth of the tapestry. In the whole range of human activities, war most closely resembles a game of cards.

22. How in General This Best Suits Human Nature

Although our intellect always longs for clarity and certainty, our nature often finds uncertainty fascinating. It prefers to day-dream in the realms of chance and luck rather than accompany the intellect on its narrow and tortuous path of philosophical enquiry and logical deduction only to arrive—hardly knowing how—in unfamiliar surroundings where all the usual landmarks seem to have disappeared. Unconfined by narrow necessity, it can revel in a wealth of possibilities; which inspire courage to take wing and dive into the element of daring and danger like a fearless swimmer into the current.

Should theory leave us here, and cheerfully go on elaborating absolute conclusions and prescriptions? Then it would be no use at all in real life. No, it must also take the human factor into account, and find room for courage, boldness, even foolhardiness. The art of war deals with living and with moral forces. Consequently, it cannot attain the absolute, or certainty; it must always leave a margin for uncertainty, in the greatest things as much as in the smallest. With uncertainty in one scale, courage and self-confidence must be thrown into the other to correct the balance. The greater they are, the greater the margin that can be left for accidents. Thus courage and self-confidence are essential in war, and theory should propose only rules that give ample scope to these finest and least dispensable of military virtues, in all their degrees and variations. Even in daring there can be method and caution; but here they are measured by a different standard.

23. But War Is Nonetheless a Serious Means to a Serious End: A More Precise Definition of War

Such is war, such is the commander who directs it, and such the theory that governs it. War is no pastime; it is no mere joy in daring and winning, no place for irresponsible enthusiasts. It is a serious means to a serious end, and all its colorful resemblance to a game of chance, all the vicissitudes of passion, courage, imagination, and enthusiasm it includes are merely its special characteristics.

When whole communities go to war—whole peoples, and especially *civilized* peoples—the reason always lies in some political situation, and the occasion is always due to some political object. War, therefore, is an act of policy. Were it a complete, untrammeled, absolute manifestation of violence (as the pure concept would require), war would of its own independent will usurp the place of policy the moment policy had brought it into being; it would then drive policy out of office and rule by the laws of its own nature, ... But in reality things are different, and this view is thoroughly mistaken. In reality war, as has been shown, is not like that. Its violence is not of the kind that explodes in a single discharge, but is the effect of forces that do not always develop in exactly the same manner or to the same degree. At times they will expand sufficiently to overcome the resistance of inertia or friction; at others they are too weak to have any effect. War is a pulsation of violence, variable in strength and therefore variable in the speed with which it explodes and discharges its energy. War moves on its goal with varying speeds; but it always lasts long enough for influence to be exerted on the goal and for its own course to be changed in one way or another—long enough, in other words, to remain subject to the action of a superior intelligence. If we keep in mind that war springs from some political purpose, it is natural that the prime cause of its existence will remain the supreme consideration in conducting it. That, however, does not imply that the political aim is a tyrant. It must adapt itself to its chosen means, a process which can radically change it; yet the political aim remains the first consideration. Policy, then, will permeate all military operations, and, in so far as their violent nature will admit, it will have a continuous influence on them.

24. War Is Merely the Continuation of Policy by Other Means

We see, therefore, that war is not merely an act of policy but a true political instrument, a continuation of political intercourse, carried on with other means. What remains peculiar to war is simply the peculiar nature of its means. War in general, and the commander in any specific instance, is entitled to require that the trend and designs of policy shall not be inconsistent with these means. That, of course, is no small demand; but however much it may affect political aims in a given case, it will never do more than modify them. The political object is the goal, war is the means of reaching it, and means can never be considered in isolation from their purpose.

25. The Diverse Nature of War

The more powerful and inspiring the motives for war, the more they affect the belligerent nations and the fiercer the tensions that precede the outbreak, the closer will war approach its abstract concept, the more important will be the destruction of the enemy, the more closely will the military aims and the political objects of war coincide, and the more military and less political will war appear to be. On the other hand, the less intense the motives, the less will the military element's natural tendency to violence coincide with political directives. As a result, war will be driven further from its natural course, the political object will be more and more at variance with the aim of ideal war, and the conflict will seem increasingly *political* in character. . . .

26. All Wars Can Be Considered Acts of Policy

It is time to return to the main theme and observe that while policy is apparently effaced in the one kind of war and yet is strongly evident in the other, both kinds are equally political. If the state is thought of as a person, and policy as the product of its brain, then among the contingencies for which the state must be prepared is a war in which every element calls for policy to be eclipsed by violence. Only if politics is regarded not as resulting from a just appreciation of affairs, but—as it conventionally is—as cautious, devious, even dishonest, shying away from force, could the second type of war appear to be more "political" than the first.

27. The Effects of This Point of View on the Understanding of Military History and the Foundations of Theory

First, therefore, it is clear that war should never be thought of as *something autonomous* but always as an *instrument of policy;* otherwise the entire history of war would contradict us. Only this approach will enable us to penetrate the problem intelligently. *Second,* this way of looking at it will show us how wars must vary with the nature of their motives and of the situations which give rise to them.

The first, the supreme, the most far-reaching act of judgement that the statesman and commander have to make is to establish by that test the kind of war on which they are embarking; neither mistaking it for, nor trying to turn it into, something that is alien to its nature. This is the first of all strategic questions and the most comprehensive. . . .

28. The Consequences for Theory

War is more than a true chameleon that slightly adapts its characteristics to the given case. As a total phenomenon its dominant tendencies always make war a paradoxical trinity—composed of primordial violence, hatred, and enmity, which are to be regarded as a blind natural force; of the play of chance and probability within which the creative spirit is free to roam; and of its element of subordination, as an instrument of policy, which makes it subject to reason alone.

The first of these three aspects mainly concerns the people; the second the commander and his army; the third the government. The passions that are to be kindled in war must already be inherent in the people; the scope which the play of courage and talent will enjoy in the realm of probability and chance depends on the particular character of the commander and the army; but the political aims are the business of government alone.

These three tendencies are like three different codes of law, deep rooted in their subject and yet variable in their relationship to one another. A theory that ignores anyone of them or seeks to fix an arbitrary relationship between them would conflict with reality to such an extent that for this reason alone it would be totally useless.

Our task therefore is to develop a theory that maintains a balance between these three tendencies, like an object suspended between three magnets.

What lines might best be followed to achieve this difficult task will be explored in the book on the theory of war. . . . At any rate, the preliminary concept of war which we have formulated casts a first ray of light on the basic structure of theory, and enables us to make an initial, differentiation and identification of its major components.

SUMMARY

Written as a dialectic, a form of intellectual argument, Clausewitz's "What Is War?" introduces several fundamental ideas for comprehending warfare, including the dual nature of war, war as a political instrument, and the paradoxical trinity, among others. These ideas also highlight Clausewitz's thoughts on the value of military theory. He believes the role of military theory is to educate the mind. In other words, military theory provides tools for thought, but not a checklist for action. Clausewitz also recognizes that war is not performed against an inanimate object: "War, however, is not the action of a living force upon a lifeless mass . . . but always the collision of two living forces." This leads to the concept of friction that will be explored more fully in the next reading. Finally, students should note that Clausewitz's original word, *Politik,* means both politics and policy. Politics refers to the conduct of or engaging in political affairs; argument, the competition of ideas, both domestic and international; while policy refers to a course of action or a plan (i.e. the decisions that result from politics). Hence, Clausewitz is correct regardless of translation: war is both *politics* by other means and war is *policy* by other means. Although challenging to read, this passage articulates many of the key concepts used in the remainder of the course. Air, space, and cyberspace theorists must never forget that their ideas must serve the broader strategy outlined by decision makers: war is an instrument of policy.

NOTES

1. This article synthesizes a number of highly regarded texts including Carl von Clausewitz, *On War,* ed. and trans. Michael Howard and Peter Paret (Princeton, N. J.: Princeton University Press, 1976); Peter Paret, "Clausewitz," in *Makers of Modern Strategy from Machiavelli to the Nuclear Age,* ed. Peter Paret (Princeton, N. J.: Princeton University Press, 1986); Michael I. Handel, *Masters of War: Classical Strategic Thought,* 3rd rev. ed. (London: Frank Cass, 2001); Colin S. Gray, *Modern Strategy* (Oxford: Oxford University Press, 1999); and Michael Howard, *Clausewitz* (Oxford: Oxford University Press, 1983). Additionally, three introductory essays to the Howard and Paret translation of *On War* prove valuable: Peter Paret, "The Genesis of On War;" Michael Howard, "The Influence of Clausewitz;" and Bernard Brodie, "The Continuing Relevance of *On War.*"

2. Paret, "Clausewitz," 188; Howard, *Clausewitz,* 6.

3. Howard, *Clausewitz,* 6.

4. Paret, "Clausewitz," 195.

5. Peter Paret emphasizes that Clausewitz used a modified form of thesis and antithesis and not a strict dialectical structure often identified with Georg Friedrich Hegel. Peter Paret, "The Genesis of *On War,*" in Carl von Clausewitz, *On War,* 15; Paret, "Clausewitz," 194, 198; Howard, *Clausewitz,* 13-14; Handel, *Masters,* 24.

6. Handel, *Masters,* 24.

7. Clausewitz called the parts of *On·War,* "books." Experienced scholars regard Book I as the most complete and Book VIII as a summation, or synthesis, of previous discussions. Michael Howard, "The Influence of Clausewitz," in Clausewitz, *On War,* 28: Paret, "Clausewitz," 196.

8. Clausewitz, "Note of 10 July 1827," *On* War, 69; Paret, "Clausewitz," 196-197.

9. Howard, "The Influence of Clausewitz," 27; Paret, "Clausewitz," 197; Howard, *Clausewitz,* 19-21.

10. Clausewitz, *On War,* 75-76.

11. Ibid., p. 77.

12. Some scholars refer to "limited" war instead of "real" war. I will use "absolute" and "ideal" war as equivalent terms and consider "real" and "limited" war as synonyms. Paret, "The Genesis of *On War,*" 22; Paret, "Clausewitz," 199-200.

13. Clausewitz, *On War,* 87.

14. Definitions paraphrased from *The American Heritage Dictionary,* 2nd College ed. (Boston: Houghton Mifflin, 1985, 959-960; Paret, "Clausewitz," 210.

15. War as a political instrument forms a foundation for this course. In the next lesson, we will explore Clausewitz's summary of his thoughts. The excerpt will provide a sample of Clausewitz's intellectual style. Look for his dialectical approach in the passage.

16. In translating Clausewitz, Michael Howard and Peter Paret will also call the "paradoxical" trinity, the "remarkable" trinity. In the original hardback translation, they used "remarkable," but they changed it to "paradoxical" in the later paperback translation. To avoid confusion, I will only use "paradoxical" trinity for the concept. Clausewitz, *On War,* 89.

17. Ibid.

18. Clayton K. S. Chun, *War, Military Theory, and Strategy: An Introduction* (Boston: Houghton Mifflin, 2002; Paret, "Clausewitz," 201. Additionally, Michael Handel provides an interesting examination of multiple triangles and vectors in "The Trinitarian Analysis," *Masters*, 102-107.

19. Handel, *Masters*, 103.

20. Clausewitz's "recent wars" refer to the French Revolutionary Wars (1792-1801) and the Napoleonic Wars (1803-1815).

21. Remember this phrase when we read Thomas Schelling in a later lesson.

22. Compare this idea with Sun Tzu's writing.

MILITARY GENIUS: THE ANSWER TO FOG & FRICTION?

Carl von Clausewitz

Clausewitz presents another useful conceptual tool in his description of military genius. Specifically, he defines genius as "a highly developed mental aptitude for a particular occupation. . . . those gifts of mind and temperament that in combination bear on military activity. . . . Genius consists *in a harmonious combination of elements*, in which one or the other ability may predominate, but none may be in conflict with the rest."[1] Obviously, this definition differs from our use of the word, but keep in mind that psychology, as social science, was in its infancy during Clausewitz's day.[2]

What did Clausewitz mean by "military genius"? Since war is the "realm of danger," courage is the first requirement. "Courage is of two kinds: courage in the face of personal danger and courage to accept responsibility." Since war is the "realm of physical exertion and suffering," a leader must possess "a certain strength of body and soul." Clausewitz continues, "War is the realm of uncertainty; three quarters of the factors on which action in war is based are wrapped in a fog of greater or lesser uncertainty. A sensitive and discriminating judgment is called for; a skilled intelligence to scent out the truth." Moreover, since war is "the realm of chance," Clausewitz calls for a "quick recognition of a truth the mind would ordinarily miss or would perceive only after long study and reflection." He further explains the concept with a French term, *coup d'oeil*, "*an intellect, that even in the darkest hour, retains some glimmerings of the inner light which leads to truth*" (emphasis in original). Linked to this instinctive ability, Clausewitz stresses determination, "the courage to follow this faint light wherever it may lead." While Clausewitz acknowledges the importance of intelligence, his use of military genius emphasizes physical and moral courage, physical and moral strength, an instinctive grasp of truth, and determination.[3]

In Clausewitz's view, a brilliant mind may be a detriment to a military leader: "Intelligence alone is not courage; we often see that the most intelligent people are irresolute. . . . In short, we believe that determination proceeds from a special type of mind, from a strong rather than a brilliant one."[4] Since the clock rules every military plan, intelligence must be matched with resolve and the ability to make a decision.[5] Military genius combines strength of mind with strength of character. In explaining strength of mind, Clausewitz points to the mental and physical energy required to meet the unexpected. He calls for staunchness, the will's resistance to a heavy blow; endurance, the will's capability for prolonged resistance; and self-control, "the gift of keeping calm under the greatest stress."[6] He builds to the idea of strength of character, the ability to stick to convictions.[7] "Obviously a man whose opinions are constantly changing, even though this is a response to his own reflections, would not be called *a man of character*."[8] In sum, while "military genius" invokes an image of Albert Einstein's mental brilliance in contemporary readers, Clausewitz blends intelligence, temperament, and action:

> Truth in itself is rarely sufficient to make men act. Hence the step is always from cognition to volition, from knowledge to ability. The most powerful springs of action in men lie in his emotions. He derives his most vigorous support, . . . , from that blend of brains and temperament which we have learned to recognize in the qualities of determination, firmness, staunchness, and strength of character.[9]

Clausewitz articulates powerful concepts in *On War*, including the dual nature of war, war as a political instrument, the remarkable trinity, military genius, and friction. They also highlight Clausewitz's thoughts on the value of military theory. He believes the role of military theory is to educate the mind. Military theory provides tools for thought, but not a checklist for action. Clausewitz recognizes that war is not performed against an inanimate object: "War, however, is not the action of a living force upon a lifeless mass . . . but always the collision of two living forces."[10] Too often military theorists aim at fixed values and seek to reduce war to objective, quantifiable factors.[11] Clausewitz rejects this tendency and stresses the uncertain and variable. In war the enemy is a living being who thinks and reacts, quite often in unexpected ways. Therefore, theory cannot lead to complete understanding, but it can strengthen and refine judgment. In addition, military theory can show how one thing is related to another and it can separate the important from the unimportant.[12] To recap, Clausewitz provides ideas to stimulate thinking and an intellectual process to educate our minds. Those looking for formulas to solve problems or concrete principles for success will be disappointed.[13]

Despite its status as a masterpiece, *On War* contains significant flaws apparent to the modern reader. To a limited extent, these flaws reflect the incomplete, unfinished state of the manuscript upon Clausewitz's death, but more importantly, *On War* reflects Clausewitz's problem of trying to explain the unique phenomenon of Napoleon Bonaparte and two decades of Napoleonic warfare. Consequently, Clausewitz over emphasizes decisive battle between formal armies. He mentions, but does not adequately develop, irregular or guerrilla warfare.[14] Along the same lines, Clausewitz centers his analysis upon the nation state and neglects cultural, religious, tribal, or other forms or non-state war.[15] Since the Age of Napoleon represented a relatively static period of technological development, Clausewitz fails to anticipate the Industrial Revolution and the vital importance of technology in modern war. Similarly, Clausewitz's continental, Prussian perspective leads him to miss the importance of naval warfare, let alone air, space, or nuclear war.[16] Furthermore, although Clausewitz's understanding of war as politics is admirable, he neglects the important relationship between war and economics. He fails to connect politics with economics or emphasize the economic dimension of why nations go to war. Although he discusses supply, logistics, and administration in one chapter, his coverage is cursory in comparison to other topics.[17] Thus, Clausewitz's shortcomings in the material realm of war, expressed in terms of weaponry, technology, supply, and logistics to some extent offsets his brilliance in the political, emotional, and theoretical realms.

B. WAR IS AN INSTRUMENT OF POLICY[18]

Up to now we have considered the incompatibility between war and every other human interest, individual or social—a difference that derives from human nature, and that therefore no philosophy can resolve. We have examined this incompatibility from various angles so that none of its conflicting elements should be missed. Now we must seek out the unity into which these contradictory elements combine in real life, which they do by partly neutralizing each other. . . . This unity lies in *the concept that war is only a branch of political activity; that it is in no sense autonomous.*

It is, of course, well-known the only source of war is politics—the intercourse of governments and peoples; but it is apt to be assumed that war suspends that intercourse and replaces it by a wholly different condition, ruled by no law but its own.

We maintain, on the contrary, that war is simply a continuation of political intercourse, with the addition of other means. We deliberately use the phrase "with the addition of other means" because we also want to make clear that war in itself does not suspend political intercourse or change it into something entirely different. In essentials that intercourse continues, irrespective of the means it employs. The main lines along which military events progress, and to which they are restricted, are political lines that continue throughout the war into the subsequent peace. How could it be otherwise? Do political relations between peoples and between governments stop when diplomatic notes are no longer exchanged? Is war not just another expression of their thoughts, another form of speech or writing? Its grammar, indeed, may be its own, but not its logic.

If that is so, then war cannot be divorced from political life; and whenever this occurs in our thinking about war, the many links that connect the two elements are destroyed and we are left with something pointless and devoid of sense.

This conception would be ineluctable even if war were total war, the pure elements of enmity unleashed. All the factors that go to make up war and determine its salient features—the strength of each antagonist, the character of the peoples and their governments, and so forth, all the elements listed in the first chapter of Book I—are these not all political, so closely connected with political activity that it is impossible to separate the two? But it is yet more vital to bear all this in mind when studying actual practice. We will then find that war does not advance relentlessly toward the absolute, as theory would demand. Being incomplete and self-contradictory, it cannot follow its own laws, but has to be treated as a part of some other whole; the name of which is policy.[19]

. . .

So policy converts the overwhelmingly destructive element of war into a mere instrument. It changes the terrible battle-sword that a man needs both hands and his entire strength to wield, and with which he strikes home once and no more, into a light, handy rapier—sometimes just a foil for the exchange of thrusts, feints and parries. . . .

If war is part of policy, policy will determine its character. As policy becomes more ambitious and vigorous, so will war, and this may reach the point where war attains its absolute form. If we look at war in this light, we do not need to lose sight of this absolute: on the contrary, we must constantly bear it in mind.

Only if war is looked at this way does its unity reappear; only then can we see that all wars are things of the *same* nature; and this alone will provide the right criteria for conceiving and judging great designs.

Policy, of course, will not extend its influence to operational details. Political considerations do not determine the posting of guards or the employment of patrols. But they are the more influential in the planning of war, of the campaign, and often even of battle. . . .

The only question, therefore, is whether, when war is being planned, the political point of view should give way to the purely military . . . that is, should it disappear completely or subordinate itself, or should the political point of view remain dominant and the military be subordinated to it?

That the political view wholly cease to count on the outbreak of war is hardly conceivable unless pure hatred made all wars a struggle for life and death. In fact, as we have said, they are nothing but expressions of policy itself. Subordinating the political point of view to the military would be absurd, for it is policy that has created war. Policy is the guiding intelligence and war only the instrument, not vice versa. No other possibility exists, then, than to subordinate the military point of view to the political. . . .

In short, at the highest level the art of war turns into policy—but a policy conducted by fighting battles rather than by sending diplomatic notes.

We can now see that the assertion that a major military development, or the plan for one, should be a matter for *purely military* opinion is unacceptable and can be damaging. Nor indeed is it sensible to summon soldiers, as many governments do when they are planning a war, and ask them for *purely military advice.* But it makes even less sense for theoreticians to assert that all available military resources should be put at the disposal of the military commander so that on their basis he can draw up purely military plans for a war or a campaign. It is in any case a matter of common experience that despite the great variety and development of modern war its major lines are still laid down by governments; in other words, if we are to be technical about it, by a purely political and not a military body.

This is as it should be. No major proposal required for war can be worked out in ignorance of political factors; and when people talk . . . about harmful political influence on the management of war, they are not really saying what they mean. Their quarrel should be with the policy itself, not with its influence. If the policy is right—that is, successful—any intentional effect it has on the conduct of the war can only be to the good. If it has the opposite effect the policy itself is wrong.

Only if statesmen look to certain military moves and actions to produce effects that are foreign to their nature do political decisions influence operations for the worse. In the same way as a man who has not fully mastered a foreign language sometimes fails to express himself correctly; so statesmen often issue orders that defeat the purpose they are meant to serve. Time and again that has happened, which demonstrates that a certain grasp of military affairs is vital for those in charge of general policy. . . .

If war is to be fully consonant with political objectives, and policy suited to the means available for war, then unless statesman and soldier are combined in one person, the only sound expedient is to make the commander-in-chief a member of the cabinet, so that the cabinet can share in the major aspects of his activities. But that, in turn, is only feasible if the cabinet—that is, the government—is near the theater of operations, so that decisions can be taken without serious loss of time. . . .

What is highly dangerous is to let any soldier but the commander-in-chief exert an influence in the cabinet. It seldom leads to sound vigorous action. . . .

Let us conclude with some historical observations. . . .

Clearly the tremendous effects of the French Revolution abroad were caused not so much by new military methods and concepts as by radical changes in policies and administration, by the new character of government, altered conditions of the French people, and the like. The other governments did not understand these changes, that they wished to oppose new and overwhelming forces with customary means: all these were political errors. Would a purely military view of war have enabled anyone to detect these faults and cure them? It would not. . . .

It follows that the transformation of the art of war resulted from the transformation of politics. So far from suggesting that the two could be disassociated from each other, these changes are a strong proof of their indissoluble connection.

Once again: war is an instrument of policy. It must necessarily bear the character of policy and measure by its standards. The conduct of war, in its great outlines, is therefore policy itself, which takes up the sword in place of the pen, but does not on that account cease to think according to its own laws.

CHAPTER 7 FRICTION IN WAR[20]

If one has never personally experienced war, one cannot understand in what the difficulties constantly mentioned really consist, nor why a commander should need any brilliance and exceptional ability. Everything looks simple; the knowledge required does not look remarkable, the strategic options are so obvious that by comparison the simplest problem of higher mathematics has an impressive scientific dignity. Once war has actually been seen the difficulties become clear; but it is still extremely hard to describe the unseen, all-pervading element that brings about this change of perspective.

Everything in war is very simple, but the simplest thing is difficult. The difficulties accumulate and end by producing a kind of friction that is inconceivable unless one has experienced war. Imagine a traveler who late in the day decides to cover two more stages before nightfall. Only four or five hours more, on a paved highway with relays of horses: it should be an easy trip. But at the next station he finds no fresh horses, or only poor ones; the country grows hilly, the road bad, night falls, and finally after many difficulties he is only too glad to reach a resting place with any kind of primitive accommodation. It is much the same in war. Countless minor incidents—the kind you can never really foresee—combine to lower the general level of performance, so that one always falls far short of the intended goal. Iron will-power can overcome this friction; it pulverizes every obstacle, but of course it wears down the machine as well. . . .

Friction is the only concept that more or less corresponds to the factors that distinguish real war from war on paper. The military machine—the army and everything related to it—is basically very simple and therefore seems easy to manage. But we should bear in mind that none of its components is of one piece: each part is composed of individuals, everyone of whom retains his potential of friction. In theory it sounds reasonable enough: a battalion commander's duty is to carry out his orders; discipline welds the battalion together, its commander must be a man of tested capacity, and so the great beam turns on its iron pivot with a minimum offriction. In fact, it is different, and every fault and exaggeration of the theory is instantly exposed in war. A battalion is made up of individuals, the least important of whom may chance to delay things or somehow make them go wrong. The dangers inseparable from war and the physical exertions war demands can aggravate the problem to such an extent that they must be ranked among its principal causes.

This tremendous friction. . . is everywhere in contact with chance, and brings about effects that cannot be measured, just because they are largely due to chance. One, for example, is the weather. Fog can prevent the enemy from being seen in time, a gun from firing when it should, a report from reaching the commanding officer. Rain can prevent a battalion from arriving, make another late by keeping it not three but eight hours on the march, ruin a cavalry charge by bogging the horses down in mud, etc.

We give these examples simply for illustration, to help the reader follow the argument. It would take volumes to cover all difficulties. We could exhaust the reader with illustrations alone if we really tried to deal with the whole range of minor troubles that must be faced in war. The few we have given will be excused by those readers who have long since understood what we are after.

Action in war is like movement in a resistant element. Just as the simplest and most natural of movements, walking, cannot easily be performed in water, so in war it is difficult for normal efforts to achieve even moderate results. A genuine theorist is like a swimming teacher, who makes his pupils practice motions on land that are meant to be performed in water. To those who are not thinking of swimming the motions will appear grotesque and exaggerated. By the same token, theorists who have never swum, or who have not learned to generalize from experience, are impractical and even ridiculous: they teach only what is already common knowledge: how to walk.

Moreover, every war is rich in unique episodes. Each is an uncharted sea, full of reefs. The commander may suspect the reef's existence without ever having seen them; now he has to steer past them in the dark. If a contrary wind springs up, if some major mischance appears, he will need the greatest skill and personal exertion, and the utmost presence of mind, though from a distance everything may seem to be proceeding automatically. An understanding of friction is a large part of that much-admired sense of warfare which a good general is supposed to possess. To be sure, the best general is not the one who is most familiar with the idea of friction, and who takes it most to heart (he belongs to the anxious type so common among experienced commanders). The good general must know friction in order to overcome it whenever possible, and in order not to expect a standard of achievement in his operations which this very friction makes impossible. Incidentally, it is a force that theory can never quite define. Even if it could, the development of instinct and tact would still be needed, a form of judgement much more necessary in an area littered by endless minor obstacles than in great, momentous questions, . . . As with a man of the world instinct becomes almost habit so that he always acts, speaks, and moves appropriately, so only the experienced officer will make the right decision in major and minor matters—at every pulse beat of war. Practice and experience dictate the answer: "this is possible, that is not." So he rarely makes a serious mistake, such as can, in war, shatter confidence and become extremely dangerous if it occurs often.

Friction, as we choose to call it, is the force that makes the apparently easy so difficult. We shall frequently revert to this subject, and it will become evident that an eminent commander needs more than experience and a strong will. He must have other exceptional abilities as well.

CHAPTER 3 ON MILITARY GENIUS[21]

Any complex activity, if it is to be carried on with any degree of virtuosity, calls for appropriate gifts of intellect and temperament. If they are outstanding and reveal themselves in exceptional achievements, their possessor is called a "genius."

We are aware that this word is used in many senses, differing both in degree and in kind. We also know that some of these meanings make it difficult to establish the essence of genius. But since we claim no special expertise in philosophy or grammar, we may be allowed to use the word in its ordinary meaning, in which "genius" refers to a very highly developed mental aptitude for a particular occupation.

Let us discuss this faculty, this distinction of mind for a moment, setting out its claims in greater detail, so as to gain a better understanding of the concept. . . . What we must do is to survey all those gifts of mind and temperament that in combination bear on military activity. These, taken together, constitute *the essence of military genius* . . . it does not consist in a single appropriate gift—courage, for example—while other qualities of mind or temperament are wanting or are not suited to war. Genius consists *in a harmonious combination of elements,* in which one or the other ability may predominate, but none may be in conflict with the rest.

If every soldier needed some degree of military genius our armies would be very weak, for the term refers to a special cast of mental or moral powers which can rarely occur in an army when a society has to employ its abilities in many different areas. The smaller the range of activities of a nation and the more the military factor dominates, the greater will be the incidence of military genius. . . . Possession of military genius coincides with the higher degrees of civilization: the most highly developed societies produce the most brilliant soldiers, as the Romans and the French have shown us. With them, as with every people renowned in war, the greatest names do not appear before a high level of civilization has been reached.

We can already guess how great a role intellectual powers play in the higher forms of military genius. Let us now examine the matter more closely.

War is the realm of danger; therefore *courage* is the soldier's first requirement.

Courage is of two kinds: courage in the face of personal danger, and courage to accept responsibility, either before the tribunal of some outside power or before the court of one's own conscience. Only the first kind will be discussed here.

Courage in face of personal danger is also of two kinds. It may be indifference to danger, which could be due to the individual's constitution, or to his holding life cheap, or to habit. In any case, it must be regarded as a permanent *condition.* Alternatively, courage may result from such positive motives as ambition, patriotism, or enthusiasm of any kind. In that case courage is a feeling, an emotion, not a permanent state.

These two kinds of courage act in different ways. The first is the more dependable; having become second nature, it will never fail. The other will often achieve more. There is more reliability in the first kind, more boldness in the second. The first leaves the mindcalmer; the second tends to stimulate, but it can also blind. *The highest kind of courage is a compound of both.*

War is the realm of physical exertion and suffering. These will destroy us unless we can make ourselves indifferent to them, and for this birth or training must provide us with a certain strength of body and soul. If we do possess those qualities, then even if we have nothing but common sense to guide them we shall be well equipped for war: it is exactly these qualities that primitive and semi civilized peoples usually possess.

If we pursue the demands that war makes on those who practice it, we come to the region dominated by the *powers of intellect.* War is the realm of uncertainty; three quarters of the factors on which action in war is based are wrapped in a fog of greater or lesser uncertainty.

A sensitive and discriminating judgement is called for; a skilled intelligence to scent out the truth.

Average intelligence may recognize the truth occasionally, and exceptional courage may now and then retrieve a blunder; but usually intellectual inadequacy will be shown up by indifferent achievement.

War is the realm of chance. No other human activity gives it greater scope: no other has such incessant and varied dealings with this intruder. Chance makes everything more uncertain and interferes with the whole course of events.

Since all information and assumptions are open to doubt, and with chance at work everywhere, the commander continually finds that things are not as he expected. This is bound to influence his plans, or at least the assumptions underlying them. If this influence is sufficiently powerful to cause a change in his plans, he must usually work out new ones; but for these the necessary information may not be immediately available. During an operation decisions have usually to be made at once: there may be no time to review the situation or even to think it through. Usually, of course, new information and re-evaluation are not enough to make us give up our intentions: they only call them in question. We now know more, but this makes us more, not less uncertain. The latest reports do not arrive all at once: they merely trickle in. They continually impinge on our decisions, and our mind must be permanently armed, so to speak, to deal with them.

If the mind is to emerge unscathed from this relentless struggle with the unforeseen, two qualities are indispensable: *first, an intellect that, even in the darkest hour, retains some glimmerings of the inner light which leads to truth; and second, the courage to follow this faint light wherever it may lead.* The first of these qualities is described by the French term, *coup d'oeil;* the second is *determination.*

The aspect of war that has always attracted the greatest attention is the engagement. Because time and space are important elements of the engagement, and were particularly significant in the days when the cavalry attack was the decisive factor, the *idea of a rapid and accurate decision* was first based on an evaluation of time and space, and consequently received a name which refers to visual estimates only. Many theorists of war have employed the term in that limited sense. But soon it was also used of any sound decision taken in the midst of action—such as recognizing the right point to attack, etc. *Coup d'oeil* therefore refers not alone to the physical but, more commonly, to the inward eye. The expression, like the quality itself, has certainly always been more applicable to tactics, but it must also have its place in strategy, since here as well quick decisions are often needed. Stripped of metaphor and of the restrictions imposed on it by the phrase, the concept merely refers to the quick recognition of a truth that the mind would ordinarily miss or would perceive only after long study and reflection.

Determination in a single instance is an expression of courage; if it becomes characteristic, a mental habit. But here we are referring not to physical courage but to the courage to accept responsibility, courage in the face of a moral danger..This has often been called *couraged'esprit,* because it is created by the intellect. That, however, does not make it an act of the intellect: it is an act of temperament. Intelligence alone is not courage; we often see that the most intelligent people are irresolute. Since in the rush of events a man is governed by feelings rather than by thought, the intellect needs to arouse the quality of courage, which then supports and sustains it in action.

Looked at in this way, the role of determination is to limit the agonies of doubt and the perils of hesitation when the motives for action are inadequate. Colloquially, to be sure, the term "determination" also applies to a propensity for daring, pugnacity, boldness, or temerity. . . .

Determination, which dispels doubt, is a quality that can be aroused only by the intellect, and by a specific cast of mind at that. More is required to create determination than a mere conjunction of superior insight with the appropriate emotions. Some may bring the keenest brains to the most formidable problems, and may possess the courage to accept serious responsibilities; but when faced with a difficult situation they still find themselves unable to reach a decision. Their courage and their intellect work in separate compartments, not together; determination, therefore, does not result. It is engendered only by a *mental act;* the mind tells man that boldness is required, and thus gives direction to his will. This particular cast of mind, which employs the fear of *wavering* and *hesitating* to suppress all other fears, is the force that makes strong men determined. . . .

In short, we believe that determination proceeds from a special type of mind, from a strong rather than a brilliant one. We can give further proof of this interpretation by pointing to the many examples of men who show great determination as junior officers, but lose it as they rise in rank. Conscious of the need to be decisive, they also recognize the risks entailed by a *wrong* decision; since they are unfamiliar with the problems now facing them, their mind loses its former incisiveness. The more used they had been to instant action, the more their timidity increases as they realize the dangers of the vacillation that ensnares them.

Having discussed *coup d'oeil* and determination it is natural to pass to a related subject: *presence of mind.* This must play a great role in war, the domain of the unexpected, since it is nothing but an increased capacity of dealing with the unexpected. We admire presence of mind . . . as we admire quick thinking in the face of danger. Neither needs to be exceptional, so long as it meets the situation. A reaction following long and deep reflection may seem quite commonplace; as an immediate response, it may give keen pleasure. The expression "presence of mind" precisely conveys the speed and immediacy of the help provided by the intellect. . . .

Four elements make up the climate of war: danger, exertion, uncertainty, and chance. If we consider them together, it becomes evident how much fortitude of mind and character are needed to make progress in these impeding elements with safety and success. According to circumstance, reporters and historians of war use such terms as *energy, firmness, staunchness, emotional balance,* and *strength of character.* These products of a heroic nature could almost be treated as one and the same force—strength of will—which adjusts itself to circumstances: but though closely linked, they are not identical. A closer study of the interplay of psychological forces at work here may be worthwhile.

To begin with, clear thought demands that we keep one point in mind of the weight, the burden, the resistance—call it what you like—that challenges the psychological strength of the soldier, only a small part is the *direct result of the enemy's activity, his resistance, or his operations.* The direct and primary impact of enemy activity falls, initially, on the soldier's person without affecting him in his capacity as commander. If, for example, the enemy resists four hours instead of two, the commander is in danger twice as long; but the higher an officer's rank, the less significant this factor becomes, and to the commander-in-chief it means nothing at all.

A second way in which the enemy's resistance *directly* affects the commander is the loss that is caused by prolonged resistance and the influence this exerts on his sense of responsibility. The deep anxiety which he must experience works on his strength of will and puts it to the test. Yet we believe that this is not by any means the heaviest burden he must bear, for he is answerable to himself alone. All other effects of enemy action, however, are felt by the men under his command, and *through them react on him.*

So long as a unit fights cheerfully, with spirit and élan, great strength of will is rarely needed; but once conditions become difficult, as they must when much is at stake, things no longer run like awell-oiled machine. The machine itself begins to resist, and the commander needs tremendous will-power to overcome this resistance. The machine's *resistance* need not consist of disobedience and argument, though this occurs often enough in individual soldiers. It is the impact of the ebbing of moral and physical strength, of the heart-rending spectacle of the dead and wounded, that the commander has to withstand—first in himself, and then in all those who, directly or indirectly, have entrusted him with their thoughts and feelings, hopes and fears. As each man's strength gives out, as it no longer responds to his will, the inertia of the whole gradually comes to rest on the commander's will alone. The ardor of his spirit must rekindle the flame of purpose in all others; his inward fire must revive their hope. Only to the extent that he can do this will he retain his hold on his men and keep control. Once that hold is lost, once his own courage can no longer revive the courage of his men, the mass will drag him down to the brutish world where danger is shirked and shame is unknown. Such are the burdens in battle that the commander's courage and strength of will must overcome if he hopes to achieve outstanding success. The burdens increase with the number of men in his command, and therefore the higher his position, the greater the strength of character he needs to bear the mounting load.

Energy in action varies in proportion to the strength of its motive, whether the motive be the result of intellectual conviction or of emotion. Great strength, however, is not easily produced where there is no emotion.

Of all the passions that inspire man in battle, none, we have to admit, is so powerful and so constant as the longing for honour and renown. . . . In war they act as the essential breath of life that animates the inert mass. Other emotions may be more common and more venerated—patriotism, idealism, vengeance, enthusiasm of every kind—but they are no substitute for a thirst for fame and honour. They may, indeed, rouse the mass to action and inspire it, but they cannot give the commander the ambition to strive higher than the rest, as he must if he is to distinguish himself. They cannot give him, as can ambition, a personal, almost proprietary interest in every aspect of fighting, so that he turns each opportunity to best advantage—plowing with vigour, sowing with care, in the hope of reaping with abundance. It is primarily this spirit of endeavor on the part of commanders at all levels, this inventiveness, energy, and competitive enthusiasm, which vitalizes an army and makes it victorious. And so far as the commander-in-chief is con- cerned, we may well ask whether history has ever known a great general who was not ambitious; whether, indeed, such a figure is conceivable.

Staunchness indicates the will's resistance to a single blow; *endurance* refers to prolonged resistance.

Though the two terms are similar and are often used interchangeably, the difference be- tween them is significant and unmistakable. Staunchness in face of a single blow may result from strong emotion, whereas intelligence helps sustain endurance. The longer an action lasts, the more deliberate endurance becomes, and this is one of its sources of strength.

We now turn to *strength of mind,* or of *character,* and must first ask what we mean by these terms.

Not, obviously, vehement display of feeling, or passionate temperament: that would strain the meaning of the phrase. We mean the ability to keep one's head at times of exceptional stress and violent emotion. Could strength of intellect alone account for such a faculty? We doubt it. Of course the opposite does not flow from the fact that some men of outstanding intellect do lose their self-control; it could be argued that a powerful rather than a capacious mind is what is needed. But it might be closer to the truth to assume that the faculty known as *self-control*—the gift of keeping calm even under the greatest stress—is rooted in temperament. It is itself an emotion which serves to balance the passionate feelings in strong characters without destroying them, and it is this balance alone that assures the dominance of the intellect. The counterweight we mean is simply the sense of human dignity, the noblest pride and deepest need of all: the urge *to act rationally at all times.* Therefore we would argue that a strong character is one *that will not be unbalanced by the most powerful emotions. . . .*

Inflammable emotions, feelings that are easily roused, are in general of little value in practi- cal life, and therefore of little value in war. Their impulses are strong but brief. If the energy of such men is joined to courage and ambition they will often prove most useful at a modest level of command, simply because the action controlled by junior officers is of short duration. Often a single brave decision, a burst of emotional force, will be enough. A daring assault is the work of a few minutes, while a hard-fought battle may last a day, and a campaign an entire year.

Their volatile emotions make it doubly hard for such men to preserve their balance; they often lose their heads, and nothing is worse on active service. All the same, it would be untrue to say that highly excitable minds could never be strong—that is, could never keep their balance even under the greatest strain. . . . If training, self-awareness, and experience sooner or later teaches them how to be on guard against themselves, then in times of great excitement an internal counterweight will assert itself so that they too can draw on great strength of character. . . .

We repeat again: strength of character does not consist solely in having powerful feelings, but in maintaining one's balance in spite of them. Even with the violence of emotion, judgement and principle must still function like a ship's compass, which records the slightest variations however rough the sea.

We say a man has strength of character, or simply has character, if he sticks to his convictions, whether these derive from his own opinions or someone else's, whether they represent principles, attitudes, sudden insights, or any other mental force. Such *firmness* cannot show itself, of course, if a man keeps changing his mind. This need not be the consequence of external influence; the cause may be the workings of his own intelligence, but this would suggest a peculiarly insecure mind. Obviously a man whose opinions are constantly changing, even though this is in response to his own reflections, would not be called a *man of character.* The term is applied only to men whose views are *stable and constant.* This may be because they are well thought-out, clear, and scarcely open to revision; or, in the case of indolent men, because such people are not in the habit of mental effort and therefore have no reason for altering their views;and finally, because a firm decision, based on fundamental principle derived from reflection, is relatively immune to changes of opinion.

With its mass of vivid impressions and the doubts which characterize all information and opinion, there is no activity like war to rob men of confidence in themselves and in others, and to divert them from their original course of action.

In the dreadful presence of suffering and danger, emotion can easily overwhelm intellectual conviction, and in this psychological fog it is so hard to form clear and complete insights that changes of view become more understandable and excusable. Action can never be based on anything firmer than instinct, a sensing of the truth. Nowhere, in consequence, are differences of opinion so acute as in war, and fresh opinions never cease to batter at one's convictions. No degree of calm can provide enough protection: new impressions are too powerful, too vivid, and always assault the emotions as well as the intellect.

Only those general principles and attitudes that result from clear and deep understanding can provide a *comprehensive* guide to action. It is to these that opinions on specific problems should be anchored. The difficulty is to hold fast to these results of contemplation in the torrent of events and new opinions. Often there is a gap between principles and actual events that cannot always be bridged by a succession of logical deductions. Then a measure of self-confidence is needed, and a degree of skepticism is also salutary. Frequently nothing short of an imperative principle will suffice, which is not part of the immediate thought-process, but dominates it: that principle is in all doubtful cases *to stick to one's first opinion and to refuse to change unless forced to do so by a clear conviction.* A strong faith in the overriding truth of tested principles is needed; the *vividness* of transient impressions must not make us forget that such truth as they contain is of a lesser stamp. By giving precedence, in case of doubt, to our earlier convictions, by holding to them stubbornly, our actions acquire that quality of steadiness and consistency which is termed strength of character.

It is evident how greatly strength of character depends on balanced temperament; most men of emotional strength and stability are therefore men of powerful character as well.

Strength of character can degenerate into *obstinacy.* The line between them is often hard to draw in a specific case; but surely it is easy to distinguish them in theory.

Obstinacy *is not an intellectual defect;* it comes from reluctance to admit that one is wrong. . . . Obstinacy *is a fault of temperament.* Stubbornness and intolerance of contradiction result from a special kind of *egotism,* which elevates above everything else *the pleasure of its autonomous intellect, to which others must bow. . . .*

We would therefore argue that strength of character turns to obstinacy as soon as a man resists another point of view not from superior insight or attachment to some higher principle, but because he *objects instinctively.* Admittedly, this definition may not be of much practical use; but it will nevertheless help us avoid the interpretation that obstinacy is simply a more intense form of strong character. There is a basic difference between the two. They are closely related, but one is so far from being *a higher degree* of the other that we can even find extremely obstinate men who are too dense to have much strength of character.

So far our survey of the attributes that a great commander needs in war has been concerned with qualities in which mind and temperament work together. Now we must address ourselves to a special feature of military activity . . . I mean the relationship between warfare and terrain.

This relationship, to begin with, is *a permanent factor*—so much so that one cannot conceive of a regular army operating except in a definite space. Second, its importance is *decisive in the highest degree,* for it affects the operations of all forces, and at times entirely alters them. Third, its influence may be felt in the *very smallest feature of the ground,* but it can also dominate *enormous areas.*

In these ways the relationship between warfare and terraindetermines the peculiar character of military action. If we consider other activities connected with the soil—gardening, for example, farming, building, hydraulic engineering, mining, game-keeping, or forestry—none extends to more than a very limited area, and a working knowledge of that area is soon acquired. But a commander . . . can never completely reconnoiter [the terrain], and which because of the constant movement and change to which he is subject he can never really come to know. To be sure, the enemy is generally no better off; but the handicap, though shared, is still a handicap, and the man with enough talent and experience to overcome it will have a real advantage. Moreover it is only in a general sense that the difficulty is the same for both sides; in any particular case the defender usually knows the area far better than his opponent.

This problem is unique. To master it a special gift is needed, which is given the too restricted name *of a sense of locality*. It is the faculty of *quickly and accurately grasping the topography of any area* which enables a man to find his way about at any time. Obviously this is an act of the imagination. Things are perceived, of course, partly by the naked eye and partly by the mind, which fills the gaps with guess work based on learning and experience, and thus constructs a whole out of the fragments that the eye can see; but if the whole is to be vividly present to the mind, imprinted like a picture, like a map, upon the brain, without fading or blurring in detail, *it can only be achieved by the mental gift that we call imagination.* . . . We also admit that a good memory can be a great help . . . .

Scope for this talent naturally grows with increased authority. . . . A commander-in-chief, on the other hand, must aim at acquiring an overall knowledge of the configuration of a province, of an entire country. His mind must hold a vivid picture of the road-network, the river-lines and the mountain ranges, without ever losing a sense of his immediate surroundings. . . . Never the less it is true that with a quick, unerring sense of locality his dispositions will be more rapid and assured; he will run less risk of a certain awkwardness in his concepts, and be less dependent on others.

We attribute this ability to the imagination; but that is about the only service that war can demand from this frivolous goddess, who inmost military affairs is liable to do more harm than good.

With this, we believe, we have reached the end of our review of the intellectual and moral powers that human nature needs to draw upon in war. The vital contribution of intelligence is clear throughout. No wonder then, that war, though it may appear to be uncomplicated, cannot be waged with distinction except by men of outstanding intellect.

. . . It is true that we normally regard the plain, efficient soldier as the very opposite of the contemplative scholar, or of the inventive intellectual with his dazzling range of knowledge. This antithesis is not entirely unrealistic; but it does not prove that courage alone will make an efficient soldier, or that having brains and using them is nota necessary part of being a good fighting man. Once again we must insist: no case is more common than that of the officer whose energy declines as he rises in rank and fills positions that are beyond his abilities. But we must also remind the reader that outstanding effort, the kind that gives men a distinguished name, is what we have in mind. Every level of command has its own intellectual standards, its own prerequisites for fame and honour.

A major gulf exists between a commander-in-chief—a general who leads the army as a whole or commands in a theater of operations—and the senior generals immediately subordinate to him. The reason is simple: the second level is subjected to much closer control and supervision, and thus gives far less scope for independent thought. . . . We only wish to show things as they are, so that the reader should not think that a brave but brainless fighter can do anything of outstanding significance in war. . . .

Appropriate talent is needed at all levels if distinguished service is to be performed. But history and posterity reserve the name of "genius" for those who have excelled in the highest positions—as commanders-in-chief—since here the demands for intellectual and moral powers are vastly greater.

To bring a war, or one of its campaigns, to a successful close requires a thorough grasp of national policy. On that level strategy and policy coalesce: the commander-in-chief is simultaneously a states man. . . .

The great range of business that a supreme commander must swiftly absorb and accurately evaluate has been indicated in the first chapter. We argue that a commander-in-chief must also be a statesman, but he must not cease to be a general. On the one hand, he is aware of the entire political situation; on the other, he knows exactly how much he can achieve with the means at his disposal.

Circumstances vary so enormously in war, and are so indefinable, that a vast array of factors has to be appreciated—mostly in the light of probabilities alone. The man responsible for evaluating the whole must bring to his task the quality of intuition that perceives the truth at every point. Otherwise a chaos of opinions and considerations would arise, and fatally entangle judgement. . . .

What this task requires in the way of higher intellectual gifts is a sense of unity and a power of judgement raised to a marvelous pitch of vision, which easily grasps and dismisses a thousand remote possibilities which an ordinary mind would labor to identify and wear itself out in so doing. Yet even that superb display of divination, the sovereign eye of genius itself, would still fall short of historical significance without the qualities of character and temperament we have described.

Truth in itself is rarely sufficient to make men act. Hence the step is always long from cognition to volition, from knowledge to ability. The most powerful springs of action in men lie in his emotions. He derives his most vigorous support, if we may use the term, from that blend of brains and temperament which we have learned to recognize in the qualities of determination, firmness, staunchness, and strength of character. . . .

Finally, and without wishing to risk a closer definition of the higher reaches of the spirit, let us assert that the human mind (in the normal meaning of the term) is far from uniform. If we then ask what sort of mind is likeliest to display the qualities of military genius, experience and observation will both tell us that it is the inquiring rather than the creative mind, the comprehensive rather than the specialized approach, the calm rather than the excitable head to which in war we would choose to entrust the fate of our brothers and children, and the safety and honour of our country

SUMMARY

A study of Clausewitz's *On War* shows it to be a respected masterpiece, full of profound insights, but by no means an unerring, sacred text. Keeping in mind that *On War* was never finished, the three passages in this lesson reinforce three important ideas: war is subordinate to politics, "fog and friction" marks war in reality and separates it from war in theory; and the "military genius" of the commander is vital to overcoming the obstacles presented by fog and friction.

Clausewitz opens the door to lifelong study of warfare. His concepts of absolute versus real war, war as an instrument of politics, the remarkable trinity, military genius, friction, and others, offer important insights for analyzing historical and contemporary events. His dialectical approach and willingness to lead the reader through intellectual debates provide a process for how to think about war. By mastering his methods we also learn to recognize *On War's* limitations. In doing so, we fulfill Clausewitz's vision of military theory: an intellectual tool to educate a leader's mind.

NOTES

1. Carl von Clausewitz, *On War*, ed. and trans. Michael Howard and Peter Paret (Princeton, N. J.: Princeton University Press, 1976), 100.
2. Peter Paret, "Clausewitz," in *Makers of Modern Strategy from Machiavelli to the Nuclear Age*, ed. Peter Paret (Princeton, N. J.: Princeton University Press, 1986) 204.
3. Clausewitz, *On War*, 100-102.
4. Ibid., 102-103.
5. Colin S. Gray, *Modern Strategy* (Oxford: Oxford University Press, 1999), 42.
6. Clausewitz, *On War*, 105-106.
7. Ibid., 107.
8. Clausewitz, 107.
9. Clausewitz, 112.
10. Clausewitz, 77. 149.
11. Williamson Murray and Mark Grimsley, "Introduction: On Strategy," in Williamson Murray, MacGregor Knox, and A. Bernstein, eds., *The Making of Strategy: Rulers, States, and War* (Cambridge: Cambridge University Press, 1994): 1.
12. Paret, "Clausewitz," 193.
13. Ironically, many military and civilian policy makers tend to use *On War* as a book of quotations and cite passages for justifying positions and to stifle debate.
14. Clausewitz's chapter entitled, "The People in Arms," (Book Six, Chapter 26) is a relatively perceptive discussion of irregular warfare, but it consists of only five pages buried in the middle of his text. Clausewitz, *On War*, 479-483; Gray, *Modern Strategy*, 110.
15. John Keegan's *A History of Warfare* (New York: Vintage Books, 1993) launches a major attack on this point. Gray, *Modern Strategy*, 102, 104.
16. Gray, *Modern Strategy*, 108.
17. See Book Five, Chapter 14, "Maintenance and Supply." Gray, *Modern Strategy*, 107; Paret, "Clausewitz," 207-209; Paret, "Clausewitz," 208-209; Howard, *Clausewitz*, 3-4.
18. The following passage concludes Clausewitz's discussion of the relationship of war and politics. It emphasizes the subordination of the military to the political. The text is an edited form of Book Eight, "War Plans"; Carl von Clausewitz, *On War*, trans. Michael Howard and Peter Paret, ed. Beatrice Heuser (Oxford: Oxford University Press, 2006), 252-258.
19. Editor's note: Notice that Clausewitz has rejected his initial thesis (that war in theory will escalate to absolute violence) and instead of producing a synthesis called for in a classic dialectic, he now backs his original antithesis (that real war is limited by politics and fog & friction).

20. The second passage is an edited form of Book One, Chapter Seven, "Friction in War." Carl von Clausewitz, *On War*, trans. Michael Howard and Peter Paret, ed. Beatrice Heuser (Oxford: Oxford University Press, 2006), 252-258.

21. The third passage represents an assertion: Clausewitz suggests that "military genius" is a partial answer to the "fog and friction" of war. The text is an edited form of Book Eight, "War Plans"; Carl von Clausewitz, *On War*, trans. Michael Howard and Peter Paret, ed. Beatrice Heuser (Oxford: Oxford University Press, 2006), 252-258.

BRIDGING THE GAP: GRAND STRATEGY, DISLOCATION, AND THE INDIRECT APPROACH

B. H. Liddell Hart

Renowned as a journalist and historian, Basil Henry Liddell Hart stands as one of the most significant British military theorists of the twentieth century. Born of British parents in Paris in 1895 and educated in England, Liddell Hart was commissioned in 1915. During World War I, he fought at the Battle of the Somme where he was a casualty of poison gas. After partial recovery, he returned to duty as a trainer of infantry men. He rose to the rank of captain and remained in service until 1924 when the British Army granted him a medical discharge.[1]

During the 1920s and 1930s, Liddell Hart gained fame as the military correspondent of major London newspapers including the *Daily Telegraph* and *The Times*. A prolific author, Liddell Hart published 30 major books and articles dedicated to preventing a reoccurrence of trench warfare. An early advocate of mobile offensive tactics and tank warfare, Liddell Hart introduced the "expanding torrent," a combined-arms approach using mechanized infantry, tanks, and aircraft to penetrate enemy lines and strike enemy command and control facilities in the rear.[2] Liddell Hart also argued for an "indirect approach" in both strategy and tactics. On the battlefield, mechanized forces would maneuver to avoid enemy strength, while strategists would use emerging land, air, and sea technologies to strike enemy flanks. In both tactics and strategy, headfirst attacks into enemy defenses would be avoided at all costs. Combining these ideas, many writers considered Liddell Hart to be the intellectual father of "Blitzkrieg."[3] Ironically, because he argued against a major commitment of British land forces on the European continent before World War II, Liddell Hart lost favor within the British government. Consequently, Liddell Hart played a minor role during the war and is known primarily for his thoughts and writing.

In many of his works, Liddell Hart attacks Carl von Clausewitz's *On War*. He goes to great lengths to dissect the Prussian's writing, but a balanced reader will note Liddell Hart's narrow and selective interpretation of Clausewitz's work. On specific issues, Liddell Hart offers useful insights, but in general, the British theorist misses the main point of his German counterpart.[4] Along the same lines, Liddell Hart's "indirect approach" parallels Sun Tzu's *The Art of War*. Scholars vary in their interpretation along these lines, but students may benefit from the comparison. Regardless of the comparisons to other "classical strategists," Liddell Hart's extensive, astute writings rank him as one of the important, influential military thinkers of recent times.

THE THEORY OF STRATEGY
B. H. LIDDELL HART[5]

Having drawn our conclusions from an analysis of history it seems advantageous to construct on the fresh foundation a new dwelling-house for strategic thought.

Let us first be clear as to what is strategy. Clausewitz, in his monumental work, *On War*, defined it as "the art of the employment of battles as a means to gain the object of war. In other words strategy forms the plan of the war, maps out the proposed course of the different campaigns which compose the war, and regulates the battles to be fought in each."[6] .

One defect of this definition is that it intrudes on the sphere of policy, or the higher conduct of the war, which must necessarily be the responsibility of the government and not of the military leaders it employs as its agents in the executive control of operations. Another defect is that it narrows the meaning of "strategy" to the pure utilization of battle, thus conveying the idea that battle is the only means to the strategical end. It was an easy step for Clausewitz's less profound disciples to confuse the means with the end, and to reach the conclusion that in war every other consideration should be subordinated to the aim of fighting a decisive battle.

Relation to Policy

To break down the distinction between strategy and policy would not matter much if the two functions were normally combined in the same person, as with a Frederick [the Great of Prussia] or a Napoleon. But as such autocratic soldier-rulers have been rare in modern times and became temporarily extinct in the nineteenth century, the effect was insidiously harmful. For it encouraged soldiers to make the preposterous claim that policy should be subservient to their conduct of operations, and, especially in democratic countries, it drew the states man on to overstep the definite border of his sphere and interfere with his military employees in the actual use of their tools.

Moltke reached a clearer, and wiser, definition in terming strategy "the practical adaptation of the means placed at a general's disposal to the attainment of the object in view."[7]

This definition fixes the responsibility of a military commander to the government by which he is employed. His responsibility is that of applying most profitably to the interest of the higher war policy the force allotted to him within the theater of operations assigned to him. If he considers that the force allotted is in adequate for the task indicated he is justified in pointing this out, and if his opinion is over ruled he can refuse or resign the command; but he exceeds his rightful sphere if he attempts to dictate to the government what measure of force should be placed at his disposal.

On the other hand, the government, which formulates war policy, and has to adapt it to conditions which often change as a war progresses, can rightly intervene in the strategy of a campaign not merely by replacing a commander in whom it has lost confidence, but by modifying his object according to the needs of its war policy. While it should not interfere with him in the handling of his tools, it should indicate clearly the nature of his task. Thus strategy has not necessarily the simple object of seeking to over throw the enemy's military power. When a government appreciates that the enemy has the military superiority, either in general or in a particular theater, it may wisely enjoin a strategy of limited aim.

It may desire to wait until the balance of force can be changed by the intervention of allies or by the transfer of forces from another theater. It may desire to wait, or even to limit its military effort permanently, while economic or naval action decides the issue. It may calculate that the over throw of the enemy's military power is a task definitely beyond its capacity, or not worth the effort—and that the object of its war policy can be assured by seizing territory which it can either retain or use as bargaining counters when peace is negotiated.

Such a policy has more support from history than military opinion hither to has recognized, and is less in herently a policy of weakness than some apologists imply. It is, indeed, bound up with the history of the British Empire, and repeatedly proved a lifebuoy to Britain's allies as well as of permanent benefit to herself. However unconsciously followed, there is ground for inquiry whether this "conservative" military policy does not deserve to be accorded a place in the theory of the conduct of war.

The more usual reason for adopting a strategy of limited aim is that of awaiting a change in the balance of force—a change often sought and achieved by draining the enemy's force, weakening him by pricks instead of risking blows. The essential condition of such a strategy is that the drain on him should be disproportionately greater than on oneself. The object may be sought by raiding his supplies; by local attacks which annihilate or inflict disproportionate loss on parts of his force; by luring him into unprofitable attacks; by causing an excessively wide distribution of his force; and, not least, by exhausting his moral and physical energy.

This closer definition sheds light on the question, previously raised, of a general's independence in carrying out his own strategy inside his theater of operations. For if the government has decided upon a limited aim or "Fabian" grand strategy the general who, even within his strategic sphere, seeks to overthrow the enemy's military power may do more harm than good to the government's war policy.[8] Usually, a war policy of limited aim imposes a strategy of limited aim, and a decisive aim should only be adopted with the approval of the government which alone can decide whether it is "worth the candle."

We can now arrive at a shorter definition of strategy as—"the art of distributing and applying military means to fulfill the ends of policy." For strategy is concerned not merely with the movement of forces—as its role is often defined—but with the effect. When the application of the military instrument merges into actual fighting, the dispositions for and control of such direct action are termed "tactics." The two categories, although convenient for discussion, can never be truly divided into separate compartments because each not only influences but merges into the other.

Higher, or Grand Strategy

As tactics is an application of strategy on a lower plane, so strategy is an application on a lower plane of "grand strategy." While practically synonymous with the policy which guides the conduct of war, as distinct from the more fundamental policy which should govern its object, the term "grand strategy" serves to bring out the sense of "policy in execution." For the role of grand strategy—higher strategy—is to co-ordinate and direct all the resources of a nation, or band of nations, towards the attainment of the political object of the war—the goal defined by fundamental policy.

Grand strategy should both calculate and develop the economic resources and man-power of nations in order to sustain the fighting services. Also the moral resources—for to foster the people's willing spirit is often as important as to possess the more concrete forms of power. Grand strategy, too, should regulate the distribution of power between the several services, and between the services and industry. Moreover, fighting power is but one of the instruments of grand strategy—which should take account of and apply the power of financial pressure, of diplomatic pressure, of commercial pressure, and, not least of ethical pressure, to weaken the opponent's will. A good cause is a sword as well as armor. Likewise, chivalry in war can be a most effective weapon in weakening the opponent's will to resist, as well as augmenting moral strength.

Furthermore, while the horizon of strategy is bounded by the war, grand strategy looks beyond the war to the subsequent peace. It should not only combine the various instruments, but so regulate their use as to avoid damage to the future state of peace for its security and prosperity. The sorry state of peace, for both sides, that has followed most wars can be traced to the fact that, unlike strategy, the realm of grand strategy is for the most part *terra incognita*—still awaiting exploration, and understanding.

Pure, or Military, Strategy

Having cleared the ground, we can build up our conception of strategy on its proper plane and original basis—that of "the art of the general."

Strategy depends for success, first and most, on a sound *calculation and co-ordination of the end and the means.* The end must be proportioned to the total means, and the means used in gaining each intermediate end which contributes to the ultimate must be proportioned to the value and needs of that inter mediate end whether it be to gain an objective or to fulfill a contributory purpose. An excess may be as harmful as a deficiency.

A true adjustment would establish a perfect *economy of force,* in the deeper sense of that oft-distorted military term. But, because of the nature and uncertainty of war, an uncertainty increased by lack of scientific study, even the greatest military ability could not achieve a true adjustment, and success lies in the closest approximation to truth.

This relativity is inherent because, however far our knowledge of the science of war be extended, it will depend on art for its application. Art cannot only bring the end nearer to the means, but by giving a higher value to the means, enable the end to be extended.

This complicates calculation, because no man can exactly calculate the capacity of human genius and stupidity, nor the incapacity of will.

Elements and Conditions

In strategy, however, calculation is simpler and a closer approximation to truth possible than in tactics. For in war the chief incalculable is the human will, which manifests itself in resistance, which in turn lies in the province of tactics. Strategy has not to overcome resistance, except from nature. *Its purpose is to diminish the possibility of resistance,* and it seeks to fulfill this purpose by exploiting the elements of *movement* and *surprise.*

Movement lies in the physical sphere, and depends on a calculation of the conditions of time, topography, and transport capacity. (By transport capacity is meant both the means by which, and the measure in which, force can be moved and maintained.)

Surprise lies in the psychological sphere and depends on a calculation, far more difficult than in the physical sphere, of the manifold conditions, varying in each case, which are likely to affect the will of the opponent.

Although strategy may aim more at exploiting movement than at exploiting surprise, or conversely, the two elements react on each other. Movement generates surprise, and surprise gives impetus to movement. For a movement which is accelerated or changes its direction inevitably carries with it a degree of surprise, even though it be unconcealed; while surprise smoothes the path of movement by hindering the enemy's counter-measures and counter-movements.

As regards the relation of strategy to tactics, while in execution the border line is often shadowy, and it is difficult to decide exactly where a strategical movement ends and a tactical movement begins, yet in conception the two are distinct. Tactics lies in and fills the province of fighting. Strategy not only stops on the frontier, but has for its purpose the reduction of fighting to the slenderest possible proportions.

Aim of Strategy

This statement may be disputed by those who conceive the destruction of the enemy's armed force as the only sound aim in war, who hold that the only goal of strategy is battle, and who are obsessed with the Clause witzian saying that "blood is the price of victory." Yet if one should concede this point and meet its advocates on their own ground, the statement would remain unshaken. For even if a decisive battle be the goal, the aim of strategy must be to bring about this battle under the most advantageous circumstances. And the more advantageous the circumstances, the less, proportionately, will be the fighting.

The perfection of strategy would be, therefore, to produce a decision without any serious fighting. History, as we have seen, provides examples where strategy, helped by favourable conditions, has virtually produced such a result . . . . The most striking and catastrophic of recent examples was the way that, in 1940, the Germans cut off and trapped the Allies' left wing in Belgium, following Guderian's surprise break-through in the centre at Sedan, and thereby ensured the general collapse of the Allied armies on the Continent.[9]

While these were cases where the destruction of the enemy's armed forces was economically achieved through their disarming by surrender, such "destruction" may not be essential for a decision, and for the fulfillment of the war-aim. In the case of a state that is seeking, not conquest, but the maintenance of its security, the aim is fulfilled if the threat be removed—if the enemy is led to abandon his purpose. . . .

While such blood less victories have been exceptional, their rarity enhances rather than detracts from their value—as an indication of latent potentialities, in strategy and grand strategy. Despite many centuries' experience of war, we have hardly begun to explore the field of psychological warfare.

From deep study of war, Clausewitz was led to the conclusion that—"All military action is permeated by intelligent forces and their effects." Nevertheless, nations at war have always striven, or been driven by their passions, to disregard the implications of such a conclusion. Instead of applying intelligence, they have chosen to batter their heads against the nearest wall.

It rests normally with the government, responsible for the grand strategy of a war, to decide whether strategy should make its contribution by achieving a military decision or otherwise. Just as the military means is only one of the means to the end of grand strategy—one of the instruments in the surgeon's case—so battle is only one of the means to the end of strategy. If the conditions are suitable, it is usually the quickest in effect, but if the conditions are unfavorable it is folly to use it.

Let us assume that a strategist is empowered to seek a military decision. His responsibility is to seek it under the most advantageous circumstances in order to produce the most profitable result. Hence *his true aim is not so much to seek battle as to seek a strategic situation so advantageous that if it does not of itself produce the decision, its continuation by a battle is sure to achieve this.* In other words, dislocation is the aim of strategy; its sequel may be either the enemy's dissolution or his easier disruption in battle. Dissolution may involve some partial measure of fighting, but this has not the character of a battle.

Action of Strategy

How is the strategic dislocation produced? In the physical, or "logistical," sphere it is the result of a move which (*a*) upsets the enemy's dispositions and, by compelling a sudden "change of-front," dislocates the distribution and organization of his forces;
(*b*) separates his forces; (*c*) endangers his supplies; (*d*) menaces the route or routes by which he could retreat in case of need and reestablish himself in his base or homeland.

A dislocation may be produced by one of these effects, but is more often the consequence of several. Differentiation, indeed, is difficult because a move directed towards the enemy's rear tends to combine these effects. Their respective influence, however, varies and has varied throughout history according to the size of armies and the complexity of their organization. With armies which "live on the country," drawing their supplies locally by plunder or requisition, the line of communication has negligible importance. Even in a higher stage of military development, the smaller a force the less dependent it is on the line of communication for supplies. The larger an army, and the more complex its organization, the more prompt and serious in effect is a menace to its line of communication.

Where armies have not been so dependent, strategy has been correspondingly handicapped, and the tactical issue of battle has played a greater part. Nevertheless, even thus handicapped, able strategists have frequently gained a decisive advantage previous to battle by menacing the enemy's line of retreat, the equilibrium of his dispositions, or his local supplies.

To be effective, such a menace must usually be applied at a point closer, in time and space, to the enemy's army than a menace to his communications; and thus in early warfare it is often difficult to distinguish between the strategical and tactical maneuver.

In the psychological sphere, dislocation is the result of the impression on the commander's mind of the physical effects which we have listed. The impression is strongly accentuated if his realization of his being at a disadvantage is sudden, and if he feels that he is unable to counter the enemy's move. Psychological dislocation fundamentally springs from this sense of being trapped.

This is the reason why it has most frequently followed a physical move on to the enemy's rear. An army, like a man, cannot properly defend its back from a blow without turning round to use its arms in the new direction. "Turning" temporarily unbalances an army as it does a man, and with the former the period of instability is inevitably much longer. In consequence, the brain is much more sensitive to any menace to its back.

In contrast, to move directly on an opponent consolidates his balance, physical and psychological, and by consolidating it increases his resisting power. For in the case of an army it rolls the enemy back towards their reserves, supplies, and reinforcements, so that as the original front is driven back and worn thin, new layers are added to the back. At the most, it imposes a strain rather than producing a shock.

Thus a move round the enemy's front against his rear has the aim not only of avoiding resistance on its way but in its issue. In the profoundest sense, it takes the *line of least resistance*. The equivalent in the psychological sphere is the *line of least expectation*. They are the two faces of the same coin, and to appreciate this is to widen our understanding of strategy. For if we merely take what obviously appears the line of least resistance, its obviousness will appeal to the opponent also; and this line may no longer be that of least resistance.

In studying the physical aspect we must never lose sight of the psychological, and only when both are combined is the strategy truly an indirect approach, calculated to dislocate the opponent's balance.

The mere action of marching indirectly towards the enemy and on to the rear of his disposi-tions does not constitute a strategic indirect approach. Strategic art is not so simple. Such an approach may start by being indirect in relation to the enemy's front, but by the very directness of its progress towards his rear may allow him to change his dispositions, so that it soon becomes a direct approach to his new front.

Because of the risk that the enemy may achieve such a change of front, it is usually neces-sary for the dislocating move to be preceded by a move, or moves, which can best be defined by the term "distract" in its literal sense of "to draw asunder." The purpose of this "distraction" is to *deprive the enemy of his freedom of action,* and it should operate in both the physical and psychological spheres. In the physical, it should cause a distension of his forces or their diver-sion to unprofitable ends, so that they are too widely distributed, and too committed elsewhere, to have the power of interfering with one's own decisively intended move. In the psychological sphere, the same effect is sought by playing upon the fears of, and by deceiving, the opposing command. "Stonewall" Jackson aptly expressed this in his strategical motto—"Mystify, mis-lead, and surprise."[10] For to mystify and to mislead constitutes "distraction," while surprise is the essential cause of "dislocation." It is through the "distraction" of the commander's mind that the distraction of his forces follows. The loss of his freedom of action is the sequel to the loss of his freedom of conception.

A more profound appreciation of how the psychological permeates and dominates the physi-cal sphere has an indirect value. For it warns us of the fallacy and shallowness of attempting to analyze and theorize about strategy in terms of mathematics. To treat it quantitatively, as if the issue turned merely on a superior concentration of force at a selected place, is as faulty as to treat it geometrically: as a matter of lines and angles.

Even more remote from truth—because in practice it usually leads to a dead end—is the tendency of textbooks to treat war as mainly a matter of concentrating superior force. In his celebrated definition of economy of force Foch termed this—"The art of pouring out *all* one's resources at a given moment on one spot; of making use there of *all* troops, and, to make such a thing possible, of making those troops permanently communicate with each other, instead of dividing them and attaching to each fraction some fixed and invariable function; its second part, a result having been attained, is the art of again so disposing the troops as to converge upon, and act against, a new single objective."[11]

It would have been more exact, and more lucid, to say that an army should always be so distributed that its parts can aid each other and combine to produce the maximum *possible* con-centration of force at one place, while the minimum force *necessary* is used elsewhere to prepare the success of the concentration.

To concentrate *all* is an unrealizable ideal, and dangerous even as a hyperbole. Moreover, in practice the "minimum necessary" may form a far larger proportion of the total than the "maxi-mum possible." It would even be true to say that the larger the force that is effectively used for *distraction* of the enemy, the greater is the chance of the concentration succeeding in its aim. For otherwise it may strike an object too solid to be shattered.

Superior weight at the intended decisive point does not suffice unless that point cannot be reinforced *in time* by the opponent. It rarely suffices unless that point is not merely weaker numerically but has been weakened morally. Napoleon suffered some of his worst checks because he neglected this guarantee—and the need for distraction has grown with the delaying power of weapons.

Basis of Strategy

A deeper truth to which Foch and other disciples of Clausewitz did not penetrate fully is that in war every problem, and every principle, is a duality. Like a coin, it has two faces. Hence the need for a well-calculated compromise as a means to reconciliation. This is the inevitable consequence of the fact that war is a two-party affair, so imposing the need that while hitting one must guard. Its corollary is that, in order to hit with effect, the enemy must be taken off his guard. Effective concentration can only be obtained when the opposing forces are dispersed; and, usually, in order to ensure this, one's own forces must be widely distributed. Thus, by an outward paradox, true concentration is the product of dispersion.

A further consequence of the two-party condition is that to ensure reaching an objective one should have *alternative objectives*. Herein lies a vital contrast to the single-minded nineteenth century doctrine of Foch and his fellows—a contrast of the practical to the theoretical. For if the enemy is certain as to your point of aim he has the best possible chance of guarding himself—and blunting your weapon. If, on the other hand, you take a line that threatens alternative objectives, you distract his mind and forces. This, moreover, is the most economic method of *distraction,* for it allows you to keep the largest proportion of your force available on your real line of operation—thus reconciling the greatest possible concentration with the necessity of dispersion.

The absence of an alternative is contrary to the very nature of war. It sins against the light which Bourcet shed in the eighteenth century by his most penetrating dictum that "every plan of campaign ought to have several branches and to have been so well thought out that one or other of the said branches cannot fail of success."[12]. . . Seventy years later [American Civil War General William T.] Sherman was to re-learn the lesson from experience, by reflection, and to coin his famous maxim about 'putting the enemy on the horns of a dilemma'. In any problem where an opposing force exists, and cannot be regulated, one must foresee and provide for alternative courses. Adaptability is the law which governs survival in war as in life—war being but a concentrated form of the human struggle against environment.

To be practical, any plan must take account of the enemy's power to frustrate it; the best chance of overcoming such obstruction is to have a plan that can be easily varied to fit the circumstances met; to keep such adaptability, while still keeping the initiative, the best way is to operate along a line which offers alternative objectives. For thereby you put your opponent on the horns of a dilemma, which goes far to assure the gaining of at least one objective—whichever is least guarded—and may enable you to gain one after the other.

In the tactical field, where the enemy's dispositions are likely to be based on the nature of the ground, it may be more difficult to find a choice of dilemma—producing objectives than it is in the strategical field, where the enemy will have obvious industrial and railway centers to cover. But you can gain a similar advantage by adapting your line of effort to the degree of resistance that is met, and exploiting any weakness that is found. A plan, like a tree, must have branches—if it is to bear fruit. A plan with a single aim is apt to prove a barren pole.

Cutting Communications

In the planning of any stroke at the enemy's communications, either by maneuver round his flank or by rapid penetration of a breach in his front, the question will arise as to the most effective point of aim—whether it should be directed against the immediate rear of the opposing force, or further back.

When studying this question at the time that experimental mechanized forces were first created, and their strategic use was under consideration, I sought guidance on it by an analysis of cavalry raids carried out in the past, especially in the more recent wars since railways came into use. While such cavalry raids had more limited potentialities than a deep strategic penetration of mechanized forces seemed to me to promise, this difference emphasized rather than detracted from the significance of the evidence which they provided. Making the necessary adjustment, the following deductions could be drawn:

> In general, the nearer to the force that the cut is made, the *more immediate* the effect; the nearer to the base, the *greater* the effect. In either case, the effect becomes much greater and more quickly felt if made against a force that is in motion, and in course of carrying out an operation, than against a force that is stationary.

In deciding the direction of a mobile stroke, much depends on the strategic position and supply conditions of the enemy forces, i.e. the number of their lines of supply, the possibility of adopting alternative lines of supply, the amount of supplies likely to be accumulated in advanced depots close behind their front. After these factors have been considered, they should be reconsidered in the light of the *accessibility* of the various possible objectives, i.e. the distance, the natural obstacles, and the opposition likely to be met. In general, the longer the distance that has to be covered, the greater the ratio of natural obstacles, but the less the ratio of opposition.

Thus, unless the natural obstacles are very severe, or the enemy has unusual independence of supplies from base, more success and more effect is to be expected from cutting his communications as far back as possible.

A further consideration is that while a stroke close in rear of the·enemy force may have more effect on the minds of the enemy troops, a stroke far back tends to have more effect on the mind of the enemy commander.

Cavalry raids in the past had often forfeited their effect by lack of care in carrying out the demolition side of their task. As a result the prospective value of mobile raids on communications had been unduly discounted. It should be realized, too, that the flow of supplies may be interrupted not only by demolition son the route, but by actual or threatened interception of trains and lorry convoys. This form of interruption was increased in potentiality by the development of mechanized forces—because of their flexibility and power of cross-country maneuver.

These deductions were confirmed by the experience of the Second World War—above all by the catastrophically paralyzing effect, physically and psychologically, that was produced when Guderian's panzer forces, racing far ahead of the main German armies, severed the Allied armies' communications where these crossed the far back line of the. . . [French in 1940].

The Method of Advance

Until the end of the eighteenth century, a physically concentrated advance, both strategic (*to* the battlefield) and tactical (*on* the battlefield) was the rule. Then Napoleon, exploiting Bourcet's ideas and the new divisional system, introduced a *distributed* strategic advance—the army moving in independent fractions. But the tactical advance was still, in general, a concentrated one.[13]

. Towards the end of the nineteenth century, with the development of fire weapons, the tactical advance became dispersed, i.e. in particles, to diminish the effect of fire. But the strategic advance had again become concentrated—this was due partly to the influence of railways and the growth of masses, partly to the misunderstanding of the Napoleonic method.

A revival of the distributed strategic advance was required in order to revive the art and effect of strategy. Moreover, new conditions—air power and motor power—point to its further development into a *dispersed strategic advance.* The danger of air attack, the aim of mystification, and the need of drawing full value from mechanized mobility, suggest that advancing forces should not only be distributed as widely as is compatible with combined action, but be dispersed as much as is compatible with cohesion. This becomes essential in face of atomic weapons. The development of radio is a timely aid towards reconciling dispersion with control.

Instead of the simple idea of a concentrated stroke by a concentrated force, we should choose according to circumstance between these variants:

(i) Dispersed advance with concentrated single aim, i.e. against one objective.

(ii) Dispersed advance with concentrated serial aim, i.e. against successive objectives.

(These will each demand preliminary moves to distract the enemy's attention and forces, unless the possibility of taking alternative objectives enables us to rely on such distracting effect being produced already by the enemy's perplexity.)

(iii)   Dispersed advance with distributed aim, i.e. against a number of objectives simultaneously.

(Under the new conditions of warfare, the *cumulative* effect of partial success, or even mere threat, at a number of points may be greater than the effect of complete success at one point.)

The effectiveness of armies depends on the development of such new methods—methods which aim at permeating and dominating areas rather than capturing lines; at the practicable object of paralyzing the enemy's action rather than the theoretical object of crushing his forces. Fluidity of force may succeed where concentration of force merely entails a perilous rigidity.

SUMMARY

In his "Theory of Strategy," British military theorist B. H. Liddell Hart introduces many fundamental concepts that form the basis of today's air, space, and cyberspace power. Students will see the link between Liddell Hart's ideas and those of Sun Tzu and Clausewitz. Additionally, later air and space theorists will draw from Liddell Hart's writing for ideas relating to grand strategy, strategic dislocation, and the indirect approach. Liddell's strategic concepts include the concept of grand strategy: to coordinate and direct all the resources of a nation toward the political object of war, i.e. the goal defined by fundamental policy. He defines the "instruments of grand strategy" as applying financial, diplomatic, commercial, and ethical pressure, as well as military. This concept serves as the source of DIME (Diplomatic, Informational, Military, and Economic instruments of power) used in contemporary doctrine. Air, space, and cyberspace thinkers would agree with Liddell Hart's idea that grand strategy looks beyond war to the subsequent peace. Likewise early air power theorists paralleled Liddell Hart's concept that strategy seeks to diminish enemy resistance through movement and surprise, ideally to win without serious fighting. Contemporary thinkers John Boyd and John Warden built upon Liddell Hart's maxim: the true aim of strategy is not to seek battle, but strategic advantage, and in turn strategic dislocation. This directly led to the idea of strategic paralysis. Boyd and Warden also learned three other concepts from Liddell Hart: 1) Psychological dislocation stems from the sense of being trapped; 2) Distract the enemy to deprive his freedom of action; and 3) Adaptability governs survival in war as well as life. Unfortunately, B. H. Liddell Hart is often overlooked by today's doctrine, but astute students recognize that Liddell Hart forms the bridge between classic military theory and modern theories of air, space, and cyberspace power.

NOTES

1. Paraphrased from Tim Travers, "Liddell Hart, B. H." in *The Officer's Companion to Military History*, Paul E. Bauman, ed. (New York: Houghton Mifflin, 1999), 265.

2. Another British military thinker, J. F. C. Fuller, is also credited with this concept. Ibid. and Alex Danchev, "Liddell Hart, Capt Sir Basil Henry," in *The Oxford Companion to Military History*, Richard Holmes, ed. (Oxford: Oxford University Press, 2001), 505-506.

3. Following World War II, some scholars list Erwin Rommel and George S. Patton as students of Liddell Hart. This claim should be viewed carefully since many military thinkers developed similar ideas about armored warfare in the 1930s. For a readable account, see Dennis E. Showalter, *Patton and Rommel: Men of War in the Twentieth Cenury* (New York: Berkley Caliber, 2005).

4. Please note, this sentence represents an assertion—the statement of my opinion as if it were a fact. If this were a formal paper, I would cite specific evidence to support this assertion, but in consideration of your time, I will leave it as is.

5. B. H. Liddell Hart, *Strategy*, 2d ed. (New York: Frederick A. Praeger, 1967), 333-346.

6. Editor's note: In his original work, Liddell Hart used the English style of spelling and punctuation. To minimize student confusion, the editor changed the text to American standards.

7. Editor's note: Liddell Hart refers to Helmuth von Moltke, the elder, a noted nineteenth century military theorist. Von Moltke served as Chief of Staff of the Prussian Army during the Wars of German Unification (1864-1871). He should not be confused with his nephew, Helmuth von Moltke, the younger, who served as Chief of the German General Staff from 1906-1914 and associated with the Schlieffen Plan of World War I. Caleb Carr, "Moltke, Helmuth Karl von," and Daniel Moran, "Moltke, Helmuth von (the Younger)," in *The Officer's Companion to Military* History, Paul E. Bauman, ed. (New York: Houghton Mifflin Custom Publishing, 1999), 306-308.

8. Editor's note: "Fabian strategy" (or "Fabian tactics") calls for the weaker side to avoid pitched battle with the stronger side. Instead, the weaker foe harasses, raids, or fights smaller engagements in order to wear down and defeat the will of the stronger side. The phrase is named for the Roman leader Quintus Fabius Maximus who faced Hannibal during the Second Punic War (217 BCE). Josiah Ober, "Fabius Maximus Cunctator," in *The Officer's Companion to Military* History, Paul E. Bauman, ed. (New York: Houghton Mifflin Custom Publishing, 1999), 159; Kennedy Hickman, "Fabian Strategy: Wearing Down the Enemy," http://militaryhistory.about.com/od/militarystrategies/p/fabian.htm, (Accessed 13 August 2013).

9. Editor's note: Liddell Hart refers to German general Heinz Guderian who is credited with the German breakthrough of the Allied lines which led to the Fall of France during World War II. Gerhard L. Weinberg, "Guderian, Heinz," in *The Officer's Companion to Military* History, Paul E. Bauman, ed. (New York: Houghton Mifflin Custom Publishing, 1999), 191-192.

10. Editor's note: Liddell Hart refers to Confederate general Thomas J. "Stonewall" Jackson of US Civil War fame.

11. Editor's note: A well-known, pre-war French military theorist and successful writer, General Ferdinand Foch commanded French armies on the Western Front during World War I.

12. Editor's note: Pierre de Bourcet (1700-1780) advocated breaking down the unwieldy armies of eighteenth-century Europe into smaller, more manageable units, known as divisions. Theodore Ropp, *War in the Modern World* (New York and London: Collier Macmillan, 1959, 1962), 101.

13. Editor's note: Armies of the French Revolution adopted Pierre de Bourcet's ideas, among others, that eventually led to Napoleon's corps system. Theodore Ropp, *War in the Modern World* (New York and London: Collier Macmillan, 1959, 1962), 101.

THE SCIENCE OF GUERRILLA WARFARE: TIME, SPACE, AND IDEAS AS WEAPONS

T. E. Lawrence

T. E. Lawrence's "Science of Guerrilla Warfare" opens a series of chapters examining asymmetric, or irregular, warfare. The block intends to provide sufficient theoretical background and context for today's Air Force officer to understand the broad political, economic, and social issues surrounding the challenges of irregular warfare (also called guerrilla war, counterinsurgency, revolutionary war, small wars, and other terms with varying specific definitions, but inherently related for our purposes).[1] The section will highlight the changes and continuities of both guerrilla warfare and theories of counterinsurgency to provide perspective for the airman called upon to support operations. Although American forces in Iraq have withdrawn and those in Afghanistan are winding down their presence, the Department of Military & Strategic Studies believes that it is imperative for officer candidates to grasp the basic concepts behind this important and difficult form of warfare. Hence, the block begins with a study of a classic, thought-provoking article.

Lawrence of Arabia is one of the truly fascinating "military" figures of the twentieth century. He possessed a unique background and unmatched talents. Oxford educated in literature and the classics, he had learned several dialects of Arabic, as well as Latin and Greek. In 1909-1910, Lawrence walked to old Crusader castles in Palestine, Lebanon, Syria, and Turkey. In 1911-1913, he participated in archaeological digs in Egypt, Syria, and present-day Iraq. In 1914, Lawrence volunteered to serve the British Army. Commissioned an intelligence officer and stationed in Cairo, Lawrence frequently interrogated Arab prisoners who had been recruited into the Turkish Army. Of this duty, he wrote, "I always knew their districts, and asked about my friends in them. Then they always told me everything!"[2] For our purposes, the point to emphasize is that Lawrence's study of the classics, archaeology, and Middle Eastern languages made him uniquely qualified. He knew and appreciated the subtleties of Bedouin tribal culture (he would argue that the concept of being "Arab" as we understand it today did not apply to Middle Eastern peoples of his day). He strongly advocated the creation of Arab nationalism and an Arab state. Because he understood that the Bedouin tribes represented family units and were largely unaffected by the broader issues of World War I, Lawrence realized that his "Arab" forces could not absorb casualties. Instead, he emphasized raiding Turkish railroads...attacking the enemy's material resources. Conversely, with a huge land area to defend, the Turks would always be on the defensive, vulnerable, and susceptible to hit and run attacks.

More than an astute military theorist, T. E. Lawrence became an international star. In contrast to the blood and mud of the Western Front's trench warfare, Lawrence's exploits gained him global fame. Unfortunately, at times Lawrence forgot his role as a British officer. During his talks with Bedouin tribal leaders, Lawrence committed on a personal level to the creation of a postwar Arab state that did not reflect the official position of the British government. Hence, Lawrence felt personally dishonored, discredited, and depressed when the United Kingdom did not back his promises to Arab leaders at the postwar conferences that eventually created European mandates to replace the Ottoman Empire. Consequently, Lawrence withdrew from public and political life; although it should be noted that he kept a private correspondence with Winston Churchill for many years while working as an enlisted aircraft mechanic in the Royal Air Force! Lawrence represents the epitome of a military amateur with a perceptive, open mind willing to look at the unique circumstances of the war he faced. Well-read and with unmatched cultural expertise, he created innovative, "out-of-the-box" approaches to the military, political, and cultural challenges of his day.

"SCIENCE OF GUERRILLA WARFARE"[3]

T.E. Lawrence

GUERRILLA, a term currently used to denote war carried on by bands in any irregular and unorganized manner; erroneously written "guerilla," being the diminutive of the Span. guerra, war. The position of irregular combatants was one of the subjects dealt with at the Peace Conference of 1899, and the rules there adopted were reaffirmed at the conference of 1907.[4] They provide that irregular bands in order to enjoy recognition as belligerent forces shall (a) have at their head a person responsible for his subordinates, (b) wear some fixed distinctive badge recognizable at a distance, (c) carry arms openly and (d) conform in their operations to the laws and customs of war. The rules, however, also provide that in case of invasion the inhabitants of a territory who on the approach of the invading enemy spontaneously take up arms to resist it, shall be regarded as belligerent troops if they carry arms openly and respect the laws and customs of war, although they may not have had time to become organized in accordance with the above provisions.... [Forward to Lawrence's 1929 *Encyclopedia Britannica* article by Sir Thomas Barclay, vice president of the International Law Association, 1929]

This study of the science of guerrilla, or irregular, warfare is based on the concrete experience of the Arab Revolt against the Turks 1916-1918.[5] But the historical example in turn gains value from the fact that its course was guided by the practical application of the theories here set forth.

The Arab Revolt began in June, 1916, with an attack by the half-armed and inexperienced tribesmen upon the Turkish garrisons in Medina and about Mecca.[6] They met with no success, and after a few days' effort withdrew out of range and began a blockade. This method forced the early surrender of Mecca, the more remote of the two centers. Medina, however, was linked by railway to the Turkish main army in Syria, and the Turks were able to reinforce the garrison there. The Arab forces which had attacked it then fell back gradually and took up a position across the main road to Mecca.

At this point the campaign stood still for many weeks.... [with the Turks possessing Mecca, but unable to leave the city due to supply shortages. The following describes Lawrence's "lessons learned" from the campaign.]

Strategy and Tactics. However, the author was unfortunately as much in charge of the campaign as he pleased, and lacking a training in command sought to find an immediate equation between past study of military theory and the present movements—as a guide to, and an intellectual basis for, future action.[7] The text books gave the aim in war as "the destruction of the organized forces of the enemy" by "the one process battle." Victory could only be purchased by blood.[8] This was a hard saying, as the Arabs had no organized forces, and so a Turkish Foch would have no aim: and the Arabs would not endure casualties, so that an Arab Clausewitz could not buy his victory.[9] These wise men must be talking metaphors, for the Arabs were indubitably winning their war...and further reflection pointed to the deduction that they had actually won it. They were in occupation of 99% of the Hejaz. The Turks were welcome to the other fraction till peace or doomsday showed them the futility of clinging to the window pane. This part of the war was over, so why bother about Medina? The Turks sat in it on the defensive, immobile, eating for food the transport animals which were to have moved them to Mecca, but for which there was no pasture in their now restricted lines. They were harmless sitting there; if taken prisoner, they would entail the cost of food and guards in Egypt: if driven out northward into Syria, they would join the main army blocking the British in Sinai. On all counts they were best where they were, and they valued Medina and wanted to keep it. Let them!

This seemed unlike the ritual of war of which Foch had been priest, and so it seemed that there was a difference of kind. Foch called his modern war "absolute." In it two nations professing incompatible philosophies set out to try them in the light of force. A struggle of two immaterial principles could only end when the supporters of one had no more means of resistance. An opinion can be argued with: a conviction is best shot. The logical end of a war of creeds is the final destruction of one, and Salammbo the classical textbook-instance.[10] These were the lines of the struggle between France and Germany, but not, perhaps, between Germany and England, for all efforts to make the British soldier hate the enemy simply made him hate war.[11] Thus the "absolute war" seemed only a variety of war; and beside it other sorts could be discerned, as Clausewitz had numbered them, personal wars for dynastic reasons, expulsive wars for party reasons, commercial wars for trading reasons.

Now the Arab aim was unmistakably geographical, to occupy all Arabic-speaking lands in Asia. In the doing of it Turks might be killed, yet "killing Turks" would never be an excuse or aim. If they would go quietly, the war would end. If not, they must be driven out: but at the cheapest possible price, since the Arabs were fighting for freedom, a pleasure only to be tasted by a man alive.[12] The next task was to analyze the process, both from the point of view of strategy, the aim in war, the synoptic —regard which sees everything by the standard of the whole, and from the point of view called tactics, the means towards the strategic end, the steps of its staircase. In each were found the same elements, one algebraical, one biological, a third psychological. The first seemed a pure science, subject to the laws of mathematics, without humanity. It dealt with known invariables, fixed conditions, space and time, inorganic things like hills and climates and railways, with mankind in type-masses too great for individual variety, with all artificial aids, and the extensions given our faculties by mechanical invention. It was essentially formulable.

In the Arab case the algebraic factor would take first account of the area to be conquered. A casual calculation indicated perhaps 140,000 square miles. How would the Turks defend all that—no doubt by a trench line across the bottom, if the Arabs were an army attacking with banners displayed...but suppose they were an influence, a thing invulnerable, intangible, without front or back, drifting about like a gas? Armies were like plants, immobile as a whole, firm-rooted, nourished through long stems to the head. The Arabs might be a vapor, blowing where they listed. It seemed that a regular soldier might be helpless without a target. He would own the ground he sat on, and what he could poke his rifle at. The next step was to estimate how many posts they would need to contain this attack in depth, sedition putting up her head in every unoccupied one of these 100,000 square miles. They would have need of a fortified post every four square miles, and a post could not be less than 20 men. The Turks would need 600,000 men to meet the combined ill wills of all the local Arab people. They had 100,000 men available. It seemed that the assets in this sphere were with the Arabs, and climate, railways, deserts, technical weapons could also be attached to their interests. The Turk was stupid and would believe that rebellion was absolute, like war, and deal with it on the analogy of absolute warfare.

Humanity in Battle. So much for the mathematical element; the second factor was biological, the breaking-point, life and death, or better, wear and tear. Bionomics [pertaining to ecology] seemed a good name for it. The war-philosophers had properly made it an art, and had elevated one item in it, "effusion of blood," to the height of a principle. It became humanity in battle, an art touching every side of our corporal being. There was a line of variability (man) running through all its estimates. Its components were sensitive and illogical, and generals guarded themselves by the device of a reserve, the significant medium of their art. Goltz had said that when you know the enemy's strength, and he is fully deployed, then you know enough to dispense with a reserve.[13] But this is never. There is always the possibility of accident, of some flaw in materials, present in the general's mind: and the reserve is unconsciously held to meet it. There is a "felt" element in troops, not expressible in figures, and the greatest commander is he whose intuitions most nearly happen. Nine-tenths of tactics are certain, and taught in books: but the irrational tenth is like the kingfisher flashing across the pool and that is the test of generals. It can only be ensued by instinct, sharpened by thought practicing the stroke so often that at the crisis it is as natural as a reflex.

Yet to limit the art to humanity seemed an undue narrowing down. It must apply to materials as much as to organisms. In the Turkish Army materials were scarce and precious, men more plentiful than equipment. Consequently the cue should be to destroy not the army but the materials. The death of a Turkish bridge or rail, machine or gun, or high explosive was more profitable than the death of a Turk. The Arab army just then was equally chary of men and materials: of men because they being irregulars were not units, but individuals, and an individual casualty is like a pebble dropped in water: each may make only a brief hole, but rings of sorrow widen out from them. The Arab army could not afford casualties. Materials were easier to deal with. Hence its obvious duty to make itself superior in some one branch, guncotton or machine guns, or whatever could be most decisive. Foch had laid down the maxim, applying it to men, of being superior at the critical point and moment of attack.[14] The Arab army might apply it to materials, and be superior in equipment in one dominant moment or respect.

For both men and things it might try to give Foch's doctrine a negative twisted side, for cheapness' sake, and be weaker than the enemy everywhere except in one point or matter. Most wars are wars of contact, both forces striving to keep in touch to avoid tactical surprise. The Arab war should be a war of detachment: to contain the enemy by the silent threat of a vast unknown desert, not disclosing themselves till the moment of attack. This attack need be only nominal, directed not against his men, but against his materials: so it should not seek for his main strength or his weaknesses, but for his most accessible material. In railway cutting this would be usually an empty stretch of rail. This was a tactical success. From this theory came to be developed ultimately an unconscious habit of never engaging the enemy at all. This chimed with the numerical plea of never giving the enemy's soldier a target. Many Turks on the Arab front had no chance all the war to fire a shot, and correspondingly the Arabs were never on the defensive, except by rare accident. The corollary of such a rule was perfect "intelligence," so that plans could be made in complete certainty. The chief agent had to be the general's head (de Feuquière said this first), and his knowledge had to be faultless, leaving no room for chance.[15] The headquarters of the Arab army probably took more pains in this service than any other staff.

The Crowd in Action. The third factor in command seemed to be the psychological, that science (Xenophon called it diathetic) of which our propaganda is a stained and ignoble part.[16] It concerns the crowd, the adjustment of spirit to the point where it becomes fit to exploit in action. It considers the capacity for mood of the men, their complexities and mutability, and the cultivation of what in them profits the intention. The command of the Arab army had to arrange their men's minds in order of battle, just as carefully and as formally as other officers arranged their bodies: and not only their own men's minds, though them first: the minds of the enemy, so far as it could reach them: and thirdly, the mind of the nation supporting it behind the firing-line, and the mind of the hostile nation waiting the verdict, and the neutrals looking on.

It was the ethical in war, and the process on which the command mainly depended for victory on the Arab front. The printing press is the greatest weapon in the armory of the modern commander, and the commanders of the Arab army being amateurs in the art, began their war in the atmosphere of the 20th century, and thought of their weapons without prejudice, not distinguishing one from another socially. The regular officer has the tradition of 40 generations of serving soldiers behind him, and to him the old weapons are the most honored. The Arab command had seldom to concern itself with what its men did, but much with what they thought, and to it the diathetic was more than half command. In Europe it was set a little aside and entrusted to men outside the General Staff. But the Arab army was so weak physically that it could not let the metaphysical weapon rust unused. It had won a province when the civilians in it had been taught to die for the ideal of freedom: the presence or absence of the enemy was a secondary matter.

These reasonings showed that the idea of assaulting Medina, or even of starving it quickly into surrender, was not in accord with the best strategy. Rather, let the enemy stay in Medina, and in every other harmless place, in the largest numbers. If he showed a disposition to evacuate too soon, as a step to concentrating in the small area which his numbers could dominate effectively, then the Arab army would have to try and restore his confidence, not harshly, but by reducing its enterprises against him. The ideal was to keep his railway just working, but only just, with the maximum of loss and discomfort to him.

The Turkish army was an accident, not a target. Our true strategic aim was to seek its weakest link, and bear only on that till time made the mass of it fall. The Arab army must impose the longest possible passive defence on the Turks (this being the most materially expensive form of war) by extending its own front to the maximum. Tactically it must develop a highly mobile, highly equipped type of force, of the smallest size, and use it successively at distributed points of the Turkish line, to make the Turks reinforce their occupying posts beyond the economic minimum of 20 men. The power of this striking force would not be reckoned merely by its strength. The ratio between number and area determined the character of the war, and by having five times the mobility of the Turks the Arabs could be on terms with them with one-fifth their number.

Range over Force. Success was certain, to be proved by paper and pencil as soon as the proportion of space and number had been learned. The contest was not physical, but moral, and so battles were a mistake. All that could be won in a battle was the ammunition the enemy fired off. Napoleon had said it was rare to find generals willing to fight battles. The curse of this war was that so few could do anything else. Napoleon had spoken in angry reaction against the excessive finesse of the 18th century, when men almost forgot that war gave license to murder. Military thought had been swinging out on his dictum for 100 years, and it was time to go back a bit again. Battles are impositions on the side which believes itself weaker, made unavoidable either by lack of land-room, or by the need to defend a material property dearer than the lives of soldiers. The Arabs had nothing material to lose, so they were to defend nothing and to shoot nothing. Their cards were speed and time, not hitting power, and these gave them strategical rather than tactical strength. Range is more to strategy than force. The invention of bully-beef [canned meat] had modified land-war more profoundly than the invention of gunpowder.[17]

The British military authorities did not follow all these arguments, but gave leave for their practical application to be tried. Accordingly the Arab forces went off first to Akaba and took it easily. Then they took Tafileh and the Dead Sea; then Azrak and Deraa, and finally Damascus, all in successive stages worked out consciously on these theories. The process was to set up ladders of tribes, which should provide a safe and comfortable route from the sea-bases (Yenbo, Wejh or Akaba) to the advanced bases of operation. These were sometimes 300 miles away, a long distance in lands without railways or roads, but made short for the Arab Army by an assiduous cultivation of desert-power, control by camel parties of the desolate and unmapped wilderness which fills up all the centre of Arabia, from Mecca to Aleppo and Baghdad.

The Desert and the Sea. In character these operations were like naval warfare, in their mobility, their ubiquity, their independence of bases and communications, in their ignoring of ground features, of strategic areas, of fixed directions, of fixed points. "He who commands the sea is at great liberty, and may take as much or as little of the war as he will": he who commands the desert is equally fortunate.[18] Camel raiding-parties, self-contained like ships, could cruise securely along the enemy's land-frontier, just out of sight of his posts along the edge of cultivation, and tap or raid into his lines where it seemed fittest or easiest or most profitable, with a sure retreat always behind them into an element which the Turks could not enter.

Discrimination of what point of the enemy organism to disarrange came with practice. The tactics were always tip and run; not pushes, but strokes.[19] The Arab army never tried to maintain or improve an advantage, but to move off and strike again somewhere else. It used the smallest force in the quickest time at the farthest place. To continue the action till the enemy had changed his dispositions to resist it would have been to break the spirit of the fundamental rule of denying him targets.

The necessary speed and range were attained by the frugality of the desert men, and their efficiency on camels. In the heat of summer Arabian camels will do about 250 miles comfortably between drinks: and this represented three days' vigorous marching. This radius was always more than was needed, for wells are seldom more than 100 miles apart. The equipment of the raiding parties aimed at simplicity, with nevertheless a technical superiority over the Turks in the critical department. Quantities of light machine guns were obtained from Egypt for use not as machine guns, but as automatic rifles, snipers' tools, by men kept deliberately in ignorance of their mechanism, so that the speed of action would not be hampered by attempts at repair. Another special feature was high explosives, and nearly everyone in the revolt was qualified by rule of thumb experience in demolition work.

Armored Cars. On some occasions tribal raids were strengthened by armored cars, manned by Englishmen. Armored cars, once they have found a possible track, can keep up with a camel party. On the march to Damascus, when nearly 400 miles off their base, they were first maintained by a baggage train of petrol-laden camels, and afterwards from the air. Cars are magnificent fighting machines, and decisive whenever they can come into action on their own conditions. But though each has for main principle that of "fire in movement," yet the tactical employments of cars and camel-corps are so different that their use in joint operations is difficult. It was found demoralizing to both to use armored and unarmored cavalry together.

The distribution of the raiding parties was unorthodox. It was impossible to mix or combine tribes, since they disliked or distrusted one another. Likewise the men of one tribe could not be used in the territory of another. In consequence, another canon of orthodox strategy was broken by following the principle of the widest distribution of force, in order to have the greatest number of raids on hand at once, and fluidity was added to speed by using one district on Monday, another on Tuesday, a third on Wednesday. This much reinforced the natural mobility of the Arab army, giving it priceless advantages in pursuit, for the force renewed itself with fresh men in every new tribal area, and so maintained its pristine energy. Maximum disorder was, in a real sense its equilibrium.

An Undisciplined Army. The internal economy of the raiding parties was equally curious. Maximum irregularity and articulation were the aims. Diversity threw the enemy intelligence off the track. By the regular organization in identical battalions and divisions information builds itself up, until the presence of a corps can be inferred on corpses from three companies. The Arabs, again, were serving a common ideal, without tribal emulation, and so could not hope for any esprit de corps. Soldiers are made a caste either by being given great pay and rewards in money, uniform or political privileges; or, as in England, by being made outcasts, cut off from the mass of their fellow-citizens. There have been many armies enlisted voluntarily: there have been few armies serving voluntarily under such trying conditions, for so long a war as the Arab revolt. Any of the Arabs could go home whenever the conviction failed him. Their only contract was honor.

Consequently the Arab army had no discipline, in the sense in which it is restrictive, submergent of individuality, the Lowest Common Denominator of men. In regular armies in peace it means the limit of energy attainable by everybody present: it is the hunt not of an average, but of an absolute, a 100-per-cent standard, in which the 99 stronger men are played down to the level of the worst. The aim is to render the unit a unit, and the man a type, in order that their effort shall be calculable, their collective output even in grain and in bulk. The deeper the discipline, the lower the individual efficiency, and the more sure the performance. It is a deliberate sacrifice of capacity in order to reduce the uncertain element, the bionomic factor, in enlisted humanity, and its accompaniment is compound or social war, that form in which the fighting man has to be the product of the multiplied exertions of long hierarchy, from workshop to supply unit, which maintains him in the field.

The Arab war, reacting against this, was simple and individual. Every enrolled man served in the line of battle, and was self-contained. There were no lines of communication or labor troops. It seemed that in this articulated warfare, the sum yielded by single men would be at least equal to the product of a compound system of the same strength, and it was certainly easier to adjust to tribal life and manners, given elasticity and understanding on the part of the commanding officers. Fortunately for its chances nearly every young Englishman has the roots of eccentricity in him. Only a sprinkling were employed, not more than one per 1,000 of the Arab troops. A larger proportion would have created friction, just because they were foreign bodies (pearls if you please) in the oyster: and those who were present controlled by influence and advice, by their superior knowledge, not by an extraneous authority.

The practice was, however, not to employ in the firing line the greater numbers which the adoption of a "simple" system made available theoretically. Instead, they were used in relay:

otherwise the attack would have become too extended. Guerrillas must be allowed liberal work-room. In irregular war if two men are together one is being wasted. The moral strain of isolated action makes this simple form of war very hard on the individual soldier, and exacts from him special initiative, endurance and enthusiasm. Here the ideal was to make action a series of single combats to make the ranks a happy alliance of commanders-in-chief. The value of the Arab army depended entirely on quality, not on quantity. The members had to keep always cool, for the excitement of a blood-lust would impair their science, and their victory depended on a just use of speed, concealment, accuracy of fire. Guerrilla war is far more intellectual than a bayonet charge.

The Exact Science of Guerrilla Warfare. By careful persistence, kept strictly within its strength and following the spirit of these theories, the Arab army was able eventually to reduce the Turks to helplessness, and complete victory seemed to be almost within sight when General Allenby by his immense stroke in Palestine threw the enemy's main forces into hopeless confusion and put an immediate end to the Turkish war.[20] His too-greatness deprived the Arab revolt of the opportunity of following to the end the dictum of Saxe that a war might be won without fighting battles.[21] But it can at least be said that its leaders worked by his light for two years, and the work stood. This is a pragmatic argument that cannot be wholly derided. The experiment, although not complete, strengthened the belief that irregular war or rebellion could be proved to be an exact science, and an inevitable success, granted certain factors and if pursued along certain lines.

Here is the thesis: Rebellion must have an unassailable base, something guarded not merely from attack, but from the fear of it: such a base as the Arab revolt had in the Red Sea ports, the desert, or in the minds of men converted to its creed. It must have a sophisticated alien enemy, in the form of a disciplined army of occupation too small to fulfill the doctrine of acreage: too few to adjust number to space, in order to dominate the whole area effectively from fortified posts. It must have a friendly population, not actively friendly, but sympathetic to the point of not betraying rebel movements to the enemy. Rebellions can be made by 2% active in a striking force, and 98% passively sympathetic. The few active rebels must have the qualities of speed and endurance, ubiquity and independence of arteries of supply. They must have the technical equipment to destroy or paralyze the enemy's organized communications, for irregular war is fairly Willisen's definition of strategy, "the study of communication," in its extreme degree, of attack where the enemy is not. **In 50 words: Granted mobility, security (in the form of denying targets to the enemy), time, and doctrine (the idea to convert every subject to friendliness), victory will rest with the insurgents, for the algebraical factors are in the end decisive, and against them perfections of means and spirit struggle quite in vain.**

SUMMARY

Lawrence personified Sun Tzu's charge to "know the enemy and know yourself…." Like B. H. Liddell Hart, this text linked both Sun Tzu and Clausewitz (granted a largely negative view) to the modern era. Students should grasp the value of Lawrence's insights for the recent wars in Iraq and Afghanistan. Did insurgents not use Lawrence's ideas against the US? Are IEDs nothing more than a modern version of Lawrence's raids on Turkish trains? Would a profound understanding of Lawrence's "in 50 words" not provide a blueprint for the counterinsurgent (i.e. take away each of the "givens")? Many students may be frustrated by the article's occasional wandering; but, as the final page shows, few writers summarize their thoughts more effectively.

The "Science of Guerrilla Warfare" has not been surpassed for brevity and astute observation. Often students struggle with Lawrence's description of the "algebraic, biological, and psychological dimensions of war. In brief, remember:

- Algebraic – those elements that can be measured, physical, size and space
- Biological – tough to explain: humanity in battle, the irrational, intuitive, the enemy as organism, the Arabs as individuals and families not an army, never give the enemy a target
- Psychological – the crowd in action, propaganda, arranging men's minds for battle, fighting for ideas

Perhaps reflecting his education in the classics, where he would have been intimately familiar with Thucydides, Lawrence added additional concepts:

- In guerrilla war, the contest is not physical, but moral.
- An undisciplined army of individuals is an asset in guerrilla war; individual talents, creativity, and non-conformity are virtues.
- Conventional armies struggle to fight an idea. The guerrilla must not give the enemy a target and must not fight battles.

Lawrence's final page of "The Science of Guerrilla War" provided a tremendous conceptual summary and identified a remarkable thesis. Likewise, Lawrence's concluding sentence, "in 50 words…," is unsurpassed as a blueprint for both the insurgent and the counter in surgent.

NOTES

1. MSS 200 will not emphasize the narrow differences between the various terms and will use them interchangeably. Academic specialists will recognize that terms vary over time and although some authors will attach precise definitions to each, the essence of the concepts remains remarkably similar. The challenges confronting Americans in the Philippine Insurrection (1899-1911) would be familiar to their great-grandchildren in Iraq or Afghanistan.

2. Jeremy Wilson, *Lawrence of Arabia: The Authorized Biography of T. E. Lawrence* (New York: Atheneum, 1990), 189.

3. T. E. Lawrence, "The Science of Guerrilla Warfare," Encyclopedia Britannica, 14th ed. (1929), http://www. britannica.com/original/print?content_id=1365, Accessed 5 Jun 2008. The original website referenced is no longer functioning, but a similar article appears at http://pegasus.cc.ucf.edu/~eshaw/lawrence.htm. Accessed 19 Jun 2012.

4. Refers to the Hague Conference of 1899 and 1907 which codified the laws of war, identified lawful combatants and members of armies, provided for rights of neutral powers and persons, and prohibited indiscriminate or cruel weaponry (dum-dum bullets, submerged contact mines, etc.). These conferences rank with the Geneva Conventions as foundations for today's Law of Armed Conflict (LOAC).

5. The Arabian Peninsula was formally part of the Ottoman Empire during World War I, but the Ottoman Turks had largely left the Bedouin Arabs alone.

6. See the introduction for biographical information on Lawrence largely based on Jeremy Wilson, *Lawrence of Arabia: The Authorized Biography of T. E. Lawrence* (New York: Atheneum, 1990).

7. Lawrence was a classical scholar well versed in the texts of the Greeks and Romans, read in their original languages. Keep in mind that the books he studied dealt primarily with war and included Thucydides, Caesar, Polybius, Xenophon, and other military writers.

8. He associated these phrases with Ferdinand Foch, but they were found in a number of French authors who wrote in the early 1900s. A well-known, pre-war French military theorist and successful writer, General Ferdinand Foch commanded French armies on the Western Front during World War I. Before the war he wrote two influential books: *The Principles of War* (1903) and *The Conduct of War* (1905). Foch emphasized massing all resources at a given moment at a single spot. He is associated with the "French School" that emphasized offensive warfare, also known as "war to the utmost," where resolute bravery and offensive spirit would overcome machine gun fire. In fairness, Foch learns and grows during the horrific experience of trench warfare, but Lawrence holds him to his early writings. By the end of World War I, Foch was named generalissimo (supreme commander) of Allied armies on the Western Front. Stefan T. Possony and Etienne Mantoux, "Du Picq and Foch: The French School," in *Makers of Modern Strategy: Military Thought from Machiavelli to Hitler,* Edward Mead Earle, ed. (Princeton: Princeton University Press, 1943, 1971), 206-233.

9. A number of British military writers held a very negative view of Carl von Clausewitz, referring to him as the "apostle of death" and attribute Germany's militarism in World War I to Clausewitz's influence. Lawrence blames Clausewitz and Foch for the carnage of the Western Front. But, Lawrence's point is very astute: without an army to fight, how could the Turks win?

10. Lawrence refers to a battle during the Punic Wars between Rome and Carthage, where Rome utterly destroyed Carthage—burning the city, slaughtering or selling the inhabitants into slavery, and sowing salt into the ashes of the destroyed city. Salammbo exemplifies "absolute war" in the ancient world.

11. A powerful anti-war movement developed in Britain (and most of Western Europe) both during and following World War I.

12. Although not authorized by his government, Lawrence will pledge freedom to the Arabs in return for their revolt against the Turks. He worked hard to convince the British government of this cause, but fails.

13. Lawrence alludes to Colmar von der Goltz, an influential German military theorist who wrote *The Nation in Arms* and who served as a German advisor to the Turks during World War I. He eventually commanded a Turkish army in Mesopotamia and died in Baghdad in 1916.

14. Also found in Napoleon's *Maximes* and Jomini's *The Art of War.* See Gérard Chaliand, ed., *The Art of War in World History: From Antiquity to the Nuclear Age* (Berkeley: University of California Press, 1994), 646-651, 724-743.

15. "deFeuquière" refers to Antoine de Pas, Marquis de Feuquière (1648-1711), a French general who served Louis XIV and who wrote on military affairs. This relatively obscure reference demonstrates Lawrence's broad knowledge. Interestingly, de Feuquière emphasized the expense of war and the economic dimension of warfare. He advocated financing an army through "hostile contributions," forcing enemy inhabitants to pay money or face

pillage, i.e. military extortion. John M. Wright, "Military Contributions During the Eighteenth Century," *Journal of the American Military Institute* 3(Spring 1939): 7.

16. Xenophon's *Anabasis* (or *Retreat of the Ten Thousand*) is one of the most famous heroic action stories, as well as military theoretical writings of the ancient world. Xenophon tells an amazing tale of suffering and survival of ten thousand Greek mercenaries stranded deep in the Persian Empire in 401 B.C. Dr. James Tucci (University of Wisconsin, Ph. D. in the classics) explained that a "diathesis" was a course of action that would lead to a certain conclusion or situation (usually bad).

17. "Bully-beef" is an informal English term for canned meat. In this sentence, Lawrence makes a profound observation.

18. See Francis Bacon, "Of the Greatness of Kingdoms and Estates," *Essays, Civil and Moral*, Vol. 3, Part 1, The Harvard Classics (New York: P. F. Collier & Son, 1909-1914); Bartleby.com, 2001; http://bartleby.com/3/1/29.html [Accessed 15 August 2012].

19. Americans would use the phrase "hit and run."

20. In September 1918, British General Sir Edmund Allenby launched a conventional assault on Damascus that succeeded in driving the Turkish Army out of Palestine and southern Syria. It also dashed Lawrence's vision of an independent triumph for his Arab forces. Allenby used the Arab irregulars to protect his flank and harass Turkish supply lines.

21. Lawrence cites Maurice de Saxe (1696-1750), one of the first and most famous European military writers of the age of limited warfare. Incidentally, de Saxe's theories of training officer candidates in military academies ultimately resulted in the founding of West Point, Annapolis, and the Air Force Academy.

POWER TO THE PEOPLE: POLITICAL MOBILIZATION AND PROTRACTED WAR

Mao Tse-tung

Mao Zedong (or Mao Tse-tung, Mao Tsetung . . . the differences are linked to the transliteration system of rendering Chinese phonetic sounds into English) stands as one of the most influential military thinkers in history. In terms of sheer numbers, probably more people have read Mao than all other military theorists combined. Students will notice similarities between Mao and Sun Tzu and Mao and Clausewitz. Keep in mind that Mao was from a relatively prosperous peasant family and enjoyed a good education that emphasized classical Chinese works. Equally important, Mao read Lenin and Clausewitz as a young revolutionary. Although we do not study Lenin in this course, Clausewitz greatly influenced Lenin's political and military writings. In his voluminous works, Lenin repeats and expands upon many of Clausewitz's ideas. At their core, they link war and politics. In fact, Lenin will go so far as to reverse Clausewitz; to Lenin, politics is an instrument of class war. Ironically, even though many scholars believed Mao was also heavily influenced by Sun Tzu, recent scholarship shows that Mao first read Sun Tzu when he was forty years old.[1]

Born in 1893 and raised during a period of revolutionary turmoil, Mao writes extensively both in volume and range of topics. Specialists emphasize Mao's awareness of the political nature of war, the role of the military as a political instrument in revolutionary war (i.e. the Red Army *is* the Chinese Communist Party during the Chinese Revolution), the advantages of a protracted war for the revolutionary, the need for transitioning from guerrilla war to conventional war, and the primacy of ideas over weapons. "Winning the hearts and minds of the people" emerges as a major theme as well as "time is on the side of the Communism."

The lesson readings emphasize Mao's theories on politics and war; protracted warfare, and strategies in applying guerrilla war. The first two excerpts come from one of his most famous essays, "On Protracted War" (1938). The third excerpt presents "Problems of Strategy in Guerrilla War" (1938). They represent the thoughts of an experienced, mature guerrilla leader. From 1927 until 1937, Mao's Red Army faced the Chinese Nationalist forces (translated as either

Kuomintang or Guomindang) led by Chiang Kai-shek (also known as Jiang Jieshi). Mao's agrarian-based Chinese Communist Party had established base areas in remote interior provinces. The Nationalist Army sought to crush the Red Army in a series of "encirclement" or "punitive" campaigns. In 1934-1935, the Mao's Communist forces broke out of the Kuomintang's noose and conducted the Long March, a year-long, 6,000-mile trek, fighting over two hundred days of pitched battles and skirmishes until finally establishing another safe base area in remote northwest China.

In 1937, the Japanese invaded China, taking most of the major cities and all the significant sea ports and large sections of territory. The Nationalists and Communists declared a "united front" to oppose the Japanese, although neither trusted the other. Chiang Kai-shek always considered Mao a more dangerous and important foe than the Japanese, while Mao saw the opportunity of fighting Japan as a means of building popular support that could later be used against the Nationalists. After Pearl Harbor, the United States played a major role in supplying both the Nationalists and Communists (although most supplies went to Chiang Kai-shek's forces). As US military power grew, Chiang Kai-shek reasoned that American power would defeat Japan, and hence the Nationalist Army hoarded US-supplied equipment in preparation for his primary foe. On the other hand, Mao's Red Army gained fame for its effective guerrilla campaign. During World War II, both the Soviets and the United States provided limited aid to Mao's forces. Upon the surrender of Japan, the Red Army received large stocks of surrendered Japanese equipment.

Within a few months of World War II's end, the Chinese Civil War resumed in earnest. Mao's battle-hardened, well-equipped forces eventually defeated the Nationalists who withdrew to the island of Taiwan. By 1949, Mao established the People's Republic of China, although Chiang Kai-shek maintained claim as leader of the Republic of China, which in turn leads to a major political issue today.

By the 1970s, many people throughout the world viewed the Vietnam War as the triumph of Mao's theories of revolutionary war over American technical and military prowess. Hence, the symbolic importance of Mao should emerge from this lesson. Mao offers a non-Western challenge to superior Western technological resources. Many would argue that the United States still does not have an answer to Mao's ideology. In a sense, this is asymmetrical warfare in contrast to American military strengths. But also keep in mind, that although Mao understood the unique circumstances faced by the Communists in China during the 1930s and 40s, his ideas did not always export. Ernesto "Che" Guevara, of college dorm poster fame, tried to foment a Communist peasant rebellion in Bolivia and learned the hard way that the local government, backed by US advisors, won the "hearts and minds" of the peasantry.

Mao wrote prodigious amounts; these selections provide a small sample to give you a feel for his blended military and political thoughts. The excerpts capture only a small portion of Mao's theories, but they provide insight into his thinking and style. Because Mao is extremely thorough, repetitious, and wordy, significant amount of his text were edited, hopefully without losing significant concepts. This was a debatable and perhaps flawed move, but with Mao's writings, "less is more."

War and Politics[2]

63. "War is the continuation of politics." In this sense war is politics and war itself is a political action; since ancient times there has never been a war that did not have a political character. The anti-Japanese war is a revolutionary war waged by the whole nation, and victory is inseparable from the political aim of the war--to drive out Japanese imperialism and build a new China of freedom and equality--inseparable from the general policy of persevering in the War of Resistance and in the united front, from the mobilization of the entire people, and from the political principles of the unity between officers and men, the unity between army and people and the disintegration of the enemy forces, and inseparable from the effective application of united front policy, from mobilization on the cultural front, and from the efforts to win international support and the support of the people inside Japan. In a word, war cannot for a single moment be separated from politics. Any tendency among the anti-Japanese armed forces to be little politics by isolating war from it and advocating the idea of war as an absolute is wrong and should be corrected.

64. But war has its own particular characteristics and in this sense it cannot be equated with politics in general. "War is the continuation of politics by other . . . means."[3] When politics develops to a certain stage beyond which it cannot proceed by the usual means, war breaks out to sweep the obstacles from the way. For instance, the semi-independent status of China is an obstacle to the political growth of Japanese imperialism, hence Japan has unleashed a war of aggression to sweep away that obstacle. What about China? Imperialist oppression has long been an obstacle to China's bourgeois-democratic revolution, hence many wars of liberation have been waged in the effort to sweep it away. Japan is now using war for the purpose of oppressing China and completely blocking the advance of the Chinese revolution, and therefore China is compelled to wage the War of Resistance in her determination to sweep away this obstacle. When the obstacle is removed, our political aim will be attained and the war concluded. But if the obstacle is not completely swept away, the war will have to continue till the aim is fully accomplished. Thus anyone who seeks a compromise before the task of the anti-Japanese war is fulfilled is bound to fail, because even if a compromise were to occur for one reason or another, the war would break out again, since the broad masses of the people would certainly not submit but would continue the war until its political objective was achieved. It can therefore be said that politics is war without bloodshed while war is politics with bloodshed.

65. From the particular characteristics of war there arise a particular set of organizations, a particular series of methods and a particular kind of process. The organizations are the armed

forces and everything that goes with them. The methods are the strategy and tactics for direct-ing war. The process is the particular form of social activity in which the opposing armed forces attack each other or defend themselves against one another, employing strategy and tactics favorable to themselves and unfavorable to the enemy. Hence war experience is a particular kind of experience. All who take part in war must rid themselves of their customary ways and accustom themselves to war before they can win victory.

Political Mobilization for the War of Resistance

66. A national revolutionary war as great as ours cannot be won without extensive and thor-oughgoing political mobilization. Before the anti-Japanese war there was no political mobili-zation for resistance to Japan, and this was a great drawback, as a result of which China has already lost a move to the enemy. After the war began, political mobilization was very far from extensive, let alone thoroughgoing. It was the enemy's gunfire and the bombs dropped by en-emy airplanes that brought news of the war to the great majority of the people. That was also a kind of mobilization, but it was done for us by the enemy, we did not do it ourselves. Even now the people in the remoter regions beyond the noise of the guns are carrying on quietly as usual. This situation must change, or otherwise we cannot win in our life-and-death struggle. We must never lose another move to the enemy; on the contrary, we must make full use of this move, political mobilization, to get the better of him. This move is crucial; it is indeed of primary importance, while our inferiority in weapons and other things is only secondary. The mobilization of the common people throughout the country will create a vast sea in which to drown the enemy, create the conditions that will make up for our inferiority in arms and other things, and create the prerequisites for overcoming every difficulty in the war. To win victory, we must persevere in the War of Resistance, in the united front and in the protracted war. But all these are inseparable from the mobilization of the common people. To wish for victory and yet neglect political mobilization is like wishing to "go south by driving the chariot north," and the result would inevitably be to forfeit victory.

67. What does political mobilization mean? First, it means telling the army and the people about the political aim of the war. It is necessary for every soldier and civilian to see why the war must be fought and how it concerns him. The political aim of the war is "to drive out Japanese imperialism and build a new China of freedom and equality"; we must proclaim this aim to everybody, to all soldiers and civilians, before we can create an anti-Japanese upsurge and unite hundreds of millions as one man to contribute their all to the war. Secondly, it is not enough merely to explain the aim to them; the steps and policies for its attainment must also be given, that is, there must be a political program.... Without a clear-cut, concrete political program it is impossible to mobilize all the armed forces and the whole people to carry the war against Ja-pan through to the end. Thirdly, how should we mobilize them? By word of mouth, by leaflets

and bulletins, by newspapers, books and pamphlets, through plays and films, through schools, through the mass organizations and through our cadres.... Fourthly, to mobilize once is not enough; political mobilization for the War of Resistance must be continuous. Our job is not to recite our political program to the people, for nobody will listen to such recitations; we must link the political mobilization for the war with developments in the war and with the life of the soldiers and the people, and make it a continuous movement. This is a matter of immense importance on which our victory in the war primarily depends.

The Object of War

68. Here we are not dealing with the political aim of war; the political aim of the War of Resistance Against Japan has been defined above as "to drive out Japanese imperialism and build a new China of freedom and equality." Here we are dealing with the elementary object of war, war as "politics with bloodshed," as mutual slaughter by opposing armies. The object of war is specifically "to preserve oneself and destroy the enemy"...

small revolutionary groups to fight the power of the state

ON PROTRACTED WAR[4]

Why a Protracted War?

30. Let us now examine the problem of protracted war. A correct answer to the question "Why a protracted war?" can be arrived at only on the basis of all the fundamental contrasts between China and Japan. For instance, if we say merely that the enemy is a strong imperialist power while we are a weak semi-colonial and semi-feudal country, we are in danger of falling into the theory of national subjugation.[5] For neither in theory nor in practice can a struggle become protracted by simply pitting the weak against the strong. Nor can it become protracted by simply pitting the big against the small, the progressive against the reactionary, or abundant support against meager support.... Therefore when we say that the War of Resistance Against Japan is a protracted war, our conclusion is derived from the interrelations of all the factors at work on both sides.[6] The enemy is strong and we are weak, and the danger of subjugation is there. But in other respects the enemy has shortcomings and we have advantages. The enemy's advantage can be reduced and his shortcomings aggravated by our efforts.... Hence, we can win final victory and avert subjugation, while the enemy will ultimately be defeated and will be unable to avert the collapse of his whole imperialist system.

31. Since the enemy has advantages only in one respect but shortcomings in all others and we have shortcomings in only one respect but advantages in all others, why has this produced not a balance, but, on the contrary, a superior position for him and an inferior position for us at the present time?... The fact is that the disparity between the enemy's strength and our own is

now so great that the enemy's shortcomings have not developed, and for the time being cannot develop, to a degree sufficient to offset his strength, while our advantages have not developed, and for the time being cannot develop, to a degree sufficient to compensate for our weakness. Therefore there can as yet be no balance, only imbalance.

32. Although our efforts in persevering in the War of Resistance and the united front have somewhat changed the enemy's strength and superiority as against our weakness and inferiority, there has as yet been no basic change. Hence during a certain stage of the war, to a certain degree the enemy will be victorious and we shall suffer defeat.... In comparison with the original situation, the enemy is still strong, but unfavorable factors have reduced his strength, although not yet to a degree sufficient to destroy his superiority, and similarly we are still weak, but favourable factors have compensated for our weakness, although not yet to a degree sufficient to transform our inferiority.... Therefore, in this stage the enemy's victory and our defeat are definitely restricted in degree, and hence the war becomes protracted.

33. But circumstances are continually changing. In the course of the war, provided we employ correct military and political tactics, make no mistakes of principle and exert our best efforts, the enemy's disadvantages and China's advantages will both grow as the war is drawn out, with the inevitable result that there will be a continual change in the difference in comparative strength and hence in the relative position of the two sides. When a new stage is reached, a great change will take place in the balance of forces, resulting in the enemy's defeat and our victory.

34. At present the enemy can still manage to exploit his strength, and our War of Resistance has not yet fundamentally weakened him. The insufficiency in his manpower and material resources is not yet such as to prevent his offensive; on the contrary, they can still sustain it to a certain extent. The reactionary and barbarous nature of his war, a factor which intensifies both class antagonisms within Japan and the resistance of the Chinese nation, has not yet brought about a situation which radically impedes his advance. The enemy's international isolation is increasing but is not yet complete. In many countries which have indicated they will help us, the capitalists dealing in munitions and war materials and bent solely on profit are still furnishing Japan with large quantities of war supplies,[7] and their governments[8] are still reluctant to join the Soviet Union in practical sanctions against Japan. From all this it follows that our War of Resistance cannot be won quickly and can only be a protracted war.... Neither the abolition of corruption and the acceleration of progress at home, nor the curbing of the pro-Japanese forces and the expansion of the anti-Japanese forces abroad, are yet accomplished facts. From all this it follows that our war cannot be won quickly but can only be a protracted war.

The Three Stages of the Protracted War

35. Since the Sino-Japanese war is a protracted one and final victory will belong to China, it can reasonably be assumed that this protracted war will pass through three stages. The first stage

covers the period of the enemy's strategic offensive and our strategic defensive. The second stage will be the period of the enemy's strategic consolidation and our preparation for the counter-offensive. The third stage will be the period of our strategic counter-offensive and the enemy's strategic retreat. It is impossible to predict the concrete situation in the three stages, but certain main trends in the war may be pointed out in the light of present conditions. The objective course of events will be exceedingly rich and varied, with many twists and turns, and nobody can cast a horoscope for the Sino-Japanese war; nevertheless it is necessary for the strategic direction of the war to make a rough sketch of its trends....

36. The first stage has not yet ended.... To accomplish this aim the enemy will have to use at least fifty divisions, or about one and a half million men, spend from one and a half to two years, and expend more than ten thousand million yen. In penetrating so deeply, he will encounter immense difficulties, with consequences disastrous beyond imagination.... In this stage the form of fighting we should adopt is primarily mobile warfare, supplemented by guerrilla and positional warfare.[9] Through the subjective errors of the Kuomintang military authorities, positional warfare was assigned the primary role in the first phase of this stage, but it is nevertheless supplementary from the point of view of the stage as a whole. In this stage, China has already built up a broad united front and achieved unprecedented unity.... [I]n spite of considerable losses, China will make considerable progress, which will become the main basis for her continued resistance in the second stage....On the enemy side, there are already signs of flagging morale, and his army's momentum of attack is less in the middle phase of this stage than it was in the initial phase, and it will diminish still further in the concluding phase. Signs of exhaustion are beginning to appear in his finances and economy; war-weariness is beginning to set in among his people and troops; and within the clique at the helm of the war, "war frustrations" are beginning to manifest themselves and pessimism about the prospects of the war is growing.

37. The second stage may be termed one of strategic stalemate. At the tail end of the first stage, the enemy will be forced to fix certain terminal points to his strategic offensive owing to his shortage of troops and our firm resistance, and upon reaching them he will stop his strategic offensive and enter the stage of safeguarding his occupied areas. In the second stage, the enemy will attempt to safeguard these areas and to make them his own by the fraudulent method of setting up puppet governments, while plundering the Chinese people to the limit; but again he will be confronted with stubborn guerrilla warfare. Taking advantage of the fact that the enemy's rear is unguarded, our guerrilla warfare will develop extensively in the first stage, and many base areas will be established, seriously threatening the enemy's consolidation of the occupied areas, and so in the second stage there will still be widespread fighting. In this stage, our form of fighting will be primarily guerrilla warfare, supplemented by mobile warfare....Except for the troops engaged in frontal defence against the enemy, our forces will be switched in large numbers to the enemy's rear in comparatively dispersed dispositions, and, basing themselves on

all the areas not actually occupied by the enemy and coordinating with the people's local armed forces, they will launch extensive, fierce guerrilla warfare against enemy-occupied areas, keeping the enemy on the move as far as possible in order to destroy him in mobile warfare . . . . The fighting in the second stage will be ruthless, and the country will suffer serious devastation. But the guerrilla warfare will be successful, and if it is well conducted the enemy may be able to retain only about one-third of his occupied territory, with the remaining two-thirds in our hands, and this will constitute a great defeat for the enemy and a great victory for China. . . .

The duration of this stage will depend on the degree of change in the balance of forces between us and the enemy and on the changes in the international situation; generally speaking, we should be prepared to see this stage last a comparatively long time and to weather its hardships. It will be a very painful period for China; the two big problems will be economic difficulties and the disruptive activities of the traitors. The enemy will go all out to wreck China's united front, and the traitor organizations in all the occupied areas will merge into a so-called "unified government." Owing to the loss of big cities and the hardships of war, vacillating elements within our ranks will clamor for compromise, and pessimism will grow to a serious extent. Our tasks will then be to mobilize the whole people to unite as one man and carry on the war with unflinching perseverance, to broaden and consolidate the united front, sweep away all pessimism and ideas of compromise, promote the will to hard struggle and apply new wartime policies, and so to weather the hardships. In the second stage, we will have to call upon the whole country resolutely to maintain a united government, we will have to oppose splits and systematically improve fighting techniques, reform the armed forces, mobilize the entire people and prepare for the counter-offensive. The international situation will become still more unfavorable to Japan and the main international forces will incline towards giving more help to China, . . . Japan's threat to Southeast Asia and Siberia will become greater, and there may even be another war.[10] As regards Japan, scores of her divisions will be inextricably bogged down in China. Widespread guerrilla warfare and the people's anti-Japanese movement will wear down this big Japanese force, greatly reducing it and also disintegrating its morale by stimulating the growth of homesickness, war-weariness and even anti-war sentiment. . . . This second stage will be the transitional stage of the entire war; it will be the most trying period but also the pivotal one. Whether China becomes an independent country or is reduced to a colony will be determined not by the retention or loss of the big cities in the first stage but by the extent to which the whole nation exerts itself in the second. If we can persevere in the War of Resistance, in the united front and in the protracted war, China will in that stage gain the power to change from weakness to strength. . . .

38. The third stage will be the stage of the counter-offensive to recover our lost territories. Their recovery will depend mainly upon the strength which China has built up in the preceding stage and which will continue to grow in the third stage. But China's strength alone will not be sufficient, and we shall also have to rely on the support of international forces and on the

changes that will take place inside Japan, or otherwise we shall not be able to win; this adds to China's tasks in international propaganda and diplomacy. In the third stage, our war will no longer be one of strategic defensive, but will turn into a strategic counter-offensive manifesting itself in strategic offensives; and it will no longer be fought on strategically interior lines, but will shift gradually to strategically exterior lines....The third stage will be the last in the protracted war, and when we talk of persevering in the war to the end, we mean going all the way through this stage. Our primary form of fighting will still be mobile warfare, but positional warfare will rise to importance. While positional defence cannot be regarded as important in the first stage because of the prevailing circumstances, positional attack will become quite important in the third stage because of the changed conditions and the requirements of the task. In the third stage guerrilla warfare will again provide strategic support by supplementing mobile and positional warfare, but it will not be the primary form as in the second stage.

39. It is thus obvious that the war is protracted and consequently ruthless in nature. The enemy will not be able to gobble up the whole of China but will be able to occupy many places for a considerable time. China will not be able to oust the Japanese quickly, but the greater part of her territory will remain in her hands. Ultimately the enemy will lose and we will win, but we shall have a hard stretch of road to travel.

40. The Chinese people will become tempered in the course of this long and ruthless war. The political parties taking part in the war will also be steeled and tested. The united front must be persevered in; only by persevering in the united front can we persevere in the war; and only by persevering in the united front and in the war can we win final victory. Only thus can all difficulties be overcome. After traveling the hard stretch of road we shall reach the highway to victory. This is the natural logic of the war.

41. In the three stages the changes in relative strength will proceed along the following lines. In the first stage, the enemy is superior and we are inferior in strength. With regard to our inferiority we must reckon on changes of two different kinds from the eve of the War of Resistance to the end of this stage. The first kind is a change for the worse. China's original inferiority will be aggravated by war losses, namely, decreases in territory, population, economic strength, military strength and cultural institutions. Towards the end of the first stage, the decrease will probably be considerable, especially on the economic side. This point will be exploited by some people as a basis for their theories of national subjugation and of compromise. But the second kind of change, the change for the better, must also be noted. It includes the experience gained in the war, the progress made by the armed forces, the political progress, the mobilization of the people, the development of culture in a new direction, the emergence of guerrilla warfare, the increase in international support, etc....

42. In the first stage, changes of two kinds are also occurring on the enemy's side. The first kind is a change for the worse and manifests itself in hundreds of thousands of casualties, the drain on arms and ammunition, deterioration of troop morale, popular discontent at home,

shrinkage of trade, the expenditure of over ten thousand million yen, condemnation by world opinion, etc. This trend also provides a basis for our ability to fight a protracted war and win final victory. But we must likewise reckon with the second kind of change on the enemy's side, a change for the better, that is, his expansion in territory, population and resources. This too is a basis for the protracted nature of our War of Resistance and the impossibility of quick victory, but at the same time certain people will use it as a basis for their theories of national subjugation and of compromise....The vigorous growth of guerrilla warfare in China will restrict her actual occupation to narrow zones. Moreover, her occupation of Chinese territory has created and intensified contradictions between Japan and other foreign countries....

43. In the second stage, the above changes on both sides will continue to develop. While the situation cannot be predicted in detail, on the whole Japan will continue on the downgrade and China on the upgrade.[11] For example, Japan's military and financial resources will be seriously drained by China's guerrilla warfare, popular discontent will grow in Japan, the morale of her troops will deteriorate further, and she will become more isolated internationally. As for China, she will make further progress in the political, military and cultural spheres and in the mobilization of the people; guerrilla warfare will develop further; there will be some new economic growth on the basis of the small industries and the widespread agriculture in the interior; international support will gradually increase; and the whole picture will be quite different from what it is now. This second stage may last quite a long time, during which there will be a great reversal in the balance of forces, with China gradually rising and Japan gradually declining....There upon, China will in general have completed her preparations for the strategic counter-offensive and will enter the stage of the counter-offensive and the expulsion of the enemy. It should be reiterated that the change from inferiority to superiority and the completion of preparations for the counter-offensive will involve three things, namely, an increase in China's own strength, an increase in Japan's difficulties, and an increase in international support; it is the combination of all these forces that will bring China's superiority and the completion of her preparations for the counter-offensive.

44. Because of the unevenness in China's political and economic development, the strategic counter-offensive of the third stage will not present a uniform and even picture throughout the country in its initial phase but will be regional in character, rising here and subsiding there. During this stage, the enemy will not relax his divisive tricks to break China's united front, hence the task of maintaining internal unity in China will become still more important, and we shall have to ensure that the strategic counter-offensive does not collapse halfway through internal dissension. In this period the international situation will become very favourable to China. China's task will be to take advantage of it in order to attain complete liberation and establish an independent democratic state, which at the same time will mean helping the world anti-fascist movement....

48. This is the so-called theory that "weapons decide everything," in which constitutes a mechanical approach to the question of war and a subjective and one-sided view. Our view is

opposed to this; we see not only weapons but also people. Weapons are an important factor in war, but not the decisive factor; it is people, not things, that are decisive. The contest of strength is not only a contest of military and economic power, but also a contest of human power and morale. Military and economic power is necessarily wielded by people....If Japan's enemy is not just China, if in future one or more other countries make open use of their considerable military and economic power defensively or offensively against Japan and openly help us, then will not our superiority be still greater? Japan is a small country, her war is reactionary and barbarous, and she will become more and more isolated internationally; China is a large country, her war is progressive and just, and she will enjoy more and more support internationally. Is there any reason why the long-term development of these factors should not definitely change the relative position between the enemy and ourselves?

49. The exponents of quick victory, however, do not realize that war is a contest of strength, and that before a certain change has taken place in the relative strength of the belligerents, there is no basis for trying to fight strategically decisive battles and shorten the road to liberation. Were their ideas to be put into practice, we should inevitably run our heads into a brick wall. Or perhaps they are just talking for their own pleasure without really intending to put their ideas into practice. In the end Mr. Reality will come and pour a bucket of cold water over these chatterers, showing them up as mere windbags who want to get things on the cheap, to have gains without pains....

50. That the war will be protracted is certain, but nobody can predict exactly how many months or years it will last, as this depends entirely upon the degree of the change in the balance of forces. All those who wish to shorten the war have no alternative but to work hard to increase our own strength and reduce that of the enemy. Specifically, the only way is to strive to win more battles and wear down the enemy's forces, develop guerrilla warfare to reduce enemy-occupied territory to a minimum, consolidate and expand the united front to rally the forces of the whole nation, build up new armies and develop new war industries, promote political, economic and cultural progress, mobilize the workers, peasants, businessmen, intellectuals and other sections of the people, disintegrate the enemy forces and win over their soldiers, carry on international propaganda to secure foreign support, and win the support of the Japanese people and other oppressed peoples. Only by doing all this can we reduce the duration of the war. There is no magic short-cut.

PROBLEMS OF STRATEGY IN GUERRILLA WAR AGAINST JAPAN[12]

The Basic Principle of War Is to Preserve Oneself and Destroy the Enemy[13]

Before discussing the question of strategy in guerrilla warfare in concrete terms, a few words are needed on the fundamental problem of war.

All the guiding principles of military operations grow out of the one basic principle: to strive to the utmost to preserve one's own strength and destroy that of the enemy. In a revolutionary war, this principle is directly linked with basic political principles. For instance, the basic political principle of China's War of Resistance Against Japan, i.e., its political aim, is to drive out Japanese imperialism and build an independent, free and happy new China. In terms of military action this principle means the use of armed force to defend our motherland and to drive out the Japanese invaders. To attain this end, the operations of the armed units take the form of doing their utmost to preserve their own strength on the one hand and destroy the enemy's on the other.... From this basic principle stems the series of principles guiding military operations, all of which--from the principles of shooting (taking cover to preserve oneself, and making full use of fire-power to destroy the enemy) to the principles of strategy-- are permeated with the spirit of this basic principle. All technical, tactical and strategic principles represent applications of this basic principle. The principle of preserving oneself and destroying the enemy is the basis of all military principles....

The Establishment of Base Areas

The third problem of strategy in anti-Japanese guerrilla warfare is the establishment of base areas, which is important and essential because of the protracted nature and ruthlessness of the war. The recovery of our lost territories will have to await the nation-wide strategic counter-offensive; by then the enemy's front will have extended deep into central China and cut it in two from north to south, and a part or even a greater part of our territory will have fallen into the hands of the enemy and become his rear. We shall have to extend guerrilla warfare all over this vast enemy-occupied area, make a front out of the enemy's rear, and force him to fightcease-lessly throughout the territory he occupies. Until such time as our strategic counteroffensive is launched and so long as our lost territories are not recovered, it will be necessary to persist in guerrilla warfare in the enemy's rear, certainly for a fairly long time, though one cannot say definitely for how long. This is why the war will be a protracted one. And in order to safeguard his gains in the occupied areas, the enemy is bound to step up his anti-guerrilla measures and, especially after the halting of his strategic offensive, to embark on relentless suppression of the guerrillas. With ruthlessness thus added to protractedness, it will be impossible to sustain guerrilla warfare behind the enemy lines without base areas.

What, then, are these base areas? They are the strategic bases on which the guerrilla forces rely in performing their strategic tasks and achieving the object of preserving and expanding themselves and destroying and driving out the enemy. Without such strategic bases, there will be nothing to depend on in carrying out any of our strategic tasks or achieving the aim of the war. It is a characteristic of guerrilla warfare behind the enemy lines that it is fought without a rear, for the guerrilla forces are severed from the country's general rear. But guerrilla warfare could not last long or grow without base areas. The base areas, indeed, are its rear.

History knows many peasant wars of the "roving rebel" type, but none of them ever succeeded. In the present age of advanced communications and technology, it would be all the
more groundless to imagine that one can win victory by fighting in the manner of roving
rebels....Therefore the struggle against the roving-rebel ideology is an inevitable process. Only
when this ideology is thoroughly overcome and the policy of establishing base areas is initiated
and applied will there be conditions favourable for the maintenance of guerrilla warfare over a
long period....

SUMMARY

Although known primarily by reputation and little-read today, Mao Zedong provides a theory
of asymmetric warfare that appeals to the materially weak and technologically backward. Drawing from Lenin and Clausewitz, Mao understands the relation of war and politics. He emphasizes the mobilizing of the masses, explaining why they should fight, why they have a stake in
the war. Like Lawrence, Mao uses time; protracted war is the advantage of the revolutionary.
His three stages of protracted war (strategic defensive, strategic stalemate, and strategic counter-
offensive) provide a system and process for success. To Mao, base areas provide the key to
political mobilization and winning the "hearts and minds." Establishing base areas in the first
stage (strategic defensive) is paramount and represents a political goal, of even greater importance than a purely military objective. Nevertheless, Mao never loses sight of the object of war:
"topreserve oneself and destroy the enemy." Although foreign to the Western tradition, in Mao's
Chinese Revolution, the Red Army is the Communist Party. The army is primarily a political
instrument. While this coincides with the thinking of Clausewitz, Lenin's influence resounds
with Mao's bold statement: "It can therefore be said that politics is war without bloodshed
while war is politics with bloodshed." Today's American officer must remember that Mao's ideas
triumphed in both the Chinese Revolution and Vietnam. Some argue that the United States still
does not have a counter to his theories. Likewise, USAF officers must understand the political
context behind Mao's thinking, the need to mobilize the masses, and protracted warfare as key
ideas for successfully waging counterinsurgency. In order to be more than a supporting player
on the joint team, air, space, and cyberspace professionals must understand the big picture.

NOTES

1. Prof. Alastair Iain Johnston, "Miscellaneous Impressions of the Status of Sun Zi's Teachings in the PLA,"
   Remarks presented at "The Art of War" Sun Zi Conference, 6 Oct 2009, National Defense University,
   Washington, DC.
2. Mao Tse-tung, "On ºtProtracted War," *Selected Military Writings of Mao Tsetung*(Peking: Foreign Languages
   Press, 1972), 226-229.
3. V. I. Lenin, "Socialism and War," *Collected Works*, Eng. ed., (Moscow: Progress Publishers, 1964), Vol. XXI, p.
   304.

4. Mao Tse-tung, "On Protracted War," *Selected Military Writings of Mao Tsetung*(Peking: Foreign Languages Press, 1972), 208-219.

5. Editor's note: Mao uses the phrase "theory of national subjugation" to refer to those who believed that Japan would win, that China was too primitive, disunited, and weak to defeat a modern, progressive enemy.

6. Editor's note: The Japanese invaded the central provinces of China in 1937 and occupied most of China's coastal cities. Eventually, Japan will expand its control over most of China's major cities and most modern regions. The Sino-Japanese War is called "the War of Resistance Against Japan" by Mao. Mao will call for a "united front" against the Japanese, a truce in the Chinese Civil War between the Nationalists (Kuomintang) and the Communists that began in 1927. Although the Nationalists and Communists will declare the "united front," neither will trust the other side. Their cooperation is more symbolic than genuine.

7. Original text footnote: The capitalists referred to here are chiefly those of the United States.

8. Original text footnote: By "Their governments" Comrade Mao Tsetung is here referring to the governments of the imperialist countries—Britain, the United States and France.

9. Editor's note: In this text, Mao does not define these terms, but in other works he will use "mobile warfare" to mean regular forces using maneuver and surprise to fight the enemy without being tied down to fixed positions (or simply running away to stay alive if the enemy forces are superior); "guerrilla warfare" refers to irregular revolutionary groups fighting classic "hit and run" warfare; and "positional warfare" means conventional forces fighting to take or defend territory.

10. Editor's note: Remember, Mao is writing this in May 1938, over a year before the start of World War II in Europe.

11. Original footnote: Comrade Mao Tsetung's prediction that there would be an upswing in China during the stage of stalemate in the War of Resistance Against Japan was completely confirmed in the case of the Liberated Areas under the leadership of the Chinese Communist Party. But there was actually a decline instead of an upswing in the Kuomintang areas, because the ruling clique headed by Chiang Kai-shek was passive in resisting Japan and active in opposing the Communist Party and the people. This roused opposition among the broad masses of the people and raised their political consciousness.

12. Mao Tsetung, "Problems of Strategy in Guerrilla War," *Selected Military Writings of Mao Tsetung*(Peking: Foreign Languages Press, 1972), 155-156 and 167-168.

13. Editor's note: For brevity's sake, the text of this edited article consists only of chapter II: "The Basic Principle of War Is to Preserve Oneself and Destroy the Enemy" and chapter VI: "The Establishment of Base Areas." Although the other chapters are important, in many ways they simply rephrase material already covered.

THE PREREQUISITES FOR SUCCESSFUL INSURGENCY

David Galula

One of the important themes of the Counterinsurgency block is simple: Counterinsurgency/Guerrilla war/Revolutionary war/Irregular war/ Asymmetric war/ Small war...(or whatever term is fashionable for any particular period) is not new. There are tremendous benefits for studying past experiences. Of course, by comprehending the character of war, we understand that every war is unique as time, culture, technology, historical circumstances, religion, geography, and other aspects change and appear in distinct, new combinations. However, from comprehending the nature of war, we know that much of irregular, guerrilla war, or insurgency is timeless and unchanging. Hence, reading David Galula's classic *Counterinsurgency Warfare: Theory and Practice* prepares our mind for the complexities and difficulties inherent in today's campaigns. We are not looking for a checklist, but a tool for thinking.

David Galula's work enters our course based on the recommendations of both institutional and individual experts to include the US Army's Strategic Studies Institute, Gen David Petraeus, and John Nagl. Although Galula is writing to counter the threat of Communist revolutionary war that dominated the late 1940s through the early 1970s, students should recognize similarities with recent struggles in Iraq and Afghanistan. Even though many might think the anti-colonial aspect of Galula's experiences no longer applies today, Al Qaida writings play heavily upon perceived injustices by Western colonialism upon the Islamic world. Along similar lines, David Galula's emphasis on securing the population emerges as the counterinsurgent's key to success.

David Galula offers a valuable perspective based upon a unique background. Born in French Tunisia, Galula attended Saint Cyr, the French equivalent of West Point, graduating shortly before the outbreak of World War II. After the German invasion, in 1941 the collaborationist Vichy French government expelled Galula from the French Army for being a Jew. He then joined the Free French forces and fought in North Africa, Italy, and France. Following the war, Galula served as a French attaché to Hong Kong, where he observed Mao's Red Army in the Chinese civil war, including a week's captivity that he writes about in this passage. He also observed the

the failure of the Communist revolution in Greece and a successful counterinsurgency in the Philippines against the Communist Hukbalahap movement. Interestingly, Galula's biography states that he did not participate in fighting the Viet Minh during the French Indochina War. This is most curious since Indochina (1946-1954) dominated the French Army's counterinsurgency experience. Later, the "lessons learned" from losing to the Viet Minh were applied with a vengeance against the Algerian independence movement. Galula commanded a company of French colonial infantry in a successful pacification campaign from 1956-1958. Despite Galula's success in his provincial area, the French Army gained a reputation for ruthlessness during the Algerian revolution. Counterinsurgent terror, torture, and heavy-handed tactics effectively broke the Algerian guerrilla forces, but alienated the French populace and brought international condemnation. Hence, the French Army won the battles, but lost the war, because as we all know, "war is politics by other means." In 1962, Lieutenant Colonel Galula left the French Army and became a research associate at Harvard University, where he wrote *Counterinsurgency Warfare*. Before his death in 1967, Galula had earned a reputation as a genuine expert in counterinsurgency and based on his observation of almost every major counterinsurgency campaign of his era. In exploring ideas to counter insurgents in Iraq and Afghanistan, American military theorists and commentators found Galula's concepts of counterinsurgency, politics, and population control to be insightful and valuable.[1]

CHAPTER 1

REVOLUTIONARY WAR: NATURE AND CHARACTERISTICS

A revolutionary war is primarily an internal conflict, although external influences seldom fail to bear upon it. Although in many cases, the insurgents have been easily identifiable national groups—Indonesians, Vietnamese, Tunisians, Algerians, Congolese, Angolans today—this does not alter the strategically important fact that they were challenging a *local* power controlling the existing administration, police, and armed forces. In this respect, colonial revolutionary wars have not differed from purely indigenous ones, such as those in Cuba and South Vietnam.

The conflict results from the action of the insurgent aiming to seize power—or splitting off from the existing country,... and from the reaction of the counterinsurgent aiming to keep his power. At this point, significant differences begin to emerge between the two camps. Whereas in conventional war, either side can initiate the conflict, only one—the insurgent—can initiate a revolutionary war, for counterinsurgency is only an effect of insurgency. Furthermore, counterinsurgency cannot be defined except by reference to its cause.

Paraphrasing Clausewitz, we might say that "Insurgency is the pursuit of the policy of a party, inside a country, by every means." It is not like an ordinary war—"a continuation of the policy by other means"—because an insurgency can start long before the insurgent resorts to the use of force.

REVOLUTION, PLOT, INSURGENCY

Revolution, plot (or *coupd'état*), and insurgency are the three ways to take power by force. It will be useful to our analysis to try to distinguish among them.

A revolution usually is an explosive upheaval—sudden, brief, spontaneous, unplanned (France, 1789; China, 1922, Russia, 1917; Hungary, 1956). It is an *accident*, which can be explained afterward but not predicted other than to note the existence of a revolutionary situation. How and exactly when the explosion will occur cannot be forecast.... Who can tell what will happen, whether there will be an explosion, and if so, how and when it will erupt?

In a revolution, masses move and then leaders appear. Sun Yat-sen was in England when the Manchu dynasty was overthrown [China, 1911], and Lenin was in Switzerland when the Romanovs fell [Russia, 1917].

A plot is a clandestine action of an insurgent group directed at the overthrow of the top leadership in its country. Because of its clandestine nature, a plot cannot and does not involve the masses. Although preparations for the plot may be long, the action itself is brief and sudden. A plot is always a *gamble*....

On the other hand, an insurgency is a *protracted struggle* conducted methodically, step by step, in order to attain specific intermediate objectives leading finally to the overthrow of the existing order (China, 1927-1949; Greece, 1945-1950; Indochina, 1945-1954; Malaya, 1948-60; Algeria, 1954-62). To be sure, it can no more be predicted than a revolution; in fact, its beginnings are so vague that to determine exactly when an insurgency starts is a difficult legal, political, and historical problem.... But though it cannot be predicted, an insurgency is usually slow to develop and is no accident, for in an insurgency leaders appear and then the masses are made to move. . . .

INSURGENCY AND CIVIL WAR

An insurgency is a civil war. Yet there is a difference in the form the war takes in each case.

A civil war suddenly splits a nation into two or more groups which, after a brief period of initial confusion, find themselves in control of part of both the territory and the existing armed forces that they proceed immediately to develop....

ASSYMETRY BETWEEN THE INSURGENT AND THE COUNTER INSURGENT

There is an asymmetry between the opposite camps of a revolutionary war. This phenomenon results from the very nature of the war, from the disproportion of strength between the opponents at the outset, and from the difference in essence between their assets and their liabilities.

Since the insurgent alone can initiate the conflict (which is not to say that he is necessarily the first to use force), strategic initiative is his by definition. He is free to choose his hour, to wait safely for a favorable situation, unless external factors force him to accelerate his moves....

Until the insurgent has clearly revealed his intentions by engaging in subversion or open violence, he represents nothing but an imprecise, potential menace to the counterinsurgent and does not offer a concrete target that would justify a large effort. Yet an insurgency can reach a high degree of development by legal and peaceful means, at least in countries where political opposition is tolerated. This greatly limits pre-emptive moves on the part of the counterinsurgent. Usually, the most he can do is try to eliminate or alleviate the conditions propitious for an insurgency.

An appraisal of the contending forces at the start of a revolutionary war shows an overwhelming superiority in tangible assets in favor of the counterinsurgent. Endowed with the normal foreign and domestic perquisites of an established government, he has virtually everything—diplomatic recognition; legitimate power in the executive, legislative, and judicial branches; control of the administration and police; financial resources; industrial and agricultural resources at home or ready access to them abroad; transport and communications facilities; use and control of the information and propaganda media; command of the armed forces and the possibility of increasing their size. He is *in* while the insurgent, being *out*, has none or few of these assets.

The situation is reversed in the field of intangibles. The insurgent has a formidable asset—the ideological power of a cause on which to base his action. The counterinsurgent has a heavy liability—he is responsible for maintaining order throughout the country. The insurgent's strategy will naturally aim at converting his intangible assets into concrete ones, the counterinsurgent's strategy at preventing his intangible liability from dissipating his concrete assets.

The insurgent thus has to grow in the course of the war from small to large, from weakness to strength, or else he fails. The counterinsurgent will decline from large to small, from strength to weakness, in direct relation to the insurgent's success....

OBJECTIVE: THE POPULATION

Afflicted with his congenital weakness, the insurgent would be foolish if he mustered whatever forces were available to him and attacked his opponent in a conventional fashion, taking as his objective the destruction of the enemy's forces and the conquest of the territory. Logic forces him instead to carry the fight to a different ground where he has a better chance to balance the physical odds against him.

The population represents this new ground. If the insurgent manages to dissociate the population from the counterinsurgent, to control it physically, to get its active support, he will win the war because, in the final analysis, the exercise of political power depends on the tacit or explicit agreement of the population or, at worst, on its submissiveness.

Thus the battle for the population is a major characteristic of the revolutionary war.

REVOLUTIONARY WAR IS A POLITICAL WAR

All wars are theoretically fought for a political purpose, although in some cases the final political outcome differs greatly from the one intended initially.

In the conventional war, military action, seconded by diplomacy, propaganda, and economic pressure, is generally the principal way to achieve the goal. Politics *as an instrument of war* tends to take a back seat and emerges again—as an instrument—when the fighting ends. We are not implying that politics vanishes entirely as the main directing force but rather that, in the course of the conventional war, once political goals have been set (although the government may change them), once directives have been given to the armed forces (although the government may modify them), military action becomes foremost.... Nevertheless, military action remains the principal instrument of the conventional war.

As a result, it is relatively easy to allocate tasks and responsibilities among the government, which directs operations, the population, which provides the tools, and the soldier, who utilizes them.

The picture is different in the revolutionary war. The objective being the population itself, the operations designed to win it over (for the insurgent) or to keep it at least submissive (for the counterinsurgent) are essentially of a political nature. In this case, consequently, political action remains foremost throughout the war. It is not enough for the government to set political goals, to determine how much military force is applicable, to enter into alliances or to break them; *politics becomes an active instrument of operation.* And so intricate is the interplay between the political and the military actions that they cannot be tidily separated; on the contrary, every military move has to be weighed with regard to its political effects, and vice versa.

The insurgent, whose political establishment is a party and whose armed forces are the party's forces, enjoys an obvious advantage over his opponent, whose political establishment is the country's government, which may or may not be supported by a party or by a coalition of parties with their centrifugal tendencies, and whose army is the nation's army, reflecting the consensus or the lack of consensus in the nation.

GRADUAL TRANSITION FROM PEACE TO WAR

In the conventional war, the aggressor who has prepared for it within the confines of his national territory, channeling his resources into the preparation, has much to gain by attacking suddenly with all his forces. The transition from peace to war is as abrupt as the state of the art allows; the first shock may be decisive.

This is hardly possible in the revolutionary war because the aggressor—the insurgent—lacks sufficient strength at the outset. Indeed, years may sometimes pass before he has built up significant political, let alone military, power. So there is usually little or no first shock, little or no surprise, no possibility of a nearly decisive battle.

Infact, the in surgent has no interest in producing a shock until he feels fully able to with stand the enemy's expected reaction. By delaying the moment when the in surgency appears as a serious challenge to the counter insurgent, the in surgent delays there action. The delay may be further prolonged by exploiting the fact that the population realizes the danger even later than the counter in surgent leadership.

REVOLUTIONARY WAR IS A PROTRACTED WAR

The protracted nature of are volutionary war does not result from a design by either side; it is imposed on the insurgent by his initial weakness. It takes time for a small group of insurgent leaders to organize are volutionary movement, to raise and to develop armed forces, to reach a balance with the opponent, and to overpower him. A revolutionary war is short only if the counter insurgency collapses at a nearly stage . . . or if, somehow, a political settlement is reached . . . .

The revolutionary war in China lasted twenty-two years, if 1927 is taken as the starting year. The war lasted five years in Greece, nine in Indo china, nine in the Philippines, five in Indonesia, twelve in Malaya, three in Tunisia, four in Morocco, eight in Algeria. . . .

INSURGENCY IS CHEAP, COUNTER INSURGENCY COSTLY

Promoting disorder is a legitimate objective for the insurgent. It helps to disrupt the economy, hence to produce discontent; it serves to undermine the strength and the authority of the counter insurgent. Moreover, disorder—the normal state of nature—is cheap to create and very costly to prevent. The insurgent blows up a bridge, so every bridge has to be guarded; he throws a grenade in a movie theater, so every person entering a public place has to be searched. When the insurgent burns a farm, all the farmers clamor for protection; if they do not receive it, they may be tempted to deal privately with the insurgent, as happened in Indo china and Algeria, to give just two examples. Merely by making anonymous phone calls warning of bombs planted in luggage, the insurgent can disrupt civilian airline schedules and scare a way tourists.

Because the counter insurgent cannot escape the responsibility for maintaining order, the ratio of expenses between him and the insurgentis high. It may be ten or twenty to one, or higher. The figure varies greatly, of course, from case to case, and in each situation during the course of the revolutionary war. It seems to apply particularly when the insurgent reaches the initial stages of violence and resorts to terrorism and guerrilla warfare. . . .

There is, it seems, an upper limit to this ratio. When the insurgent increases his terror is morguerrilla activity by a factor of two, three, or five, he does not force the counter insurgent to multiply his expenditures by the same factor. Sooner or later, as a turation point is reached, a point where the law of diminishing returns operates for both sides.

Once the insurgent has succeeded in acquirings table geographical bases . . . he be comes *ipsofacto* a strong promoter of order with in his own area, in order to show the difference between the effectiveness of his rule and the inadequacy of his opponent's.

Because of the disparity in cost and effort, the insurgent can thus accept a protracted war; the counter insurgent should not.

FLUIDITY OF THE INSURGENT, RIGIDITY OF THE COUNTER INSURGENT

The insurgent is fluid because he has neither responsibility nor concrete assets; the counterinsurgent is rigid because he has both, and no amount of wailing canalter this fact for either side. Each must accept the situation as it is and make the best of it.

If the counter insurgent wanted to rid himself of his rigidity, he would have to renounce to some extent his claim to the effective rule of the country, or dispose of his concrete assets. One way of doing this, of course, would be to handover everything to the insurgent, and then start an insurgency against him, but no counter insurgent on record has dared apply this extreme solution.

On the other hand, the insurgent is obliged to remain fluid atleast until he has reached a balance of forces with the counter insurgent. However desirable for the insurgent to possess territory, large regular forces, and powerful weapons, to possess the mandtorely on them prematurely could spell his doom.. . .

In the revolutionary war, therefore, and until the balance of forces has reached, only the insurgent can consistently wage profitable hit-and-run operations because the counter insurgent alone offers profitable and targets; only the insurgent, as a rule, is free to accept or refuse battle, the counter insurgent being bound by his responsibility. On the other hand, only the counter insurgent can use substantial means because he alone possesses them.

Fluidity for one side and rigidity for the other are further determined by the nature of the operations. They are relatively simple for the insurgent—promoting disorder in every way until he assumes power; they are complicated for the counter insurgent, who has to take into account conflicting demands (protection of the population and the economy, and offensive operations against the insurgent) and who has to coordinate all the components of his forces—the administrator, the policeman, the soldier, the social worker, etc. The insurgent can afford a loose, primitive organization; he can delegate a wide margin of initiative, but his opponent cannot.

THE POWER OF IDEOLOGY

The insurgent cannot seriously embark on an insurgency unless he has a well-grounded cause with which to attract supporters among the population. A cause, as we have seen, is his sole asset at the beginning, and it must be a powerful one if the insurgent is to overcome his weakness.

Can two explosive but antagonistic causes exist simultaneously in a single country—one for the insurgent, the other for his opponent? Such a situation has happened occasionally, for example, in the United States, when the antislavery movement clashed with the doctrine of states' rights. The most likely result in this case is a civil war, not an insurgency.

The probability is that only one cause exists. If the insurgent has preempt edit, then the force of ideology works for him and not for the counter insurgent. However, this is true largely in the early parts of the conflict. Later on, as the war develops, war itself becomes the paramount issue, and the original cause consequently loses some of its importance.

It has been asserted that a counter insurgent confronted by a dynamic insurgent ideology is bound to meet defeat, that no a mount of tactics and technique can compensate for his ideological handicap. This is not necessarily so because the population's attitude in the middle stage of the war is dictated not so much by the relative popularity and merits of the opponents as by the more primitive concern for safety. Which side gives the best protection, which one threatens the most, which one is likely to win, these are the criteria governing the population's stand. So much the better, of course, if popularity and effectiveness are combined.

PROPAGANDA—A ONE-SIDED WEAPON

The asymmetrical situation has important effects on propaganda. The insurgent, having no responsibility, is free to use every trick; if necessary, he can lie, cheat, exaggerate. He is not obliged to prove; he is judged by what he promises, not by what he does. Consequently, propagan da is a powerful weapon for him. With no positive policy but with good propaganda the insurgent may still win.

The counter insurgent is tied to his responsibilities and to his past, and for him, facts speak louder than words. He is judged on what he does, not on what he says. If he lies, cheats, exaggerates, and does not prove, he may achieve some temporary successes, but at the price of being discredited for good. And he cannot cheat much unless his political structures a remonolithic, for the legitimate opposition in his own camp would so on disclose his every psychological maneuver. For him, propaganda can be no more than a secondary weapon, valuable only if intended to inform and not to fool. A counter insurgent can seldom cover bad or non existent policy with propaganda.

REVOLUTIONARY WAR REMAINS UNCONVENTIONAL UNTIL THE END

Once the insurgent has acquired strength and possesses significant regular forces, it would seem that the war should become a convention alone, a sort of civil war in which each camp holds a portion of the national territory from which he directs blows at the other. But if the insurgent has understood his strategic problems well, revolutionary war never reverts to a conventional form.

For one reason, the creation of a regular army by the insurgent does not mean an end to subversion and guerrilla activity. On the contrary, they increase in scope and intensity in order to facilitate the operations of the regular army and to amplify their effects.

For another reason, the insurgent has involved the population in the conflicts ice its beginning; the active participation of the population was indeed a *sin qua non* for his success. Having acquired the decisive advantage of a population organized and mobilized on his side, why should he cease to make use of an asset that gives his regular forces the fluidity and the freedom of action that the counter insurgent cannot achieve? As long as the population remains under his control, the insurgent retains his liberty to refuse battle excepton his own terms. . . .

We have indicated above the general characteristics of revolutionary war. They are an ineluctable product of the nature of this war. An insurgent or a counter insurgent who would conduct his war in opposition to any of these characteristics, going against the grain, so to speak, would certainly not increase his chances for success.

CHAPTER 2

THE PREREQUISITES FOR A SUCCESSFUL INSURGENCY

The cause of most recent insurgencies can easily be attributed to revolutionary situations that might have exploded into spontaneous revolutions, but bred instead, a group of leaders who then proceeded to organize and conduct the insurgencies. In view of this fact, it would be wrong and unjust to conclude that insurgencies are merely the product of personal ambitions on the part of their leaders who developed the whole movement, artificially, so to speak.

For the sake of demonstration, let us suppose that in country X a small group of discontented men—possessing the attributes of leadership, inspired by the success of so many insurgencies in the past twenty years, well aware of the strategic and tactical problems involved in such an enterprise—have met and decided to overthrow the existing order by the path of insurgency.

In light of the counterinsurgent's material superiority at the outset, their chances of victory will obviously depend on whether certain preliminary conditions are met. What conditions? Are these conditions a must? In other words, what are the prerequisites for a successful insurgency?

Knowing what they are would help in assessing, from a counterinsurgent's point of view, how vulnerable a country would be to an insurgency.

A Cause

Necessity of a Cause

How can the insurgent ever hope to pry the population away from the counterinsurgent, to control it, and to mobilize it? By finding supporters among the population, people whose support will range from active participation in the struggle to passive approval. The first basic need for an insurgent who aims at more than simply making trouble is an attractive cause, particularly in view of the risks involved and in view of the fact that the early supporters and the active supporters—not necessarily the same persons—have to be recruited by persuasion.

With a cause, the insurgent has a formidable, if intangible, asset that he can progressively transform into concrete strength. A small group of men *sans* cause can seize power by a lucky plot—this has happened in history—but then a plot is not an insurgency. The lack of an attractive cause is what restrains a priori apolitical crime syndicates from attempting to assume power, for they realize that only criminals will follow them. . . .

Strategic Criteria of a Cause

The best cause for the insurgent's purpose is one that, by definition, can attract the largest number of supporters and repel the minimum of opponents. Thus, a cause appealing to the proletariat in an industrialized country (or to the peasants in an underdeveloped one) is a good cause. . . . Independence from colonial rule was automatically a good cause in Indonesia, Tunisia, Morocco, Algeria, Cyprus, the Belgian Congo, and now Angola.

The insurgent must, of course, be able to identify himself totally with the cause or, more precisely, with the entire majority of the population theoretically attracted by it. . . .

To be perfectly sound, the cause must be such that the counterinsurgent cannot espouse it too or can do so only at the risk of losing his power, which is, after all, what he is fighting for. Land reform looked like a promising cause to the Hukbalahaps after the defeat of Japan and the accession of the Philippines to independence; but when the government offered land to the Huks' actual and potential supporters, the insurgents lost their cause and the game.[2] . . .

A cause, finally, must also be lasting, if not for the duration of the revolutionary war, at least until the movement is well on its feet. This differentiates a strategic cause from a tactical one, a deep-seated cause from a temporary one resulting from the exploitation of an ephemeral difficulty, such as, for instance, the high price and the scarcity of food after a year of natural calamities.

The nature of the cause

What is a political problem? It is "an unsolved contradiction," according to Mao Tse-tung. If one accepts this definition, then a political cause is the championing of one side of the contradiction. In other words, where there is no problem, there is no cause, but there are always problems in any country. What makes one country more vulnerable than another to insurgency is the depth and acuity of its existing problems.

Problems of all natures are exploitable for an insurgency, provided the causes they lead to meet the above criteria. The problem may be essentially political, related to the national or international situation of the country.... It follows that any country where the power is invested in an oligarchy, whether indigenous or foreign, is potential ground for a revolutionary war.

The problem may be social, as when one class is exploited by another or denied any possibility of improving its lot.... The problem becomes particularly dangerous when the society does not integrate those who, by the level of their education or by their achievements, have proved to belong to the true elite. For it is among this rejected elite that the insurgents can find the indispensable leaders.

The problem may be economic, such as the low price of agricultural products in relation to industrial goods, or the low price of raw material in relation to finished products, or the import of foreign goods rather than the development of a national industry....

The problem may be racial,.... Or religious,.... Or cultural....

The problem may even be artificial so long as it has a chance to be accepted as a fact. The lot of the Chinese farmers—victims of exactions by the authorities and of the rapacity of the local usurers—was no doubt a hard one. The Chinese Communists did exploit this problem. However, their chief cause... was land reform....a class war on the issue would theoretically bring to their side the majority of the farmers. The sole comprehensive work on the subject...contradicted the Communist picture of the situation, but this fact did not decrease in the slightest the psychological value of the slogan "Land to the Tiller." An efficient propaganda machine can turn an artificial problem into a real one.

It is not absolutely necessary that the problem be acute, although the insurgent's work is facilitated if such is the case. If the problem is merely latent, the first task of the insurgent is to make it acute by "raising the political consciousness of the masses." Terrorism may be a quick means of producing this effect....

Tactical Manipulation of the Cause

The insurgent is not restricted to the choice of a single cause. Unless he has found an over-all cause, like anticolonialism, which is sufficient in itself because it combines all the political, social, economic, racial, religious, and cultural issues described above, he has much to gain by selecting an assortment of causes especially tailored for the various groups in the society that he is seeking to attract.

Let us suppose that the revolutionary movement is tentatively made up, as it was in China, of the Communist Party...and its allies.... The insurgent has to appeal to the whole, and a cause is necessary for that. Since it is easier to unite "against" than "for," particularly when the components are so varied, the general cause will most probably be a negative one, something like "throw the rascals out"...In addition, the insurgent must appeal to each component of the movement, and in this aspect, the various causes will probably contain a constructive element....

Nothing obligates the insurgent to stick to the same cause if another one looks more profitable. Thus, in China, the Communists initially took the classic Marxist stand in favor of the workers (1921-1925). Then they actively espoused the national cause of the Kuomintang, for the unification of China against the warlords (1925-1927). After the Kuomintang-Communist split, they largely dropped the workers in favor of the poor peasants, advocating land reform by radical means (1928-1934). Then Japanese aggression became the central issue in China, and the Communists advocated a patriotic united front against Japan (1927-45), adopting meanwhile a moderate agrarian policy: Land redistribution would be ended, but instead, the Communists would impose strict control of rents and interest rates. After the Japanese surrender, they finally reverted to land reform with the temperate proviso that landlords themselves would be entitled to a share of the land (1945-49). What the Communists actually did after their victory, between 1950 and 1952, was to carry out their land reform "through violent struggles" in order to conduct a class war among the rural population.... Once this was achieved, the Party buried land reform for good and started collectivizing the land.

Thus, if idealism and a sense of ethics weigh in favor of a consistent stand, tactics pull toward opportunism.

Diminishing Importance of the Cause

The importance of a cause, an absolute essential at the outset of an insurgency, decreases progressively as the insurgent acquires strength. The war itself becomes the principal issue, forcing the population to take sides, preferably the winning one....

WEAKNESS OF THE COUNTER INSURGENT

Let us assume now that our minute group of insurgent leaders in Country X has found several good causes, some acute, some latent, some artificial, on which to base their insurgency. They all have agreed on a potent platform. Can they start operating? Not unless another preliminary condition has been met. The insurgent, starting from almost zero while his enemy still has every means at his disposal, is as vulnerable as a new-born baby. He cannot live and grow without some sort of protection, and who but the counterinsurgent himself can protect him? Therefore, we must analyze what makes a body politic resistant to infection.

Strengths and Weaknesses of the Political Regime

1. *Absence of problems.* A country fortunate enough to know no problem is obviously immune from insurgency. But since we have assumed that our potential insurgent leaders

have fund a cause, let us eliminate these countries—if there are any—from our consideration.

2. *National consensus.* The solidity of a regime is primarily based upon this factor. Thailand may live under a dictatorship or a democratic system, but her national consensus...has so far always strengthened the regime in power. . . .

3. *Resoluteness of the counterinsurgent leadership.* Resoluteness is a major factor in any sort of conflict, but particularly so in a revolutionary war for the reasons that (a) the insurgent has the initial benefit of a dynamic cause; (b) an insurgency does not grow suddenly into a national danger and the people's reaction against it is slow. Consequently, the role of the counterinsurgent leaders is paramount.

4. *Counterinsurgent leaders' knowledge of counterinsurgency warfare.* It is not enough for the counterinsurgent leaders to be resolute; they must also be aware of the strategy and tactics required in fighting an insurgency. . . .

5. *The machine for the control of the population.* Four instruments of control count in a revolutionary war situation: the political structure, the administrative bureaucracy, the police, and the armed forces.

   a. *The political structure.* If Country X is located behind the Iron Curtain, where political opposition is not tolerated and where the population is kept under a system of ·terror and mutual suspicion, the initial group of insurgents has no chance to develop; at best, the group will be able to survive in total secrecy...while waiting for better times. . . .

A control of this order rules out the possibility of launching an insurgency. As long as there is no privacy, as long as every unusual move or event is reported and checked, as long as parents are afraid to talk in front of their children, how can contacts be made, ideas spread, recruiting accomplished? . . .

At the other extreme, if anarchy prevails in Country X, the insurgent will find all the facilities he needs in order to meet, to travel, to contact people, to make known his program, to find and organize the early supporters, to receive and to distribute funds, to agitate and to subvert, or to launch a widespread campaign of terrorism.

In between these extremes lies a wide range of political structures that in varying degrees facilitate or hinder the task of the insurgent...

   b. *The administrative bureaucracy.* A country is run in its day-to-day life by its bureaucracy, which has a work force of its own that has sometimes no relation to the strength or weakness of the top political leadership. France under the Third and Fourth Republics had a weak leadership but a strong administrative apparatus...

c. *The police.* The eye and arm of the government in all matters pertaining to internal order, the police are obviously a key factor in the early stages of an insurgency; they are the first counterinsurgent organization that has to be infiltrated and neutralized.

Their efficiency depends on their numerical strength, the competency of their members, their loyalty toward the government, and last but not least, on the backing they get from the other branches of government—particularly the judicial system. If insurgents, though identified and arrested by the police, take advantage of the many normal safeguards built into the judicial system and are released, the police can do little. Prompt adaptation of the judicial system to the extraordinary conditions of an insurgency, an agonizing problem at best, is a necessity. . . .

d. *The armed forces.* Leaving aside the factors of strength applicable to the armed forces in all wars, those that are relevant in a revolutionary war are:

    i.   The numerical strength of the armed forces in relation to the size and the population of the country. An insurgency is a two-dimensional war fought for the control of the population. There is no front, no safe rear. No area, no significant segment of the population can be abandoned for long—unless the population can be trusted to defend itself. This is why a force of ten or twenty to one between the counterinsurgent and the insurgent is not uncommon when the insurgency develops into guerilla warfare. . . .

    ii.   The composition of the armed forces. A conventional war today requires a modern, well-balanced force, with its air, sea, and ground components. But a revolutionary war is primarily a war of infantry. Paradoxically, the less sophisticated the counterinsurgent forces, the better they are. . . . As for an air force, whose supremacy the insurgent cannot challenge, what it needs are slow assault fighters, short take-off transport planes, and helicopters.

    iii.   The feeling of the individual soldier toward the insurgent's cause and toward the counterinsurgent regime. Whereas the insurgent initially can use only a few combatants and can therefore select volunteers, the counterinsurgent's manpower demands are so high that he is condemned to draft soldiers, and he may well be plagued by the problem of loyalty.

    iv.   The time lapse before intervention. Because of the gradual transition from peace to war in a revolutionary war, the armed forces are not ordered into action as fast as they would be in a conventional war. This delay is another characteristic of revolutionary wars. To reduce it is a political responsibility of the country's leaders.

6. *Geographic conditions.* Geography can weaken the strongest political regime or strengthen the weakest one....

It is the combination of all these factors that determine whether an insurgency is possible or not once the potential insurgent has a cause.

Crisis and Insurgency

The insurgent cannot, of course, choose his opponent; he must accept him as he is. If he is confronted by a powerful counterinsurgent, he has no recourse but to wait until his opponent is weakened by some internal or external crisis.

The recent series of colonial insurgencies is, no doubt, a consequence of World War II, which constituted a formidable crisis for the colonial powers. The record shows that no insurgency or revolt succeeded in colonial territories before 1938, although the situation then was no less revolutionary than after the war....

The Border Doctrine

Every country is divided for administrative and military purposes into provinces, counties, districts, zones, etc. The border areas are a permanent source of weakness for the counterinsurgent whatever his administrative structures, and his advantage is usually exploited by the insurgent, especially in the initial violent stages of the insurgency. By moving from one side of the border to the other, the insurgent is often able to escape pressure or, at least, to complicate operations for his opponent....

GEOGRAPHIC CONDITIONS

The role of geography, a large one in an ordinary war, may be overriding in a revolutionary war. If the insurgent, with his initial weakness, cannot get any help from geography, he may well be condemned to failure before he starts. Let us examine briefly the effects of the various geographic factors.

1. *Location.* A country isolated by natural barriers (sea, desert, forbidding mountain ranges) or situated among countries that oppose the insurgency is favorable to the counterinsurgent.
2. *Size.* The larger the country, the more difficult for a government to control it. Size can weaken even the most totalitarian regime...

3. *Configuration.* A country easy to compartmentalize hinders the insurgent.... if the country is an archipelago, the insurgency cannot easily be spread ....

4. *International borders.* The length of the borders, particularly if the neighboring countries are sympathetic to the insurgents, as was the case in Greece, Indochina, and Algeria, favors the insurgent. A high proportion of coast line to inland borders helps the counterinsurgent because maritime traffic can be controlled with a limited amount of technical means, which the counterinsurgent possesses or is usually able to acquire....

5. *Terrain.* It helps the insurgent insofar as it is rugged and difficult, either because of mountains and swamps or because of the vegetation....

6. *Climate.* Contrary to the general belief, harsh climates favor the counterinsurgent forces, which have, as a rule, better logistical and operational facilities. This will be especially favorable if the counterinsurgent soldier is a native and, therefore, accustomed to the rigors of the climate.... Merely to keep scarce weapons and ammunition in good condition when one lives continuously in the open, as the guerrilla does, is a perpetual headache.

7. *Population.* The size of the population affects the revolutionary war in the same way as does the size of the country: the more inhabitants, the more difficult to control them. But this factor can be attenuated or enhanced by the density and distribution of the population. The more scatted the population, the better for the insurgent; .... A high ratio of rural to urban population gives an advantage to the insurgent; ... The control of a town, which is extremely dependent on outside supplies, requires smaller forces than the control of the same number of people spread over the countryside—except in the case of a mass uprising, which can never last long in any event.

8. *Economy.* The degree of development and sophistication of the economy can work both ways. A highly developed country is very vulnerable to a short and intense wave of terrorism. But if terrorism lasts, the disruption becomes such that the population may not be able to endure it and, consequently, may turn against the insurgent even when it was not initially hostile to him.

   An underdeveloped country is less vulnerable to terrorism but much more open to guerrilla warfare, if only because the counterinsurgent cannot count on a good network of transport and communication facilities and because the population is more autarchic.

To sum up, the ideal situation for the insurgent would be a large land-locked country shaped like a blunt tipped star, with jungle-covered mountains along the borders and scattered swamps in the plains, in a temperate zone with a large and dispersed rural population and a primitive economy. (See Figure 1.) The counterinsurgent would prefer a small island shaped like a pointed star, on which a cluster of evenly spaced towns are separated by desert, in a tropical or arctic climate, with an industrial economy. (See Figure 2.)

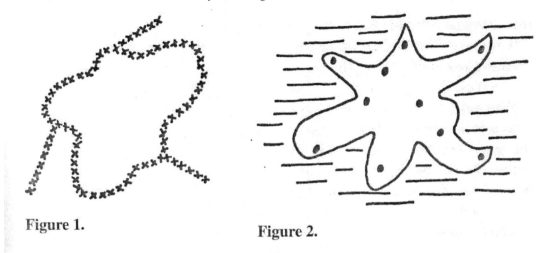

Figure 1.   **Figure 2.**

OUTSIDE SUPPORT

Outside support to an insurgency can take the form of:

1. *Moral support,* from which the insurgent will benefit without any effort on his part, provided his cause goes along with "the wind of history."...Moral support is expressed by the weight of public opinion and through various communications media. Propaganda is the chief instrument of moral support, used to sway public opinion when it is adverse, or to reinforce existing public sympathy.
2. *Political support,* with pressure applied directly on the counterinsurgent, or indirectly by diplomatic action in the international forum....
3. *Technical support,* in the form of advice to the insurgent for the organization of his movement and the conduct of his political and military operations....
4. *Financial support,* overt or covert....
5. *Military support,* either through direct intervention on the insurgent's side or by giving him training facilities and equipment.

No outside support is absolutely necessary at the start of an insurgency, although it obviously helps when available. Military support short of direct intervention, in particular, cannot be absorbed in a significant amount by the insurgent until his forces have reached a certain level of development. The initial military phase of an insurgency, whether terrorism or guerrilla warfare, requires little in the way of equipment, arms, ammunition, and explosives. These can usually be found locally or smuggled in.

When the time comes, however, for the insurgent to pass from guerrilla warfare to a higher form of operations, to create a regular army, the need for much larger and more varied supplies becomes acute. Either he is able to capture it from the counterinsurgent, or it must come from the outside. If not, the development of the insurgent military establishment is impossible. . . .

In conclusion, (1) a cause, (2) a police and administrative weakness in the counterinsurgent camp, (3) a not-too-hostile geographic environment, and (4) outside support in the middle and later stages of an insurgency—these are the conditions for a successful insurgency. The first two are musts. The last one is a help that may become a necessity.

CHAPTER 3: THE INSURGENCY DOCTRINE

STRATEGIC PATTERNS FOR INSURGENCY

Since counterinsurgency exists solely as a reaction to an insurgency, the counterinsurgent's problems and operations can be best understood in the light of what prompts them. In this chapter, we will summarize the insurgency doctrine.

Two general patterns for insurgencies emerge from the history of past revolutionary wars. One is based essentially on the theory and experience of the Chinese Communists....

The other pattern, a variation of the first in its early stage, has been followed in several nationalist insurgencies.

They will be described next, but it must be understood that they are given only as patterns build upon generalizations. While they substantially fit the actual events in their broad lines, they may be partially at variance with the history of specific insurgencies.

THE ORTHODOX PATTERN (COMMUNIST)

To the Communists, revolution consists not merely in overthrowing the existing order but also in carrying out afterward a complete Communist transformation of the country.

The First Step: Creation of a Party

The basic instrument for the entire process is a party, and the first step for the insurgent is to create it.

By definition, it should be the party of the proletariat, but since the proletariat is small or nonexistent in colonial and semi colonial countries, the lowest class of peasants must be included in it; . . . as the coming armed struggle has to be conducted in rural areas. Because the proletariat cannot produce the competent early leaders, they must be sought·for among the intellectuals and particularly among the students who can provide ardor as well as brains.

The intensity, the vicissitudes of the long struggles ahead make it imperative that the party be strong, disciplined, tested. It must not be a loose organization, which may break apart at the first sharp turn in party policy or give way under reaction to the counterinsurgent. In addition, it must not disintegrate in the aftermaths of victory... It must be and stay an elite party....

Its purity is maintained by systematic, regular weeding-out conducted in "intra-Party struggles,"... Deviators from orthodoxy are won back by conciliatory methods or expelled if they do not confess their errors.

In view of its future operations, the party must be organized into both open and clandestine apparatuses, the latter designed for a dual purpose: defensive, in the case the counterinsurgent decides to suppress the party; offensive in order to subvert and to conduct the mass struggles in the enemy's areas once the party has gone into open rebellion.

It cannot be denied that the creation and the growth of such a party is at best a slow, painstaking process.... Building a strong, reliable revolutionary party is certainly the most difficult part in the insurgency....

On the other hand, this first step can be accomplished by legal and peaceful means, at least in countries where political opposition is tolerated.

The Second Step: United Front

An elite party is perforce a minority party. It cannot overpower the counterinsurgent by itself, with its own means. Therefore, the second step, which may largely overlap with the first, consists in rallying allies around the party—the more the better. This raises several problems:

A large united front will necessarily include dubious allies whose use must be curbed short of the point where they can endanger the basic program of the insurgent. . . .

The party may lost its identify in a united front. In order to reduce risk, the party...can enter an alliance with other parties, but it must never merge with them. It cannot absorb them, either...

The party's platform at any given time during the conflict must contain something that appeals to each ally and nothing that may be too objectionable to them. So the real postwar intentions of the party must be kept secret; they need be disclosed only to the top leadership....

During this second step, the party's clandestine apparatus will engage in subversive action directed toward three main elements:

The counterinsurgent, with a view toward preventing and sabotaging an eventual reaction.

The allies, in order to channel their activity in the direction chosen by the party and to prevent any damaging split in the united front.

The masses, in order to prepare and to promote the political struggles against the counter-insurgent.

This is done by infiltration…agitation, and propaganda. Good intelligence is an important by-product of this work.

As the moment of the armed struggle approaches, the work among the masses becomes particularly important in the rural areas that have been tentatively selected as favorable grounds for the insurgent's initial military operations. A population won over to the cause and an area where the party organization is strong are essential for the success of the first guerrilla operations, on which much depends.

The insurgent's activity during the second step remains generally within the bounds of legality and nonviolence. It does not constitute an open rebellion, a clear-cut challenge to the counterinsurgent. Having the initiative, the insurgent can always slow down or retreat if a reaction threatens.

The Third Step: Guerrilla Warfare

The insurgent may seize power merely by political play and subversion. If not, then an armed struggle is the logical continuation. The Chinese Communists assert that the armed struggle is both necessary and indispensable, that victory must be won by force, that "liberation" must not be granted or gained by compromise. The reasons for their stand are these:

A local revolutionary war is part of the global war on capitalism and imperialism. Hence, a military victory against the local enemy is in fact a victory against the global enemy and contributes to his ultimate defeat.

When the insurgent seizes power after an armed struggle, his victory is complete, his authority absolute. The war has polarized the population, revealing friends and enemies, which makes it easier to implement the Communist postwar program.

Through the armed struggle, the party consolidates itself. It acquires experience, once and for all cures its infantile diseases, eliminates the weak members, is able to select the best, the true leaders. The logical implication of this is that the insurgent must win primarily through his own effort; if he is put into power by external intervention, the party's internal weakness will plague him for years.

The party assumes power with a tested, reliable military establishment which is the party's guarantor in the political transformation to come.

So, whether because it is impossible to succeed otherwise or because of his faith in the usefulness of the armed struggle, the insurgent embarks on a contest of strength. The decision being his,[3] he chooses the time when conditions seem ripe, when, *internally*, the counterinsurgent is weakened by a fortuitous or provoked crisis, when subversion is producing effects, when public opinion is divided, when the party's organization has been built up in some rural areas; and when, *externally*, direct intervention on the counterinsurgent's side is unlikely; when the insurgent can count on some moral and political support at this stage and on military aid later, if necessary.

The goal is the creation of the insurgent's military power, but it has to be accomplished progressively, step by step. Guerrilla warfare is the only possible course of action for a start. In this step, the first objective is the guerrilla's survival: the final one, the acquisition of bases in which an insurgent government and administration will be established, the human and other resources exploited, and regular forces created. Guerrilla warfare with no bases, says Mao Tse-tung, is nothing but roving banditism; unable to maintain links with the population, it cannot develop and is bound to be defeated.

Objectively, there is no difference between ordinary, everyday bandit activity in almost every country and the first guerrilla actions. What makes it possible for the guerrillas to survive and to expand? The complicity of the population. This is the key to guerrilla warfare, indeed to the insurgency, and it has been expressed in the formula of the fish swimming in the water.[4] The complicity of the population is not to be confused with the sympathy of the population; the former is active, the latter inactive, and the popularity of the insurgent's cause is insufficient by itself to transform sympathy into complicity. The participation of the population in the conflict is obtained, above all, by a political organization (the party) living among the population, backed by force (the guerrilla gangs), which eliminates open enemies, intimidates the potential ones, and relies on those among the population who actively support the insurgents. Persuasion brings a minority of supporters—they are indispensable—but force rallies the rest. There is, of course, a practical if not ethical limit to the use of force; the basic rule is never to antagonize at any one time more people than can be handled.

Just as important as the links between the insurgent's political organization and the population are the links between his armed forces and the masses. To see that they are properly maintained—and that the forces never become a rival to the party—is the task of the political commissars.

The guerrilla operations will be planned primarily not so much against the counterinsurgent as in order to organize the population. An ambush against a counterinsurgent patrol may be a military success, but if it does not bring the support of a village or implicate its population against the counterinsurgent, it is not a victory because it does not lead to expansion. In other words, attrition of the enemy is a by-product of guerrilla warfare, not its essential goal.

Where to operate? In the areas that the counterinsurgent cannot easily control and where the guerrilla gangs can consequently survive and develop. The factors in selecting the first areas of operations are:

The strength of the insurgent's organization among the population that has been achieved in preliminary work.

The remoteness of the areas from the center of the counterinsurgent's power.

Their inaccessibility due to terrain and poor communications.

Their location on both sides of administrative borders, which makes it difficult for the enemy to coordinate his reaction.

Later on, as success breeds success, the first factor becomes less important, and guerrilla warfare can be expanded geographically by injecting teams of guerrilla units and political workers in other areas, even if they are devoid of strong party structures. This underlines the importance of early success.

Armament is not a problem at this stage. The insurgent's requirements are small. Weapons (pistols, rifles, shotguns) are generally available or can be bought and smuggled in. Crude weapons (grenades, mines, even mortars) can be manufactured, and equipment can be captured from the enemy.

Demoralization of the enemy's forces is an important task. The most effective way to achieve it is by employing a policy of leniency toward the prisoners. They must be well treated and offered the choice of joining the movement or of being set free, even if this means that they will return to the counterinsurgent's side. Despite its setbacks in the early stage, this is the policy that pays the most in the long run. During a trip in western China in April, 1947, the author was captured by Communist troops.... He was treated as a prisoner the first morning, put under surveillance for the rest of the day, and considered a "guest of honor" for his week-long involuntary but highly interesting stay among the People's Liberation Army. During this week, various military and political cadres undertook to explain their policy, strategy, and tactics. A political commissar explained the Communist technique for handling Kuomintang [Nationalist—counterinsurgent] prisoners. They were offered the choice between (1) joining the Communist Army, (2) settling in Communist territory, where they would be given a share of land, (3) going back home, or (4) returning to the Nationalist Army....

In the same month, a colleague of the author visited a camp...where the Nationalists kept 5,000 Communist prisoners.... "Between you and me, we have no more than ten real Communists among these prisoners."

"Who are the others then?"

"Nationalist soldiers caught and released by the Communists. We don't want them to contaminate our army."

Thus, the Communists had achieved the trick of having the Nationalists themselves watching their own men! ...

The united-front policy remains in force throughout the conflict and must be given substance during the armed struggle. How can allies be admitted into the political structures and the guerrilla units without weakening the insurgency? The only way is by confronting the allies with the party's superior organization, discipline, doctrine, policy, leadership. The party alone must lead; forceful leaders among the allies must be won over or neutralized. The party alone must expand; the allied parties may be permitted only to stagnate....

The Fourth Step: Movement Warfare

Guerrilla warfare cannot win the decision against a resolute enemy. Protracted guerrilla activity, so cheap to carry out and so expensive to suppress, may eventually produce a crisis in the counterinsurgent camp, but it could just as well alienate the population and disintegrate the united front. The enemy must be met on his own ground; an insurgent regular army has to be created in order to destroy the counterinsurgent forces.

There is a problem with timing. If premature, the creation of this regular army, which necessarily is less elusive then guerrilla gangs, may lead to disaster. So it must not be undertaken until bases have been liberated and the enemy discouraged from invading them too frequently, and until the problem of armament is solved.

When the situation fulfills these conditions the best guerrilla units can be progressively transformed into regular troops, first of company strength, then of battalion strength, and so on up to division level or even higher....

... it is capture from the enemy that dictates the nature of the insurgent's operations.... requires an overwhelming and sudden concentration of insurgent forces against an isolated counterinsurgent unit caught in the open—not entrenched; hence a *movement warfare* in which the insurgent can exploit his fluidity, his better intelligence, and the simple but effective cross-country logistical facilities afforded by the organized population. For the sake of fluidity, heavy armament must be ruled out... the actual shock must be brief, and no sustained attack can be undertaken; for the sake of better intelligence, operations are preferably conducted in areas where the insurgent political organizations are strong and active among the population.

Supply from abroad, if such a possibility exists, imposes on the insurgent the necessity of acquiring bases on or near the international border of the country, close to the source of supply.

The insurgent units' lack of punch—their feeble logistical capacities—rule out fixed defensive operations. In fact, so precious are the regular units, particularly when they have just been created, that the defense of the bases has to be left to other insurgent forces, to the population itself with its militias, to the guerrilla units, and to the local troops, which provide a core for the defense. In offensive operations, these second-rate units will also relieve the regular troops from the task of covering and reconnoitering. . . .

In order to mobilize the population for a total war effort, every inhabitant under the insurgent's control is made to belong simultaneously to at least two organizations: one, *horizontal*, is a geographic organization, by hamlet, village, or district; the other, *vertical*, groups the inhabitants by categories of every kind, by age, by sex, by profession. The party cells crisscross the whole structure and provide the cement. An additional organization helps to keep everybody in line: the party's secret service, whose members remain unknown to the local cadres and answer only to the top hierarchy, which is thus in a position to control those who control the masses....

The expansion of the insurgent movement raises the problem of political and military cadres. They are selected on the basis, above all, of their loyalty and, secondly, of their concrete achievements in the field....

The Fifth Step: Annihilation Campaign

As the over-all strength of the insurgent grows while his opponent's decreases, a balance of forces is reached at some point. In the assessment of the insurgent's strength must be included not only his military assets but the solidity of his political structure, the fact that the population is mobilized in his areas, the subversive activity of his underground agents in the counterinsurgent's areas, and finally, the insurgent's psychological superiority.

From then on, the scope and scale of the insurgent's operations will increase swiftly; a series of offensives aiming at the complete destruction of the enemy will constitute the last and final step.

At any time during the process, the insurgent may make peace offers, provided there is more to gain by negotiating than by fighting.

THE BOURGEOIS-NATIONALIST PATTERN: A SHORTCUT

The goal of the insurgent in this case is generally limited to the seizure of power; post insurgency problems, as secondary preoccupations, are shelved for the time being. The precise and immediate aim of the initial core of insurgents, a dedicated but inevitably small group of men with no broad organization to back them, is to set up a revolutionary party rapidly.

The First Step: Blind Terrorism

The purpose is to get publicity for the movement and its cause, and by focusing attention on it, to attract latent supporters. This is done by random terrorism, bombings, arson, assassinations, conducted in as spectacular a fashion as possible, by concentrated, coordinated, and synchronized waves. Few men are needed for this sort of operation....

The Second Step: Selective Terrorism

This quickly follows the first. The aims are to isolate the counterinsurgent from the masses, to involve the population in the struggle, and to obtain as a minimum its passive complicity.

This is done by killing, in various parts of the country, some of the low-ranking government officials who work most closely with the population, such as policemen, mailmen, mayors, councilmen, and teachers. Killing high-ranking counterinsurgent officials serves no purpose since they are too far removed from the population for their deaths to serve as examples.

The early supporters are set to work collecting money from the population. Although money, the sinew of war, is interesting in itself, this operation has important side effects. The amount of money collected provides a simple standard to gauge the efficiency of the supporters and to select leader accordingly. It also implicates the mass and forces it to show its revolutionary spirit. "You give money, you are with us. You refuse money, you are a traitor." A few of those unwilling to pay are executed.... These assassinations have value only if they serve as examples; therefore they must not be hidden or committed on the sly....

The insurgent has to destroy all bridges linking the population with the counterinsurgent and his potential allies. Among these, people (generally the liberal-minded) inclined to seek a compromise with the insurgents will be targets of terrorist attacks.

When all this is achieved, conditions are ripe for the insurgent guerrillas to operate and for the population to be mobilized effectively. From there on, this pattern rejoins the orthodox one, if necessary.

Illegal and violent at the outset, dangerous for the insurgent because terrorism may backfire, this pattern may save years of tedious organizational work. By terrorism, small groups of insurgents have been catapulted overnight to the top of large revolutionary movements, and some have won the victory at that very time, without need for further action. However, the bill is paid at the end with the bitterness bred by terrorism and with the usual post victory disintegration of a party hastily thrown together.

VULNERABILITY OF THE INSURGENTS IN THE ORTHODOX PATTERN

Let us follow the insurgent who has selected the orthodox pattern as his course of action. He operates necessarily in a country where political opposition is tolerated.

During the first two steps—creation of a party and organization of a united front—his vulnerability depends directly on the tolerance of the counterinsurgent and can be correspondingly low or high. Sooner or later, the counterinsurgent realizes the danger and starts reacting. The insurgent's vulnerability rises because he has not yet acquired military power and is in no position to resist by force. If the counterinsurgent's reaction is feeble enough, the insurgent has survived his first test, has learned how far he can go, and his vulnerability decreases.

If all has proceeded well, the insurgent has created his party and organized a popular front. He decides now to initiate... guerrilla warfare (Step 3). His military power is still nil or feeble, whereas the full weight of his opponent's may be brought to bear against him. Consequently, the insurgent's vulnerability rises sharply to its highest level, and he may well be destroyed. If

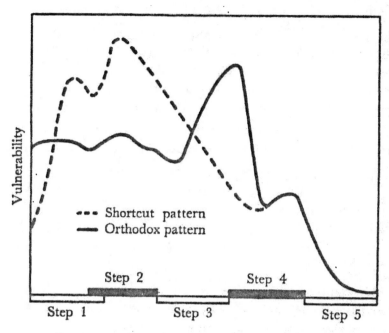

Figure 3. Vulnerability of the Insurgent in the Course of the
Revolutionary War

he survives, his vulnerability goes down until he starts organizing a regular army (Step 4): His
units, no longer small, elusive guerrilla groups, then offer better targets for the counterinsurgent's
conventional forces. Vulnerability increases once more. After this last hurdle is cleared, the insurgent is no longer vulnerable.

    If vulnerability could be measured, it might be graphically represented as shown in figure 3.

VULNERABILITY OF THE INSURGENT IN THE SHORTCUT PATTERN

In the case when the insurgent has chosen to follow the bourgeois-nationalist pattern, his vulnerability starts from a lower level since his action is clandestine at the outset. It climbs rapidly because of the danger inherent in terrorism, which the normal police force may be able to suppress
if it has not been planned and conducted on a sufficient scale. The insurgent, who needs publicity
above everything else at this stage, is also at the mercy of a tight and prompt censorship.

    However, surprise plays in his favor, and he can count on the fact that the counterinsurgent's
reaction is never immediate. If the insurgent has survived the first few days of blind terrorism,
his vulnerability decreases.

It soon arises again because the full power of the counterinsurgent begins to be mobilized against him; the armed forces, particularly, go into action much sooner than in the orthodox pattern. Vulnerability goes up to a new height. If the insurgent survives, it diminishes progressively.

When the insurgent reaches Step 3 (guerrilla warfare) and rejoins the orthodox pattern, he is less vulnerable than he would have been had he chosen the orthodox pattern at the start because he has already successfully withstood the full brunt of the counterinsurgent reaction.

NOTES

1. The information for the biographical sketch is drawn from Ann Marlowe, *David Galula: His Life and Intellectual Context* (Carlisle, PA: U.S. Army War College, Strategic Studies Institute, 2010), http://www.StrategicStudiesInstitute.army.mil/ (Accessed 11 Jun 2012).
2. The defeat of the Communist-inspired Hukbalahap Insurrection in the Philippines from 1946-1955 served as a case study for a successful counterinsurgency that featured sound political and military measures by the Philippine government supported by a small, but effective American military advisory effort. Lawrence M. Greenburg, *TheHukbalahap Insurrection: A Case Study of a Successful Anti-Insurgency Operation in the Philippines, 1946-1955* (Washington: US Army Center of Military History, 1987).
3. . . . A Communist insurgent movement may be ordered by the Communist International to step up or to slow down its action.
4. Galula is referring to Mao's quote: "The guerrilla must move amongst the people as a fish swims in the sea."

COLD AND HOT REVOLUTIONARY WAR: "LAWS" FOR COIN?

David Galula

In his chapter on strategy, Clausewitz cautions, "Everything in strategy is very simple, but that does not mean that everything is very easy. Once it has been determined, from the political conditions, what a war is meant to achieve and what it can achieve, it is easy to chart the course. But great strength of character, as well as great lucidity and firmness of mind, is required in order to follow through steadily, to carry out the plan, and not to be thrown off course by thousands of diversions."[1] This passage resounds when reading David Galula's chapters on counterinsurgency (COIN). With Galula's wide range of experiences with COIN, certainly he is aware of the pitfalls of any "step-by-step" approach. Nevertheless, Galula's chapters of counterinsurgency in "cold" and "hot" revolutionary wars provide a coherent plan of action for the counterinsurgent faced with a myriad of complex challenges.

The previous lesson outlined revolutionary warfare, insurgency, and emphasized population control as the key to an insurgent's success. This lesson focuses on the counterinsurgent's actions in "cold" revolutionary war (before insurgent violence) and "hot" revolutionary war (after the insurgents commence hostilities). Galula points out that the insurgents are materially weak, but possess the strategic initiative. The task for the counterinsurgent is to isolate the insurgent from the population. He provides four "laws" of counterinsurgency and an eight-step strategy to establish population control and regain initiative. Hence, Galula appeals because he seems practical and actionable. However, these chapters appear to ignore fog & friction and the difficulties of even doing the simplest task in war. Today's airman must analyze Galula's theories, recommendations, and perspective for their applicability to current conflicts. Nevertheless, although writing for revolutionary wars of a generation ago, David Galula earned the esteem of today's counterinsurgency theorists and provided valuable insights for our forces recently engaged in Iraq and Afghanistan.

CHAPTER 4

COUNTERINSURGENCY IN THE COLD REVOLUTIONARY WAR

From the counterinsurgent's point of view, a revolutionary war can be divided into two periods:

1. The "cold revolutionary war," when the insurgent's activity remains on the whole legal and nonviolent (as in Steps 1 and 2 in the orthodox pattern).
2. The "hot revolutionary war," when the insurgent's activity becomes openly illegal and violent (as in the other steps in the orthodox pattern and in the entire process of the shortcut pattern).

The transitions from "peace" to "war," as we have seen, can be very gradual and confusing. Even when the insurgent follows the shortcut pattern, violence is always preceded by a short period of stirrings. . . . For analytical purposes, we shall choose as a dividing line between the two periods the moment when the counterinsurgent armed forces are ordered to step in, and we shall approach the study of counterinsurgency warfare in chronological order, starting with the "cold revolutionary war."

The situation at this stage is characterized by the fact that the insurgent operates largely on the legal side, and only partly on the fringe of legality, through his subversion tactics. He may or may not have been recognized as an insurgent; if he has been identified as such, only the police and a few people in the government generally realize what is looming.

The essential problem for the counterinsurgent stems from the fact that the actual danger will always appear to the nation as out of proportion to the demands made by an adequate response. The potential danger is enormous, but how to prove it on the basis of available, objective facts? How to justify the efforts and sacrifices needed to smother the incipient insurgency? The insurgent, if he knows how to conduct his war, is banking on precisely this situation, and will see to it that the transition from peace to war is very gradual indeed. . . .

Four general courses of action are open to the counterinsurgent under these circumstances, and they are not mutually exclusive:

1. He may act directly on the insurgent leaders.
2. He may act indirectly on the conditions that are propitious to an insurgency.
3. He may infiltrate the insurgent movement and try to make it ineffective.
4. He may build up or reinforce his political machine.

DIRECT ACTION AGAINST THE INSURGENT

The direct approach consists of depriving the insurgent of any physical possibility of building up his movement. At this stage, the insurgent's movement generally has no life of its own; everything depends on its leaders, who are, consequently, the key elements. By arresting them or by restricting their ability to contact people, by impeaching them in the courts, by banning their organizations and publications if necessary, the counterinsurgent may nip the insurgency in the bud. Such a method is easy, of course, in totalitarian countries, but it is hardly feasible in democracies. One of two situations may arise: Either the counterinsurgent government may have already have equipped itself as a precautionary measure (even in the absence of pressure) with special powers and laws designed to cope with insurgencies. In this case, the main problem is to act without giving undue publicity to the insurgent, an important matter particularly if the insurgent's cause has a wide popular appeal.

The other possibility is that the counterinsurgent may not have provided himself in advance with the necessary powers. Thus when he attempts to act directly against the insurgent, he opens a Pandora's box. Arrests have to be justified. On what basis? Where is the limit to be drawn between normal political opposition, on the one hand, and subversion, which is difficult to define under the best circumstances? The arrested insurgent can count almost automatically on some support from the legitimate opposition parties and groups. Referred to the courts, he will take refuge in chicanery, exploit to the utmost every advantage provided by the existing laws. Worse yet, the trial itself will serve as a sounding board for his cause. The banned organizations will spring up again under other labels, and the counterinsurgent will bear the onus of proving their ties to the old ones.

The counterinsurgent will inevitably be impelled to amend normal procedures, but this time under pressure. . . .

Since legal changes are slow, the counterinsurgent may be tempted to go a step further and to act beyond the borders of legality. A succession of arbitrary restrictive measures will be started, the nation will soon find itself under constraint, opposition will increase, and the insurgent will thank his opponent for having played into his hands.

It can therefore be concluded with relative safety that the direct approach works well if:

1. The insurgent's cause has little appeal (but we have assumed that no wise insurgent would launch an insurgency unless the prerequisite of a good cause had been fulfilled).
2. The counterinsurgent has the legal power to act.
3. The counterinsurgent can prevent the insurgent from gaining publicity.

INDIRECT ACTION AGAINST THE INSURGENT

We have seen in Chapter 2 that insurgency cannot normally develop unless two essential prerequisites are met: the insurgent's having a cause, and his being helped initially by the weakness of his opponent. Two other conditions, although not absolutely necessary, are also helpful to the insurgent: geographic factors, and outside support. By acting on these conditions, a counterinsurgent could hope to frustrate the growth of an insurgent movement.

Geographic factors are what they are and cannot be significantly changed or influenced except by displacing the population—an absurdity in peacetime—or by building artificial fences, which is also too costly in peacetime. The question of outside support offers more leeway but rests largely outside the counterinsurgent's reach.

To deprive the insurgent of a good cause amounts to solving the country's basic problems. If this is possible, well and good, but we know now that a good cause for the insurgent is one that his opponent cannot adopt without losing his power in the process. And there are problems that, although providing a good cause to an insurgent, are not susceptible of solution. . . .

Alleviating the weaknesses in the counterinsurgent's rule seems more promising. Adapting the judicial system to the threat, strengthening the bureaucracy, reinforcing the police and the armed forces may discourage insurgency attempts, if the counterinsurgent leadership is resolute and vigilant.

INFILTRATION OF THE INSURGENT MOVEMENT

An insurgency movement in its infancy is necessarily small; hence, the views and attitudes of its members have a greater importance at the early period than at any other time. They are all, so to speak, generals with no privates to command. History is full of cases of obscure political movements that floundered and vanished soon after they were created because the founders did not agree and split the movement.

A young insurgent movement is necessarily inexperienced and should be relatively easy to infiltrate with agents who will help to disintegrate it from within and to derail it. If they do not succeed in this, they can at least report its activity. . . .

There is much merit in this idea, but it should be remembered that the longer the insurgent movement lasts, the better will be its chances to survive its infantile diseases and to take root. It may of course dwindle by itself, without outside intervention. Relying on luck, however, does not constitute a policy.

STRENGTHENING THE POLITICAL MACHINE

Most of the counterinsurgent's efforts in the "hot" revolutionary war, as we shall show, tend to build a political machine at the grass roots in order to isolate the insurgent from the population forever.

This strategy, on which we shall not elaborate now, is just as valid in the cold revolutionary war, and it should be easier to implement preventively than when the insurgent has already seized control of the population. Such a strategy, to us, represents the principal course of action for the counterinsurgent because it leaves the least to chance and makes full use of the counterinsurgent's possibilities.

It may be useful to remember that a peacetime political machine is build essentially on patronage.

CHAPTER 5

COUNTERINSURGENCY IN THE HOT REVOLUTIONARY WAR

Force, when it comes into play in a revolutionary war, has the singular virtue of clearing away many difficulties for the counterinsurgent, notably the matter of the issue. The moral fog dissipates sooner or later, the enemy stands out more conspicuously, repressive measures are easier to justify. But force adds, of course, its own difficulties.

At our point of departure in the study of the hot revolutionary war—that is, the moment when the armed forces have been ordered to step in—the situation usually conforms to the following pattern:

The insurgent has succeeded in building his political organization. He directs either an elite party leading a united front, or a large revolutionary movement bound to the cause. Although his actions other than subversion are overt, he operates clandestinely.

The country's map reveals three sorts of areas:

The "red" areas, where the insurgent effectively controls the population and carries out guerrilla warfare.

The "pink" areas, in which he attempts to expand; there are some efforts at organizing the populations and some guerrilla activity.

The "white" areas, not yet affected but nevertheless threatened; they are subjected to the insurgent's subversion but all seems quiet.

Confusion is prevalent in the counterinsurgent's camp. There is a realization that an emergency exists, but the feeling of crisis is more widely spread in government circles than among the population of the white and even the pink areas. The true allegiance of every citizen is open to doubt. The leadership and its policy are questioned. The political, the judicial, the military structures geared for ordinary days have not yet been adapted to the requirements of the situation. The economy is rapidly deteriorating; the government's expenses are rising while its income is declining. In the psychological field, the insurgent has the edge since he exploits a cause without which he would not have been able to develop so far as to engage in guerrilla warfare or terrorism. The counterinsurgent forces are torn between the necessity of guarding key areas and fixed installation, of protecting lives and property, and the urge to track the insurgent forces.

With this general picture in mind, we shall now discuss the various avenues open to the counterinsurgent.

LAWS AND PRINCIPLES OF COUNTERINSURGENCY WARFARE

Limits of Conventional Warfare

Let us assume that the political and economic difficulties have been magically solved or have proved manageable,[2] and that only one problem remains, the military one—how to suppress the insurgent forces. It is not a problem of means since the counterinsurgent forces are still largely superior to the insurgent's, even though they may be dispersed. It is primarily a problem of strategy and tactics, of methods and organization.

The strategy of conventional warfare prescribes the conquest of the enemy's territory, the destruction of his forces. The trouble here is that the enemy holds no territory and refuses to fight for it. He is everywhere and nowhere. By concentrating sufficient forces, the counterinsurgent can at any time penetrate and garrison a red area. Such an operation, if well sustained, may reduce guerrilla activity, but if the situation becomes untenable for the guerrillas, they will transfer their activity to another area and the problem remains unsolved. It may even be aggravated if the counterinsurgent's concentration was made at too great risk for other areas.

The destruction of the insurgent forces requires that they be localized and immediately encircled. But they are too small to be spotted easily by the counterinsurgent's direct means of observation. Intelligence is the principal source of information on guerrillas, and intelligence has to come from the population, but the population will not talk unless it feels safe, and it does not feel safe until the insurgent's power has been broken.

The insurgent forces are also too mobile to be encircled and annihilated easily. If the counterinsurgent, on receiving news that guerrillas have been spotted, uses ready forces immediately, chances are they will be too small for the task. If he gathers larger forces, he will have lost time and probably the benefit of surprise.

True, modern means of transportation—particularly helicopters, when available—allow the counterinsurgent to combine strength with swiftness. True, systematic large-scale operations, because of their very size, alleviate somewhat the intelligence and mobility deficiency of the counterinsurgent. Nevertheless, conventional operations by themselves have at best no more effect than a fly swatter. Some guerrillas are bound to be caught, but new recruits will replace them as fast as they are lost. If counterinsurgent operations are sustainable over a period of months, the guerrilla losses may not be so easily replaced. The question is, can the counterinsurgent operations be so sustained?

If the counterinsurgent is so strong as to be able to saturate the entire country with garrisons, military operations along conventional lines will, of course, work. The insurgent, unable to grow beyond a certain level, will slowly wither away. But saturation can seldom be afforded.

Why Insurgency Warfare Does Not Work for the Counterinsurgent

Insurgency warfare is specifically designed to allow the camp afflicted with congenital weakness to acquire strength progressively while fighting. The counterinsurgent is endowed with congenital strength; for him to adopt the insurgent's warfare would be the same as a giant to try to fit into a dwarf's clothing. How, against whom, for instance could he use his enemy's tactics? He alone offers targets for guerrilla operations. Were he to operate as a guerrilla, he would have to have the effective support of the population guaranteed by his own political organization among the masses; if so, then the insurgent would not have it and consequently could not exist; there would be no need for the counterinsurgent's guerrilla operations. This is not to say that there is no place in counterinsurgency warfare for small commando-type operations. They cannot, however, represent the main form of the counterinsurgent's warfare.

Is it possible for the counterinsurgent to organize a clandestine force able to defeat the insurgent on his own terms? Clandestine seems to be another of those obligations-turned-assets of the insurgent. How could the counterinsurgent, whose strength derives precisely from his open physical assets, build up a clandestine force except as a minor and secondary adjunct? Furthermore, room for clandestine organizations is very limited in revolutionary war. Experience shows that no rival—not to speak of hostile—clandestine movements can coexist for long; one is always absorbed by the other. . . .

Can the counterinsurgent use terrorism too? It would be self-defeating since terrorism is a source of disorder, which is precisely what the counterinsurgent aims to stop.

If conventional warfare does not work, if insurgency warfare cannot work, the inescapable conclusion is that the counterinsurgent must a apply a warfare of his own that takes into account not only the nature and characteristics of the revolutionary war, but also the laws that are peculiar to counterinsurgency and the principles deriving from them.

The First Law: The Support of the Population Is as Necessary for the Counterinsurgent as for the Insurgent

What is the crux of the problem for the counterinsurgent? It is not how to clean an area. We have seen that he can always concentrate enough forces to do it, even if he has to take some risk in order to achieve the necessary concentration. The problem is, how to keep an area clean so that the counterinsurgent forces will be free to operate elsewhere.

This can be achieved only with the support of the population. If it is relatively easy to disperse and to expel the insurgent forces from a given area by purely military action, if it is possible to destroy the insurgent political organizations by intensive police action, it is impossible to prevent the return of the guerrilla units and the rebuilding of the political cells unless the population cooperates.

The population, therefore, becomes the objective for the counterinsurgent as it was for his enemy. Its tacit support, its submission to law and order, its consensus—taken for granted in normal times—have been undermined by the insurgent's activity. And the truth is that the insurgent, with his organization at the grass roots, is tactically the strongest of opponents where it counts, at the population level.

This is where the fight has to be conducted, in spite of the counterinsurgent's ideological handicap and in spite of the head start gained by the insurgent in organizing the population.

The Second Law: Support Is Gained Through an Active Minority

The original problem becomes now: how to obtain the support of the population—support not only in the form of sympathy and approval but also in active participation in the fight against the insurgent.

The answer lies in the following proposition, which simply expresses the basic tenet of the exercise of political power:

> In any situation, whatever the cause, there will be an active minority for the cause, a neutral majority, and an active minority against the cause.

The technique of power consists in relying on the favorable minority in order to rally the neutral majority, and to neutralize or eliminate the hostile minority.

In extreme cases, when the cause and the circumstances are extraordinarily good or bad, one of the minorities disappears or becomes negligible, and there may even be a solid unanimity for or against among the population. But such cases ore obviously rare.

This holds true for every political regime, from the harshest dictatorship to the mildest democracy. What varies is the degree and the purpose to which it is applied. Mores and the constitution may impose limitations, the purpose may be good or bad, but the law remains essentially valid whatever the variations, and they can indeed be great, for the law is applied unconsciously in most countries.

It can no longer be ignored or applied unconsciously in a country beset by a revolutionary war, when what is at stake is precisely the counterinsurgent's power directly challenged by an active minority through the use of subversion and force. The counterinsurgent who refuses to use this law for his own purposes, who is bound by its peacetime limitations, tends to drag the war out without getting victory.

How far to extend the limitations is a matter of ethics, and a very serious one, but no more than bombing the civilian population in a conventional war. All wars are cruel, the revolutionary war perhaps most of all because every citizen, whatever his wish, is or will be directly and actively involved in it by the insurgent who needs him and cannot afford to let him remain neutral. The cruelty of the revolutionary war is not a mass, anonymous cruelty but a highly personalized one. No greater crime can be committed by the counterinsurgent than accepting, or resigning himself to, the protraction of the war. He would do as well to give up early.

The strategic problem of the counterinsurgent may be defined now as follows: "To find the favorable minority, to organize it in order to mobilize the population against the insurgent minority." Every operation, whether in the military field or in the political, social, economic, and psychological fields, must be geared to that end.

To be sure, the better the cause and the situation, the larger will be the active minority favorable to the counterinsurgent and the easier its task This truism dictates the main goal of the propaganda—to show that the cause and the situation of the counterinsurgent are better than the insurgent's. More important, it underlies the necessity for the counterinsurgent to come out with an acceptable countercause.

Victory in Counterinsurgency Warfare

We can now define negatively and positively what is a victory for the counterinsurgent.

A victory is not the destruction in a given area of the insurgent's forces and his political organization. If one is destroyed, it will both be re-created by a new fusion of insurgents from the outside. . . .

A victory is that plus the permanent isolation from the population, isolation not enforced upon the population but maintained by and with the population. . . .

The Third Law: Support from the Population Is Conditional

Once the insurgent has established his hold over the population, the minority that was hostile to him becomes invisible. Some of its members have been eliminated physically, thereby providing an example to others; others have escaped abroad; most have been cowed into hiding their true feelings and have thus melted within the majority of the population; a few are even making a show of their support for the insurgency. The population, watched by the active supporters of the insurgency, lives under the threat of denunciation to the political cells and prompt punishment by the guerrilla units.

The minority hostile to the insurgent will not and cannot emerge as long as the threat has not been lifted to a reasonable extent. Furthermore, even after the threat has been lifted, the emerging counterinsurgent supporters will not be able to rally the bulk of the population so long as the population is not convinced that the counterinsurgent has the will, the means, and the ability to win. When a man's life is at stake, it takes more than propaganda to budge him.

Four deductions can be made from this law. Effective political action on the population must be preceded by military and police operations against the guerrilla units and the insurgent organizations.

Political, social, economic, and other reforms, however much they ought to be wanted and popular, are inoperative when offered while the insurgent still controls the population. . . .

The counterinsurgent needs a convincing success as early as possible in order to demonstrate that he has the will, the means, and the ability to win.

The counterinsurgent cannot safely enter into negotiations except from a position of strength, or his political supporters will flock to the insurgent side.

In conventional warfare, strength must be assessed by the extent of support from the population as measured in terms of political organization at the grass roots. The counterinsurgent reaches a position of strength when his power is embodied in a political organization issuing from, and firmly supported by, the population.

The Fourth Law: Intensity of Efforts and Vastness of Means Are Essential

The operations needed to relieve the population from the insurgent's threat and to convince it that the counterinsurgent will ultimately win are necessarily of an intense nature and of long duration. They require a large concentration of efforts, resources, and personnel.

This means the efforts cannot be diluted all over the country but must be applied successively area by area.

STRATEGY OF THE COUNTERINSURGENCY

Translated into a general strategy, the principles derived from these few laws suggest the following step-by-step procedure:

In a Selected Area

1. Concentrate enough armed forces to destroy or to expel the main body of armed insurgents.
2. Detach for the area sufficient troops to oppose an insurgent's comeback in strength, install these troops in the hamlets, villages, and towns where the population lives.
3. Establish contact with the population, control its movements in order to cut off its links with the guerrillas.
4. Destroy the local insurgent political organizations.
5. Set up, by means of elections, new provisional local authorities.
6. Test these authorities by assigning them various concrete tasks. Replace the softs and the incompetents, give full support to the active leaders. Organize self-defense units.
7. Group and educate the leaders in a national political movement.
8. Win over or suppress the last insurgent remnants.

Order having been re-established in the area, the process may be repeated elsewhere. It is not necessary, for that matter, to wait until the last point has been completed.

The operations outlined above will be studied in more detail, but let us first discuss this strategy. Like every similar concept, this one may be sound in theory but dangerous when applied rigidly to a specific case. It is difficult, however, to deny its logic because the laws—or shall we say the facts—on which it is based can be easily recognized in everyday political life and in every recent revolutionary war.

The strategy is also designed to cope with the worst case that can confront a counterinsurgent, i.e., supporting an insurgency in what was called a "red" area, where the insurgent is already in full control of the population. Some of the operations suggested can obviously be skipped in the "pink" areas, most can be skipped in the "white" ones. However, the general order in which they must be conducted cannot be tampered with under normal conditions without sense. For instance, small detachments of troops cannot be installed in villages so long as the insurgent is able to gather a superior force and to overpower a detachment in a surprise attack; Step 2 obviously has to come after Step 1. Nor can elections be staged when insurgent cells still exist, for the elections would most likely bring forth the insurgent's stooges.

Economy of Forces

Because these operations are spread in time, they can be spread in space. This strategy thus conforms with the principle of economy of forces, a vital one in a war where the insurgent needs so little to achieve so much whereas the counterinsurgent needs so much to achieve so little.

While a main effort is made in the selected area, necessarily at some risk to the other areas, what results can the counterinsurgent legitimately expect from his operations in these other areas? To prevent the insurgent from developing into a higher form of warfare, that is to say, from organizing a regular army. This objective is fulfilled when the insurgent is denied safe bases, and it can be achieved by purely conventional raids that do not tie down large counterinsurgent forces.

Through this strategy, insurgency can be rolled back with increased strength and momentum, for as soon as an area has been made safe, important forces can be withdrawn and transferred to the neighboring areas, swollen with locally recruited loyal and tested personnel. The transfer of troops can begin as soon as the first step is concluded.

Irreversibility

The myth of Sisyphus is a recurrent nightmare for the counterinsurgent.[3] By following the strategy just outlined, the counterinsurgent introduces some measure of irreversibility in his operations. When troops live among the population and give it protection until the population is able to protect itself with a minimum of outside support, the insurgent's power cannot easily be rebuilt, and this in itself is no mean achievement. But the turning point really comes when leaders have emerged from the population and have committed themselves on the side of the counterinsurgent. They can be counted upon because they have proved their loyalty in deeds and not in words, and because they have everything to lose from a return of the insurgents.

Initiative

This is an offensive strategy and it inevitably aims at regaining the initiative from the insurgent. On the national scale, this is so because the counterinsurgent is free to select the area of main effort; as soon as he does it, he no longer submits himself to the insurgent's will. It is so equally on the local scale because he confronts the insurgent with a dilemma: accepting the challenge, and thus a defensive posture, or leaving the area and being powerless to oppose the counterinsurgent's action on the population.

In conventional warfare, when the Blues attack the Reds on Point A, the Reds can relieve the pressure by attacking the Blues on Point B, and the Blues cannot escape the counterpressure. In revolutionary warfare, when the insurgent exerts pressure in area A, the counterinsurgent cannot relieve the pressure by attacking the insurgent on Area B. The insurgent simply refuses to accept the fight, and he can refuse because of his fluidity. . . .

However, when the counterinsurgent applies pressure not on the insurgent directly but on the population, which is the insurgent's real source of strength, the insurgent cannot so freely refuse the fight because he courts defeat.

Full Utilization of the Counterinsurgent's Assets

If the insurgent is fluid, the population is not. By concentrating his efforts on the population, the counterinsurgent minimizes his rigidity and makes full use of his assets. His administrative capabilities, his economic resources, his information and propaganda media, his military superiority due to heavy weapons and large units, all of which are cumbersome and relatively useless against the elusive insurgent, recover their full value when applied to the task of obtaining the support of a static population. What does it matter if the counterinsurgent is unable on the whole to run as fast as the insurgent? What counts is the fact that the insurgent cannot dislodge a better-armed detachment of counterinsurgents from a village, or cannot harass it enough to make the counterinsurgent unable to devote most of his energy to the population.

Simplicity

Why is there so little intellectual confusion in conventional warfare while there has been so much in the past counterinsurgencies? Two explanations may be advanced: When a conventional war starts, the abrupt transition from peace to war and the very nature of the war clarify most of the problems for the contending sides, particularly for the defender. The issue, whatever it was, becomes now a matter of defeating the enemy. The objective, insofar as it is essentially military, is the destruction of his forces and the occupation of his territory; such an objective provides clear-cut criteria to assess gains, stagnation, or losses. The way to reach it is by military action supported by diplomacy and economic blockade. The national organization for war is simple: The government directs, the military executes, the nation provides the tools.

We have seen that this cannot be the case in counterinsurgency warfare. Transition from peace to war is very gradual, the issue is never clear, the objective is the population, military and political actions cannot be separated, and military action—essential though it is—cannot be the main form of action.

Conventional warfare has been thoroughly analyzed in the course of centuries—indeed for almost the entire extent of recorded history—and the process of battle has been sliced into distinct phases: march toward the enemy, contact with the enemy, test of the enemy's strength, attack, exploitation of success, eventually retreat, etc. The student learns in military schools what he has to do in each phase, according to the latest doctrine. Field games are staged to give him practical training in the maneuvers he may have to conduct. When he is in the field under actual war conditions, his intellectual problem amounts to determining which phase of the battle he finds himself in; then he applies to his particular situation the general rules governing the phase. His talent, his judgment come into play only here.

This has not yet been done for counterinsurgency warfare. Who indeed has heard of field games involving the task of winning the support of the population when such a task, which, in any event, requires months of continuous efforts, has no clear built-in criteria to assess the results of the games? And who is going to play the part of the population?

Simplicity in concept and in execution are (*sic*) important requirements for any counterinsurgency doctrine. The proposed strategy appears to meet them. For it is not enough to give a broad definition of the goal (to get the support of the population); it is just as necessary to show how to reach it (by finding and organizing the people who are actively in favor of the counterinsurgent), and in such a way as to allow a margin of initiative to the counterinsurgent personnel who implement the strategy—and they are a widely mixed group of politicians, civil servants, economists, social workers, soldiers—yet with enough precision to channel their efforts in a single direction. The division of the over-all action into successive steps following each other in logical order facilitates the tactical tasks of the agents; they know at each step what the intermediate objective is and what they have to do to reach it.

To Command Is to Control

With the step-by-step approach, the counterinsurgent provides himself with a way of assessing at any time the situation and the progress made. He can thus exert his control and conduct the war by switching means from an advanced area to a retarded one, by giving larger responsibilities to the subordinate leaders who have proved successful, and by removing those who have failed. In other works, he can command because he can verify.

What could happen in default of control? The general counterinsurgency effort would produce an *accidental* mosaic, a patchwork of pieces with one well pacified, next to it another one not so pacified or perhaps even under the effective insurgent's control: an ideal situation for the insurgent, who will be able to maneuver at will among the pieces, concentrating on some temporarily vanishing from others. The *intentional* mosaic created by necessity when the counterinsurgent concentrates his efforts in a selected area is in itself a great enough source of difficulties without adding to it in the selected area.

SUMMARY

Chapters 4 and 5 of David Galula's *Counterinsurgency Warfare: Theory and Practice* demonstrate the appeal of the book to counterinsurgency practitioners. Clear, concise, seemingly practical, Galula's ideas offer actionable suggestions for those "on the ground" confronted with overwhelming political and military problems. For example, Galula presents a number of short, useful concepts:

- Revolutionary war – consist of "cold revolutionary war" (insurgents remain legal and nonviolent) and "hot revolutionary war" (insurgent's become openly illegal and violent).
- In cold revolutionary war, the counterinsurgent should be open to four general courses of action: 1. Act directly against insurgent leaders; 2. Act indirectly against the conditions driving an insurgency; 3. Infiltrate the insurgent movement; 4. Build up or reinforce his political machine.
- Four laws of counterinsurgency in "hot revolutionary war": 1. The support of the population is as necessary for the counterinsurgent as the insurgent; 2. Support is gained through an active minority; 3. Support from the population is conditional; 4. Intensity of efforts and vastness of means are essential.
- A step-by-step counterinsurgency procedure (strategy):
  1. Concentrate enough armed force to destroy or to expel the main body of armed insurgents.
  2. Detach sufficient troops to oppose an insurgent's comeback . . . .
  3. Establish contact with the population, control its movements . . . .
  4. Destroy the local insurgent political organizations.
  5. Set up, by elections, new provisional local authorities.
  6. Test these authorities . . . . Replace the softs and the incompetents.
  7. Group and educate the leaders in a national political movement.
  8. Win over or suppress the last insurgent remnants.

Despite Galula's expertise and valuable insights, warnings should sound in the mind of the reader. Remember Clausewitz's observation, "Everything in strategy is very simple, but that does not mean that everything is very easy . . . "? Or Sun Tzu's famous line, "Therefore, it can be said that, one may know how to win, but cannot necessarily do so." Thus, the budding student of war should remain cautious regarding David Galula's sage advice. Fog, friction, and chance will always remain in play and populations will always remain fickle.

NOTES

1. Carl von Clausewitz, *On War*, trans. Michael Howard and Peter Paret, ed. Beatrice Heuser (Oxford and New York: Oxford University Press, 2007), 134-135.
2. Original note: Except, of course, the psychological handicap, which can be alleviated only by the protraction of the war. To solve it would require that the counterinsurgent espouse the insurgent's cause without losing his power at the same time. If it were possible to do so, then the insurgent's cause was a bad one to start with, tactically speaking.
3. Editor's note: In Greek mythology, Sisyphus was punished for his sins by having to push a boulder up a hill each day and then after reaching the summit, watch if roll down . . . repeating the pattern for eternity. http://www.mythweb.com/encyc/entries/sisyphus.html (Accessed 14 Jun 2012).

THEORY INTO DOCTRINE?

The final chapter of volume one returns to the concepts of theory (teaching how to think about war) and doctrine (accepted beliefs about how best to fight). AFDD 1, *Air Force Basic Doctrine, Organization, and Command,* represents basic, fundamental doctrine for the USAF and serves the doctrinal purposes discussed in our opening chapters. The passages "War," "The Nature of War," "Traditional and Irregular War,"and "Culture and War" summarize the concepts previously studied and provide a current Air Force perspective of the issues. Students should recognize ideas from many of the theorists encountered earlier and appreciate the link between classic thoughts about military theory and strategy and today's air, space, and cyberspace domains. Articles describing the evolution of air, space, and cyberspace thought appear in the second volume of MSS 200, corresponding conceptually with the changes in the "character of war."

WAR[1]

Every art has its rules and maxims. One must study them: theory facilitates practice. The lifetime of one man is not long enough to enable him to acquire perfect knowledge and experience. Theory helps to supplement it; it provides a youth with premature experience and makes him skillful also through the mistakes of others. In the profession of war the rules of the art are never violated without drawing punishment from the enemy, who is delighted to find us at fault.

— Frederick the Great

Because war underpins the reason for the Air Force's existence, an understanding of doctrine should also include an understanding of war. The ultimate objective of peace time preparation of forces is their employment as instruments of national power to deter or win wars. Therefore, Airmen should understand the nature and consequences of war.

War is a violent struggle between rival parties to attain competing objectives. War is just one means used by nation-states, sub-national groups, or supranational groups to achieve disputed objectives. War has been a basic aspect of human affairs throughout history. The modern Western tendency to view war as an aberration in human affairs, only occasionally necessary as an operation with limited aims or an all-out campaign to destroy a clearly recognized evil, often distorts our understanding of warfare and its purposes. Warfare is ingrained in the very nature of certain cultures. While for nation states, war is an instrument of policy aiming at political objectives, it is also, even within this context, a phenomenon involving the full range of human emotions and irrationalities. War has a dynamic of its own, often fueled by pressures of the irrational: anger, fear, revenge, and hatred. Thus, the resort to violence rarely remains for long tied to cold, clear political objectives; it can—and has—moved in unexpected directions.

Military professionals operate in war within an environment that cannot be replicated in peacetime. They are asked to perform their work perhaps only a few times in their careers and then under very different circumstances from those for which they have prepared. Moreover, the arena in which military professionals operate is a deadly one. Not only are they attempting, as General George Patton stated, to "make the other poor bastard die for his country," the enemy is attempting to do the same to us. Consequently, war is an arena characterized by extraordinary fear, pain, and suffering and is further complicated by the effects of weather and terrain.

THE NATURE OF WAR

Three enduring truths describe the nature of war. Despite technological advances and the best of plans and intentions, war will never be as straightforward in execution as planned, nor free of unintended consequences. The particular characteristics usually change from conflict to conflict, but the nature of war remains eternal.

- **War is an instrument of policy, strategy, or culture.** Victory in war is not measured by casualties inflicted, battles won or lost, number of tanks destroyed, or territory occupied, but by the achievement of (or failure to achieve) the strategy and policy objectives of nation states, and often the cultural objectives of all actors (including non- or supra-state entities). More than any other factor, these objectives—one's own and those of the enemy—shape the scope, intensity, and duration of war. To support US national policy objectives, military objectives and operations should be coordinated and orchestrated with nonmilitary and partner nation instruments of power. Prussian philosopher of war Carl von Clausewitz emphasized that war is a continuation of the policies of nations, but not all belligerents in war are organized nation states.

- **War is a complex and chaotic human endeavor.** Irrational and non-rational human impulses and human frailties shape war's nature—it is not deterministic. Uncertainty and unpredictability—what many call the "fog of war"—combine with danger, physical stress, and human fallibility to produce what Clausewitz called "friction," which makes even simple operations unexpectedly and sometimes even insurmountably difficult.

- **War is a clash of opposing wills.** War is collision of two or more living forces. War is not waged against an inanimate or static object, but against a living, calculating, interactively complex, adaptive opponent. The enemy often does not think as we think and often holds different values, motivations, and priorities than ours. Victory results from creating advantages against a thinking adversary bent on creating his own advantages. This produces a dynamic interplay of action and reaction. While physical factors are crucial in war, the will of the people and the character of their leaders are also critical components of war. Allied and enemy resolve—the determination to enforce one's will on one side and to resist on the other—can be the decisive element.

Success in war requires mastery of the art of war as well as the science of war. Warfare is one of the most complex of human activities. Success depends more on intellectual superiority, morale, and determination than it does on numerical and technological superiority. Success thus demands an intricate combination of science (that which can be measured, studied, and controlled) and art (creativity, flexibility, intuition, and the ability to adapt). Sound doctrine, good leadership, effective organization, moral values, and realistic training can lessen the effects of uncertainty, unpredictability, and unreliability that are always present in war.

TRADITIONAL AND IRREGULAR WAR

The US' overwhelming dominance in recent conventional wars has made it highly unlikely that most adversaries would choose to fight the US in a traditional, conventional manner. Thus, for relatively weaker powers (including non-state entities) irregular warfare has become an attractive, if not more necessary, option. Irregular warfare presents different challenges to our military and to the Air Force.

Traditional warfare is characterized as "a confrontation between nation-states or coalitions/ alliances of nation-states"[2] (JP 1, *Doctrine for the Armed Forces of the United States*). This confrontation typically involves force-on-force military operations in which adversaries employ a variety of conventional military capabilities against each other in the air, land, maritime, space, and cyberspace domains. The objective may be to convince or coerce key military or political decision makers, defeat an adversary's armed forces, destroy an adversary's war-making capacity, or seize or retain territory in order to force a change in an adversary's government or policies.

Irregular warfare is defined as "a violent struggle among state and non-state actors for legitimacy and influence over the relevant populations. Irregular warfare favors indirect and asymmetric approaches, though it may employ the full range of military and other capabilities in order to erode an adversary's power, influence, and will" (JP 1-02).

Traditional warfare and irregular warfare differ primarily by the approach and strategy used to achieve the effects desired. **Traditional warfare seeks a change in the policies and practices, if not in the outright existence, of a government** by coercing key government leaders or defeating them militarily. **Irregular warfare**, conversely, **seeks to undermine a group, government, and/or ideology by influencing the population, which is often the center of**

gravity. The focus of irregular warfare is not primarily on the military or destructive capability of an adversary (state or non-state).

Irregular warfare is not a lesser-included form of traditional warfare. Rather, irregular warfare encompasses a variety of operations where the nature and characteristics are significantly different from traditional war. There are principally five activities or operations that are undertaken in sequence, in parallel, or in blended form in a coherent campaign to address irregular threats: counterterrorism, unconventional warfare, foreign internal defense, counterinsurgency, and stability operations.

Traditional warfare and irregular warfare are not mutually exclusive; both forms of warfare may be present in a given conflict. Airmen should understand that the character of war may often change in the course of a conflict. This is especially true in irregular warfare where the conflict is often protracted and varies in intensity. Traditional warfare can rapidly evolve into an irregular war and vice versa, requiring the military force to adapt from one form to the other.

Refer to AFDD 3-24, *Irregular Warfare*, for detailed discussion on irregular warfare.

When one is attempting to change minds, rather than blow them away, local beliefs and attitudes assume high strategic importance.

— Colin S. Gray, *The Air power Advantage in Future Warfare*

CULTURE AND WAR

The role of culture in establishing the terms of conflict is another vital component that has increased in importance in recent operations. War among Western powers has always been seen as an adjunct to politics and commerce, and often as a dangerous distraction from them. The rewards of war are physical; psychological reinforcement comes predominantly from war's spoils, not from war itself. In general, this view has led Western powers to try to force resolution as quickly and "cheaply" as practicable (in all but comparatively rare civil and religious wars), to seek decisive engagement with the enemy when possible, and to focus warfare upon defeat of the enemy's fielded military forces. This was true even during Industrial Age conflicts, where the total moral and physical power of the nation-state was mobilized for war. This is the cultural legacy that has most heavily influenced the modern use of air power.

People in other cultures often view things differently, and Airmen should be sensitive to these differences. In a number of non-Western societies around the globe, the cultural motivation for war is more deeply felt, causing them to fight in ways and for reasons that may seem strange to Americans. Some adhere to a warrior ethos, in which the act of waging war provides its own important psychological reinforcements. Some do not separate church, state, and popular culture in the Western manner, but see religion, politics, warfare, and even trade as part of a seamless whole. Thus, the wars they wage may take on the single-mindedness and ferocity of religious or civil wars.

US commanders should consider these factors when devising strategies to deal with adversaries from such cultures. They should seek to understand how the adversary thinks and not "mirror-image." For example, during the Vietnam War the US assumed that North Vietnamese motivations, priorities, and interests were similar to our own. This incorrect assumption significantly hampered the process of devising a winning strategy and prolonged the war. The US should also carefully plan for stability and other operations that follow major combat, and constantly keep the conflict's ultimate end state in mind during combat operations, considering all possible means for creating effects and achieving objectives, not just those conventionally used for destruction of fielded forces.

NOTES

1. AFDD 1, *Air Force Basic Doctrine, Organization, and Command,* HQ USAF: LeMay Center, 14 Oct 2011, 21-25: also found at http://www.e-publishing.af.mil/shared/media/epubs/AFDD1.pdf.
2. Joint doctrine does not formally define traditional war. However, JP 1 contains this characterization.